Joy.
Love & Merry Xmas.
Chuck.
xxx
1990

BACK THE ATTACK!

Back the Attack!

Canadian Women During the Second World War — at Home and Abroad

JEAN BRUCE

Macmillan of Canada
A Division of Canada Publishing Corporation
Toronto, Ontario, Canada

CANADIAN CATALOGUING IN PUBLICATION DATA

Bruce, Jean, date.
  Back the attack!

Bibliography: p.
Includes index.
ISBN 0-7715-9682-0

1. World War, 1939–1945 — Women — Canada.
2. World War, 1939–1945 — Participation, Female.
3. World War, 1939–1945 — Personal narratives,
Canadian. I. Title.

D810.W7B78 1985   305.4'0971   C85-098871-3

Edited by Kathleen Richards
Designed by Catherine Wilson/Sunkisst Graphics
Typesetting by Compeer Typographic Services Ltd.

Macmillan of Canada
A Division of Canada Publishing Corporation
Toronto, Ontario, Canada

For Gertrude Laing of Winnipeg and Calgary,
a woman for all seasons

CONTENTS

Woman's Place Is Everywhere

In this grim and unrelenting war, when all that is precious to us hangs in the balance — woman's place is everywhere. Not only in the home or on the farm . . . not only among those whose noble task it is to nurse the wounded and comfort the afflicted . . . but among the workers in our factories . . . among those who keep the wheels of industry and transportation turning . . . among those who proudly wear the uniforms of our Navy, Army and Air Force. When only the all-out effort of all our nation can carry us through to Victory, *woman's place is everywhere!* And everywhere, in every way, Canada's women are "Carrying On!"

Advertisement in *Women at War*, compiled by J. H. Hodgins, D. B. Crombie, Eric Crawford, and R. B. Huestis, Toronto, 1943

TT 100-678

Introduction

MA 157

When I started researching *Back the Attack!* in 1979 I began to suspect there was a treasure-trove of material waiting to be discovered. But there was certainly no indication of its existence at a symposium organized that year by the Directorate of History, Department of National Defence, entitled "The Second World War as a National Experience". As far as the organizers and the participating historians were concerned, women were not considered part of that experience. In only one paper out of fourteen did I find one short reference to them (in the context of Quebec's Roman Catholic hierarchy and its attitude to women in the labour force).

One evening during that November 1979 symposium I watched a selection of wartime film footage specially assembled by the Public Archives of Canada. Here again I drew a blank. Where were the women who had served in the armed forces at home and abroad? I knew there had been nearly 50,000 of them. Where were the 4,500 nursing sisters, two-thirds of whom worked dangerously close to the front lines? What about the three-quarters of a million women in Canadian war industries, the 400,000 in the civilian labour force, the 760,000 on the farms? Where were the servicemen's wives and mothers who ran homes and families single-handed for several years? What about the four million women who, as consumers, guaranteed the success of the government's food-rationing program, the anti-inflation campaign, and hundreds of salvage drives?

These were my first basic questions, but many others, much more specific, came to mind as my research progressed. Where were the streetcar drivers and the lumberjills? The union organizers in the factories? The civil servants? The spies who worked for "Intrepid"? The ferry pilots who served in Britain, and the Red Cross and St. John Ambulance drivers overseas? Where were the entertainers, the filmmakers, and the broadcasters? The journalists and the politicians? They may have been missing from the 1979 symposium, but they were very much part of the war, and they are here in this book.

If you have ever considered the way television and radio documentaries are put together, you will find that I have used some of the same techniques, and the same sources, to produce this book about Canadian women in the Second World War. I say "produce" quite deliberately, because my early background as a CBC radio producer, followed by a period as a television researcher, interviewer, and story editor, has influenced me greatly as a writer. My book, rather like a television documentary, is a montage of personal stories, statements, and visual images within the context of a broader historical overview.

Because print is a more flexible and accommodating medium than television, I have also been able to draw freely upon letters and diaries, magazines, newspapers, books and radio scripts, political debates, and a wide variety of archival records, including the military. When all these different materials are combined with dozens of personal interviews, the result is a vivid picture of what Canadian women did during the war years. As my title, *Back the Attack!*, suggests, I have focused upon women who were active participants in the war effort as war workers, servicewomen, nursing sisters, and volunteers at home and overseas. But you will also find out what it felt like to be a woman at home during the war, "keeping the home fires burning". There were, of course, a great many men in the lives of all these women: husbands and sweethearts, sons and brothers, bosses and co-workers, fellow members of the armed forces, all seen through women's eyes.

One of my favourite novels, *The Go-Between* by L.P. Hartley, begins with the evocative sentence "The past is a foreign country: they do things differently there." To find out just how differently women did things, or regarded events during the Second World War, I have interviewed 250 women over the past five years, and extracts from those interviews provide my book with its chief narrative thread. My own role—as "producer" rather than "author"—has been to create the framework and the context, to find the supporting materials that provide the links. In the end, the selection process is a highly personal one, although I like to think that I started out with no conscious preconceptions or theories to prove.

Personal interviews were particularly important to this book because there was little previous research to go on, apart from Ruth Roach Pearson's trailblazing scholarly articles on the Canadian Women's Army Corps and women in industry, and Colonel G.W. Nicholson's history of Canada's nursing sisters. But my interviews are important for another reason as well: many of my other sources were vehicles for the propaganda which is an inevitable part of any war effort. In fact, the National Film Board, which produced many of my best photographs, was established as an agency of government propaganda at the beginning of the war.

When you look at the striking photographs of women working in munitions factories or in the armed forces, you have to remember that most were taken for specific purposes: to further the war effort by persuading other women to enlist in the services or to do their patriotic duty by working on an assembly line—or to convince the public at large that it was both essential and acceptable for women to do these things. As you might expect, these photographs project the same positive image that government posters and advertisements do, showing cheerful, resourceful women salvaging scrap metal and rubber, selling War Savings Stamps, or congratulating a son who has just joined the Air Force. You won't find pictures of weary women in sweatshops, harassed housewives, or servicewomen "out on the town", although these people certainly existed. I talked with several of them.

You will detect the propaganda in many, but not all, newspaper stories, magazine articles, and radio scripts. Most stories don't tell you frankly what it was like to be in the Army, to work in a shipyard, or to drive a streetcar. A certain "gee whiz" quality, or a coyness in the writing style—whether the journalist was male or female—often seemed to trivialize the work that women were doing. Personal letters are a more reliable source, and I had access to a good number of them. But there were some built-in inhibiting factors. If they were written by members of the armed forces, they were vetted by the censor, in case they contained information of use to the enemy. If they were written by daughters to worried parents back home, they were not always entirely frank. I did not come across many diaries. Servicewomen and nursing sisters were not supposed to keep them, but fortunately other women could, and did. I am thinking here particularly of a Vancouver aircraft-factory worker.

Of all my various sources, the personal interviews will tell you most about what it really felt like for a Canadian woman to be part of the war effort. The other material—including the photographs—provides the context and the atmosphere of a period not very far removed in time from the 1980s, but quite "foreign" in spirit in many ways. The attitudes towards the war itself, towards the British connection, towards the role of women in the family unit,

PAC PA 117565

will strike the modern reader as very different, although other things may seem surprisingly contemporary, such as the demands for equal pay for equal work and child care for working women. But beware: the way these women thought, wrote, and behaved has to be considered in the context of their time, not ours, if we want to understand their point of view.

Good oral-history interviews bring the past to life in an almost tangible way. They create a bridge between past and present, because the person responding to questions about past events acts as an interpreter for the modern listener or reader. But interviews, like all other sources, have their limitations. Memories can fade after forty-five years, or be filtered through later experiences. Certain painful or embarrassing episodes may be conveniently forgotten, while other, favourite stories have been much embellished in the retelling. As an interviewer I find it just as essential to maintain a sense of objectivity as it is to establish a comfortable rapport with the person I am interviewing. In the last resort, interviews are only as good as the research that precedes them; and however vivid the memories, they have to be checked against contemporary and later records wherever possible.

During the past few years there have been many books published about the war, television and radio programs produced, plays staged, and exhibitions mounted. But until quite recently, the wartime role of Canadian *women*, per se, has been widely neglected. CBC television producer George Robertson's documentary on women in the armed forces, "Women at War", first aired on 11 November 1982, and the Canadian War Museum's exhibition Women and War, curated by Nancy Miller Chenier, were the first significant and successful attempts to attract public

interest in this long-neglected subject area. Why has it taken so long for this important and fascinating piece of Canadian social history to receive attention? I believe it was partly because the actual fighting during the war was done by men, and all the leading military, political, and industrial figures were male. But I suspect also that women's contribution was long ignored because it was generally assumed that the things women did simply could not have been very important.

One of my major hurdles as researcher and interviewer was to overcome the self-deprecating attitude of women with remarkably interesting experiences to relate — once I could persuade them to talk. Even when they did consent to be interviewed, several chose not to speak for attribution. That is one reason why you will find very few names attached to the quotes in this book, although I have named names whenever an individual's position or experience seemed to be unique. I hope that, when they read this book, the women who took so much time to talk with me, write letters, send photographs, and show me scrapbooks, letters, and diaries, will finally be convinced that their combined efforts did indeed form a significant part of "The Second World War as a National Experience".

Jean Bruce

Jean Bruce
Ottawa
May 1985

1
Keeping the Home Fires Burning

The outbreak of war in 1939 affected a great many Canadian women directly and personally, as wives and mothers, sisters and sweethearts, of men who joined the armed forces. For some the war brought excitement and romance: a quick engagement or a hastily arranged marriage and a short, bitter-sweet honeymoon before a serviceman was posted. Any woman with a family or friends serving overseas lived with the possibility that a telegram would arrive one day to say that someone was killed, missing in action, a prisoner of war, or presumed dead. (Later, of course, there were female relatives and friends to worry about, when nursing sisters and servicewomen were posted to Britain or Europe.) Not every man was able to come home on leave, and some women didn't see their husbands or lovers for five years. In some cases the man never came back; in others a marriage or an engagement was the casualty.

If you were a young and unattached woman in 1939 the war offered unprecedented opportunities within the next few years: jobs that paid good money — unbelievable good fortune after the Depression years — and the chance to move away from home, and to

go to parties and dances in the name of patriotic duty, to keep up the morale of Canada's fighting men.

For great numbers of women, however, the war meant several years of hard work. It meant taking over a family farm or a small business, or getting a job to make ends meet — in addition to running a household as a single parent. For these women the war was an endurance test.

There were plenty of stresses and strains involved in being a homemaker, yet it was a calling of the highest national importance in wartime, women were told. "The women who keep the heart of the nation sound by doing their daily tasks in the homes and the communities are doing war service of the highest possible order," National War Services Minister J.T. Thorson told the House of Commons in November 1941. Women were responsible for maintaining the morale of men in the armed forces and in the factories, he said.

From a great many sources, women received the same urgent message: their co-operation and their participation were essential to the war effort. Women all over Canada responded to the demands made on their patriotism by knitting socks for soldiers and packing ditty bags for sailors, by selling War Savings Stamps and Certificates (and buying them, too), and by collecting money to buy bombers and mobile canteens.

War savings stamps poster. MTL

REALLY EXCITED   I remember the Sunday war was declared. My young brother was taking flying lessons that summer. He had just graduated from high school. My husband had studied aeronautical engineering. They both greeted the onset of war as if a carnival had been announced. It would be wrong to say they were ecstatic, but they were really excited. I went off alone to church to sing "O God, our help in ages past", and let a few tears trickle down my cheeks.

My husband enlisted right away in the Air Force. This was something that wasn't discussed. The fact that it was going to change my life completely somehow wasn't pertinent. I wasn't to worry my pretty little head.

Winnipeg

I NEVER SAW HIM GO   Not every man wanted to rush off to war. I met my husband at college, the year war came, and we were both pacifists. At King's College [Halifax, Nova Scotia] we were all terribly involved in politics and political discussions. We were influenced by modern poets, anti-war poets like Spender and Auden, and we all read *All Quiet on the Western Front*.

In spite of his views, Noel was in the O.T.C. [Officers' Training Corps] at university. We were all very hard up, and people did it for the money—they got a small amount for going once a week. But two years later things had changed. Many other students had joined the armed forces, and Noel said, "What am I doing here? I can't let other people fight for me." Looking back I can see the propaganda, but we all ended up being very patriotic. We were married when we graduated in 1941, and Noel joined the Army right away.

Noel was commissioned and sent to Camp Borden in Ontario for training. He came back to an Army base near Kentville [Nova Scotia] for two months, and we lived together then, but we never had an ordinary married life.

We knew Noel would be sent overseas and that he'd have to leave without telling me. We had a little signal arranged, but in the end I never saw him go. With all the censorship you didn't know when a troopship left, only afterwards.

Nova Scotia

Red Cross group, Alexandria, Ont., 1943. PAC PA 116125

WIRE THE PRIME MINISTER   "I don't know what a woman of 85 can do, but I am going to wire the Prime Minister offering my services," Mrs. John Scott, Quebec's pioneer feminist, said Saturday, knitting on socks for soldiers as she spoke.

The woman who at the age of 75 went aloft in an airplane to distribute pamphlets for the women suffrage cause has taken the news of another war in her stride and is already deciding what her actions will be.

"I knitted a pair of socks every day until Thursday of each week during the last war, for my sons and acquaintances," she said, "and the balance of the week I worked for the Red Cross."

Women, she believes, are the equal of men in all respects and they must shoulder their responsibilities in this crisis if they are to convince men that they must be accorded equal rights in all things.

She lost one son in the last war, while another was severely wounded, and has grandsons of an age to serve in the present conflict.

On the whole the most important thing a woman can do is cook, Mrs. Scott believes, and thinks that most of the troubles of the world might be solved if "everyone got three square meals a day."

"Of course," she said, "I know socks can be made more quickly by machinery. It's just the idea of being able to feel that you are doing something."

Montreal *Gazette*, 4 September 1939

AN OUTING   We used to roll bandages for the Red Cross. The women felt that this was an outing, you know. You got together and you rolled bandages and you had a cup of coffee, and you had a chat.

And we knit; we knit mitts. You had to learn to leave a hole in the front. You knit a flap that pulled off, so they could get their fingers out, I suppose for loading the guns.

Belleville, Ont.

THINGS TO SEND TO ENGLAND   I lent my living room in Thornhill to the Women's Institute, and the village women came to make things to send to England. There was the blacksmith's wife, and the village handyman's wife. Poorer people are so much more inventive; they know how to make things over.

We had a big roll of cotton to make diapers for English children, and the roll was too wide. There was eight inches or more to spare on the side. And do you know, we made children's pyjamas out of those eight-inch strips, piecing them together. They were taken to Toronto, to the [Canadian National] Exhibition, as an example of what could be done.

Thornhill, Ont.

NICE WARM QUILTS   When the students went home at Christmas, I told them to bring back any scraps of cotton or chintz they could lay hands on. The University loaned us the attic of the old Arts building, and we had a workroom there. Three kind ladies loaned me sewing machines, and we sewed the bits and pieces into big patchwork squares. I bought great rolls of grey flannelette, and my students made these nice warm quilts with flannelette backing. They went to stations on the North Sea coast [of England] where torpedoed and rescued sailors were brought in. I remember getting word back from men who said they liked our coverlets because they didn't slip off the bed!

Dean of Women, Queen's University,
Kingston, Ont.

Byrne Hope Sanders, editor of *Chatelaine* magazine for thirteen years, was appointed Director of the Consumer Branch, Wartime Prices and Trade Board, in January 1942. Price and production limits were set on many consumer items by the W.P.T.B.
Photo by Malak, courtesy David Sperry.

WILL THE WOMEN OF CANADA HELP?

Can you sew? Can you knit?
Do you want to help the gallant people of Britain?

HOW YOU CAN HELP
Will you set aside a definite time each day during the long summer days and evenings to knit or sew for these men and women who need what you can send them so much? Knit sweaters, Balaclava helmets, scarves, mittens, socks. Make warm skirts; under-clothing; slacks — anything you think would be useful for a man or woman fighting under the conditions you know they are facing.

WILL YOU ANSWER THE CALL?
The call has come direct to Canadian women!

Let Canadian women send over such a stream of warm clothing and comforts as has never been seen before in history!

Byrne Hope Sanders, Editor,
Chatelaine magazine, June 1941

Ditty-bag promotion, Eaton's, Montreal, 1943. Ditty bags contained socks, tooth powder, shaving soap, razor blades, first-aid kits, cigarettes, candy, writing paper, flashlights, and other "comforts" for men at sea. PAC PA 128910

One of the government's most urgent needs was for salvage materials — bones, rags, metals, paper, glass, waste fats and oils — needed to produce war supplies and domestic goods. Winnipeg women led the way by organizing on a block-by-block basis, and other cities followed suit. MTL

WAR WORK

RED CROSS

Jam for Britain	228 lbs
Gift of sugar	78 lbs
Clothing new	8 articles
Knitted articles	164
Hospital supplies	18
Money donations	$34.05

"V" BUNDLES FOR BRITAIN

Quilts	31
Clothing made over	35

SOLDIERS' PARCELS

1940   5 in Canada and 1 overseas (Christmas)
1941   5 in Canada and 4 overseas (Christmas)

From the Minutes of the Women's Institute,
Burton, B.C., December 1941

THE IMMEDIATE REACTION   In September 1939 when the thunder of war first crashed about our ears, the immediate reaction was an almost hysterical desire to do something....

Alice Sorby of Winnipeg, *Junior League Magazine*, New York, October 1940

OUT OF JUNK . . .   I was at the Children's Hospital as a volunteer when word got out that there were not enough small bottles to put medicine in. We all knew that our houses and our garbage pails were full of bottles, so Margaret Konantz organized this bottle drive. We hoped we might get a couple of thousand bottles to tide the Hospital over. There was an empty firehall just off Osborne St. and it was agreed that it could be our collecting point.

EVERY OUNCE OF RUBBER IS NEEDED NOW!

GREATER WINNIPEG
PATRIOTIC SALVAGE CORPS

RUBBER DRIVE
MAY 1st TO 31st

HUNT IN YOUR HOME FOR —
OLD TIRES, INNER TUBES, RUBBER BOOTS AND SHOES, GALOSHES AND OVERSHOES, HOT WATER BOTTLES, SINK MATS, KNEELING PADS, RUBBER GLOVES, BALLS, RUBBER TOYS, ANYTHING MADE OF RUBBER.

IT IS RUBBER MONTH IN WINNIPEG
PUT IT ON THE BOULEVARD ON PICK-UP DAY

● A SPRING RUBBER CLEAN-UP WILL SPEED VICTORY ●

Left: Bottle drive, Bowness, Alta. Volunteers across Canada were co-ordinated by the Voluntary Services Division of the Department of National War Services. Through a network of regional committees, appeals for help were made by Mrs. W. E. (Nell) West, Director of the Division. GANA 2934-16   *Above:* Public notice of salvage drive. Private source

An appeal went out over the radio, and the response was unbelievable. The bottles flooded in in such numbers, they were really quite unmanageable. Marg Konantz knew immediately that this was a way of tying into the war effort. This was something women could relate to. Out of junk, out of garbage, we could do something to help people on the streets of London.

We also knew that we were going to have to use paper and cans and rubber and clothes, everything, over and over again, and we needed a way of collecting this stuff. We were able to evolve a block system: there was one woman for every city block in Winnipeg, and that woman would call other people and say, ''There will be a collection of paper on Tuesday, and if you put your newspapers out at the curb, it will help the war effort.''

Winnipeg

STAMP YOUR WAY TO VICTORY   You say, ''My small contribution would be of little value.'' Do you know that $5 invested in War Savings may bring down a German plane, for it will buy one round of anti-aircraft shells?

That $5 will let a soldier fight for you with one hundred rounds of rifle ammunition, or may stop an enemy with five machine-gun bursts. We are told that $75 will provide a 500-pound bomb to be dropped over Berlin or Berchtesgaden.

''Stamp Your Way to Victory''
committee member, Saskatoon,
22 November 1944

OUR MOTHERLAND   I am thinking of that island fortress across the Atlantic — our Motherland, our England — that green and pleasant land. Let us tighten the bonds of union between her and us. Let us sacrifice for her, who has sacrificed so much for us — who bore the brunt of this conflict for so long alone; who has been the great and solid bastion of democracy, and the spearhead of freedom for all the peoples of the world. Britain, to whom the world is looking to bind up the broken-hearted, to proclaim liberty to the captives and to open the prison door to them that are bound. . . .

Mrs. A. T. Stikeman, Municipal Regent,
Montreal, speaking at the 1942 annual general
meeting of the Imperial Order Daughters of
the Empire

UNTIL HE COMES BACK!

BUY VICTORY BONDS

NA 1623-2

MUGS-IN-TIME   Our Spring Tea was held at the home of Mrs. Bunty Mellon Chown on June 6th, 1942. Proceeds $450.00. Our money this year has been sent to Women's Volunteer Services in Britain and has been used to buy Foot Pedal Carts for Bombed Areas. These carts are fitted up with a thermos jug which holds 80 to 100 cups of tea, coffee or milk — also mugs and biscuits — and are called ''Mugs-in-time''. These carts do not require gasoline or rubber for tires and can be rushed out to Bombed Areas and to Defence Workers and Fire Fighters in outlying districts. . . .

Winnipeg item in Overseas Nursing Sisters'
Association newsletter, 1942

The first object of the Order was ''to stimulate and give expression to the sentiment of patriotism that binds the women and children of the Empire around the throne and person of their Gracious and Beloved Sovereign.'' Courtesy Imperial Order Daughters of the Empire

BRITISH STOCK   Whereas the present war may be a war of extermination and hence the vital necessity of preserving British Stock:

Therefore Be It Resolved by this North Shore Local Council of Women that the National Council ask the Government of Canada, should the need arise, to offer asylum to the menaced children of Great Britain. . . .

Motion by the North Shore Local Council of Women, B.C., sent in September 1939 to the President, National Council of Women. The motion was adopted.

FLAMING RED HAIR   There were tremendous numbers of people who wanted to take British children, but sometimes their expectations were quite unreal. I sensed that a great many people who came in to register had a vision of Little Lord Fauntleroy with a cultured accent and curly hair.

I remember one girl with flaming red hair and a cockney accent. Her father was a London bus driver and he had some kind of musical combo which he took into the pubs on Saturday nights. The kids used to go along too, to sing and dance. They'd eaten nothing but fish and chips, it seemed.

Kay was sixteen and she didn't want to be a child in anyone's family. Her first foster-parents were quiet, older people. They just couldn't cope.

I took her in. I was twenty-six and I had three young children by that time. The last thing I needed was another "child", but I certainly needed help. My husband was in the Navy and I was in charge of the household. I told Kay that if she worked from four to six for me, she could earn her room and board.

We had a trial run for a week. When the week was up she asked if she could call me "Mum". She stayed with us until the end of the war.

Winnipeg

British "war guests" arrive at Montreal, July 1940. Altogether 5,858 British children were sent to Canada, 4,326 by private arrangement and the others under a British government evacuation scheme. The submarine menace to shipping in the North Atlantic prevented more children from being sent to Canada after April 1941. PAC PA 142400

"THE HOARDER"

PUBLIC ENEMY NO.1

People who buy more of anything than they currently need, and merchants who encourage them to do so, are sabotaging the war effort and are therefore public enemies.

Loyal citizens do *not* hoard. They buy only for their immediate needs. They cheerfully adjust their standard of living, realizing that their country's needs must come first. They do not try to gain unfair advantages over their neighbours.

Wartime Prices and Trade Board, Ottawa

SUGAR RATION

Now ½ LB. PER WEEK PER PERSON

Since sugar rationing was first introduced, the shipping situation has become more serious. The danger to ships and lives has increased. Consequently it has now become necessary to reduce the sugar ration from ¾ lb. to ½ lb. per week per person. Only persons in areas remote from source of supply are permitted to have more than two weeks' supply on hand at any time.

Wartime Prices and Trade Board, Ottawa

THE LIQUOR TRAFFIC The weekly meeting of the North End W.C.T.U. was held in library with the Pres. Mrs. B. presiding. Mrs. C. opened devotionals by singing hymn "Leaning on the everlasting arms" followed by reading the 34 Psalm. Mrs. C. then read a very lovely reading "Face Another Year".

Moved by Mrs. B. seconded by Mrs. C. that Company Pres. and delegates have the use of library on Jan. 24 at 2 o'clock to put their resolution on paper concerning the liquor traffic and its effect on khaki clad boys, to be forwarded to Prov. House.

> Women's Christian Temperance Union minute book, Saint John, N.B., 17 January 1940

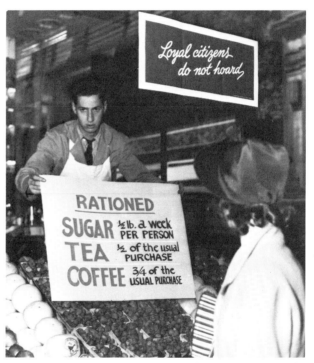

Montreal, circa 1943. When rationing was introduced in 1942 and limits were set on the purchases of sugar, tea, coffee, milk, butter, and gasoline, women's co-operation was essential to the program's success. Rationing was an inconvenience rather than a serious hardship. PAC PA 108300

THE BATTLE OF PRODUCTION Will you put yourself this question? Do I need this so much that my country must release war machinery to make it for me? Must I be so different from other women that workers and machines, needed for blankets, uniforms, and parachutes, are to be used on elaborate styles and silk stockings for me?

> Charlotte Whitton, President, Canadian Welfare Council, CBC, 18 December 1941

ONE COUPON MEATS

By M. Lois Clipsham

BRANBURGERS
(A Chatelaine Institute approved recipe)
Here's how to make six generous servings of savory meat patties. They cook in short order and give you an entirely new flavor.

One pound of minced beef — one coupon.

1 Egg
2 Teaspoonfuls of salt
¼ Teaspoonful of pepper
2 Tablespoonfuls of minced onion
1 Tablespoonful of chopped parsley
1 Cupful of milk or ½ cupful of canned evaporated milk and ½ cupful of water
¼ Cupful of catsup
1 Cupful of ready-cooked bran
1 Pound of ground beef

Beat the egg slightly, add the remaining ingredients except the beef and soak until most of the moisture is taken up. Add the meat and mix thoroughly. Shape into 12 patties (2½ inches in diameter). Bake in a hot oven—450 deg. Fahr. —for about 30 minutes or broil for 20 minutes. Gravy may be made with the pan drippings.

Chatelaine magazine, September 1943

WE USED TO PAINT OUR LEGS Stockings were very hard to get. You had to line up to buy them. There'd be notices in the paper saying such-and-such a store had them, and then there'd be line-ups around the block. You'd be there for an hour or an hour and a half, and sometimes the stockings would run out before you got to the counter. You never got more than two pairs anyway, and they were mostly rayon.

Did you know we used to paint our legs, to make them look as if we were wearing stockings? You needed a steady hand to paint the seam down the back of your leg!

Montreal

"PINK TEAS" ARE OUT Wartime Prices and Trade Board officials say that serving tea and coffee at club meetings or at garden parties is contrary to the spirit of the ration regulations.

Quoting Donald Gordon, Chairman of the WPTB, the officials declare "Ships and sailors' lives must not be risked to bring in from abroad a single pound of supplies which we can do without."

From a Halifax newspaper, 29 May 1942

COSMETIC FORECASTS "The war-conscious woman" says a beauty expert "will parsimoniously melt the stubby ends of lipsticks and pour them into a little paint pot for use with a brush. She will have a small flask of cologne or other thinning fluid to redeem her aging nail enamel. In fact, the woman of today will welcome many new things under the wartime sun—perfume in the form of a heavy cream (to save alcohol for explosives), cleansing cream in cardboard boxes, soapless shampoos that condition as they clean, lipstick in paper so hard it can't be crushed and so slick it can't be stained."

Echoes, magazine published by the Imperial Order Daughters of the Empire, Christmas 1942

FUR COAT STYLES REDUCED A THIRD

The number of styles in which fur garments may be manufactured in Canada is reduced by one-third, effective for the fall season, under an order issued by the administrator of fur skins and fur garments for the Wartime Prices and Trade Board made public today.

The order also limits the length of women's fur coats, prohibits the use of certain materials for fur linings, pockets and cuffs in fur garments, and limits the number of boxes in packing for delivery.

Canadian Press news item, 29 May 1942

ALL USED TOOTHPASTE, SHAVING CREAM TUBES GOVERNMENT PROPERTY

Samuel Godfrey [WPTB], administrator of used goods, is empowered to make such orders as necessary to collect them from drug stores, department stores and cigar stores.

250 used tubes would supply the necessary tin solder for a Bolingbroke bomber, Mr. Godfrey said.

Canadian Press news item, 3 June 1942

UNRAVELLED OLD SWEATERS   Mother was always knitting — leggings and coats and hats and dresses. She unravelled old sweaters and wound the wool into hanks. Then she washed it and dried it and wound it back into balls. Then she knitted it again.

Montreal

WORN-OUT SOCKS   One bathrobe, that was made out of the good parts of worn-out socks, made a tour of Canadian fairs as an exhibition piece. Curtains became sleeping bags for British babies, old felt hats were transformed into babies' shoes. . . .

Gertrude Laing, *A Community Organizes for War: The Story of the Greater Winnipeg Coordinating Board for War Services and Affiliated Organizations, 1939-1946*, Winnipeg, 1948

STEADFAST AND FAITHFUL   Your work, whatever it may be, is just as valuable, just as much war work, as that which is done by the bravest soldier, sailor, or airman who actually meet the enemy in battles.

In a hundred ways, you have filled the places of the men who have gone away to fight, and coping uncomplainingly with all the tedious difficulties of wartime, you, the housewives, many doing whole-time and many part-time jobs, you have kept their homes for them, against the blessed day when they come back.

These men, both at home and abroad, are counting on us at all times to be steadfast and faithful. I know that we shall not fail them.

We women as homemakers have a great part to play. Speaking as I do tonight, from my own dearly beloved home, I must say that I look forward to a great rebuilding of family life, as soon as the war ends.

Queen Elizabeth, wife of King George VI, in a broadcast from London to the Commonwealth nations, carried by the CBC, 11 April 1943

OUR FIVE CENTS' WORTH   What every woman knows is that somewhere the money for the Victory Loan must be dug out — so here is our five cents' worth to help along.

You know the odds and ends of soap that accumulate in everyone's house. If you make a small bag from an old towel with a drawstring top and drop the pieces in as you collect them, you have a perfect bathtub cleaner. Rub it over the high-water mark and it disappears.

Kate Aitken, CFRB Radio, Toronto, 18 October 1943

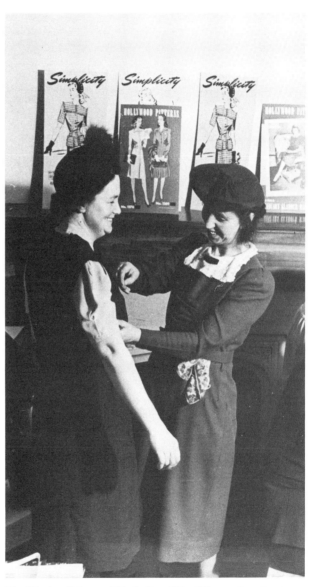

The Wartime Prices and Trade Board hired Toronto broadcaster Kate Aitken to promote the remodelling and recycling of clothes and household furnishings across Canada. GECO

PRETTY GIRLS FOR SEAMEN

NEW WESTMINSTER — The truth of the old song was brought home with a bang on Saturday night, when the prettiest girls of this city and many from Vancouver showed their keenness for the boys in blue.

Looking their loveliest, dozens of girls arrived at the Arena here to be dancing partners to the 69 men of H.M.S. Warspite who were guests of the city at a concert and dance.

Introductions were overlooked for the night as the smart navy man set his bright eyes on a pretty girl and asked her "for the honour".

Only men in uniform were allowed on the large dance floor. With the Warspites were hundreds of Rocky Mountain Rangers with their attractive girls, and the occasional airman was noticed among the dancers.

Vancouver News-Herald, 27 October 1941

1804005 LAC Donnelly P
32 S.F.T.S. R.A.F.
Moose Jaw, Sask.

To the Secretary
Empire War Services Club
Saskatoon
Saturday December 15

Dear Madam:
During a recent visit to Saskatoon, my friend and I called at the Empire Services Club, and one of the lady hostesses very kindly enquired as to our plans for Christmas leave, and suggested that in the event of our going to Saskatoon, it might be arranged that we spend Xmas with a Saskatoon family.

We are very anxious to take advantage of this wonderful offer and would greatly appreciate it if you could let us know whether the hospitality is still available. We must apologise for having left it so late, but our leave has only just been confirmed.

We are both Londoners, single, aged 20 and 21 respectively, have been in Canada four months training for airmen, are both tall and dark, enjoy dancing and any form of entertainment.

Thanking you in anticipation of any efforts on our behalf,

I Remain,
Yours Sincerely,
Patrick Donnelly

WE WERE NICE GIRLS   Some of us were hostesses at dances and entertainments for servicemen. Of course you had to be invited. They were careful about who got in. I mean, these dances were well run and chaperoned. They were organized by the Red Cross or the Women's Auxiliaries, and there'd be some middle-aged woman in your office who belonged to one of these groups. She'd invite us, and give us tickets.

We were all in our late teens, we were decently brought up, and we were nice girls. We had a wonderful time. The Air Force were the most dashing, the most daring, and some girls only went to Air Force dances. But I went to them all.

We used to say we got our feet trod on so much by army boots that we deserved decorations for war injuries!

Victoria

The Seamen's Mission, Saint John, N.B. NBM 00342

AUSTRALIANS WERE FAVOURITES   At the Y we ran the Red Triangle Hostess Club, and I was in charge of hospitality. Lots of people would have parties and they'd phone up and say, "Will you send me six boys for dinner?" or "We're having a dance. How about sending us some Air Force boys?"

Friday nights we had a dance at the Y for the boys who didn't know how to dance, then Saturday night they put it into practice. We'd have as many as seven hundred boys come in for the Saturday-night dance, and we'd provide the hostesses, junior hostesses. One hundred and fifty local girls would be invited.

I always took two boys back home to my family Saturday nights, all through the war. The Australians were my favourites. They were a little more aggressive, and if you ever said to them, "Come up and see us, or give us a ring," by Jove they were there the next day.

Y.M.C.A. volunteer, Calgary

TERRIBLE STORIES   I worked evenings behind the counter in the YMCA canteen. It was low-ceilinged and smoky and crowded, and there was always a slightly drunken sailor away in a corner playing the piano.

Some nights men told us terrible, terrible stories of bombed-out houses, dead families, occupied countries, Nazi tyranny, torpedoed ships. We'd give them some more coffee and laugh at their jokes, and go home to our comfortable beds and have nightmares, with cold winds blowing through our minds.

Halifax

H.M.C.S. *Skeena* arriving in Halifax from England, March 1941. PAC PA 105177

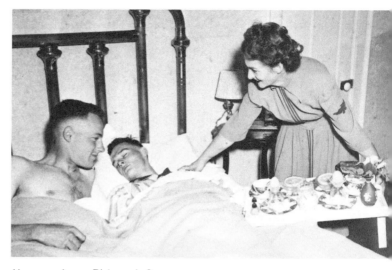

Airmen on leave, Richmond, Que. DND PL 9943

OH YIPES!   Toronto was the hub of recruiting for Ontario. It was an exciting place to be. We used to meet chaps at the canteen, there'd be soft drinks and Cokes and cigarettes and sandwiches, and they had records to dance to. And then we'd go out dancing and roller-skating. We'd go down to Sunnyside and dance at the Palais Royale. A lot of fellows were stationed at the Exhibition. Oh yipes! There were more men here than anywhere. I just went merrily along and had a very good time.

But things were different then. There was no pill and we were afraid [of getting pregnant]. You were often given that line: "This may be my last day before I'm sent overseas," but you got used to hearing it and you didn't give in. You knew there was always another town and another girl.

Toronto

SOMEBODY WROTE TO MY HUSBAND

My husband was away in the Signal Corps, and I had to do something. I would go bowling or to a show. And I went to a dance once in a while at the Y. My dad always objected, and I could see why, later on.

You could go to a dance stag, and the fellows would go along and take their pick. We danced to Frankie Laine records. Sometimes they'd want to take you home, but I didn't go along with that. I just loved to dance.

Things went wrong when somebody wrote to tell my husband about me. There was no need to. I really went off the deep end. We split up after a while. Maybe we got married too young. I was only nineteen, the first time. An awful lot of marriages broke up during the war.

Sometimes girls overseas wrote to the wives of soldiers and said, ''Your husband is the father of my child.'' I heard one time that five women got letters from the same girl!

Toronto

GAS-MASK CONTAINERS

The Arts Formal in January 1940 constituted the first Canadian University benefit dance for the Red Cross. Decorations were in a military motif, with food distributed in gas-mask containers by attendants dressed in military uniforms, while sand-bag ''dug-outs'' formed the bandstands. Air raids, complete with siren warnings, combined to portray a night in London during an air raid. . . .

Queen's University *Journal*, 16 January 1940

Victory Loan Parade, Toronto. As the Allied war effort intensified and demands on Canadian manpower increased, Prime Minister King asked Canadians to release him from his 1939 promise that there would be no conscription for overseas military service. In the April 1942 plebiscite the majority of Canadians voted in favour of ''conscription if necessary''; Quebec, however, voted strongly against it. PAC PA 115549

MAYBE THE BOY IS HOMESICK

For Canadian homes who are entertaining boys from England or Australia or New Zealand, don't spring that question ''Well, how do you like Canada?'' almost as soon as he gets inside the house. Maybe the boy is homesick and doesn't like Canada very well. Maybe it's tactful to let that subject ride for a while.

Don't entertain the boys to death. Give them homelike privileges. Offer the soldier guest a chance to take a warm, leisurely bath, and see that there's plenty of big, soft towels. And do give him pen and ink and a table to write on. Offer to wash and mend his socks and let him sprawl in the armchair and read the paper.

Jean Hinds, CBC, Winnipeg,
28 January 1942

ETIQUETTE

Now that the dating season has arrived, and many of you will have the chance to take a stroll in the company of a serviceman or an officer of the Army, the Navy or the Air Force, it would be good to know a little about military etiquette, in order to know how to conduct yourself.

Whether or not he is a commissioned officer, a serviceman must always keep his right arm at his side ready to salute. On principle he is not allowed to give his arm to his companion or to take her arm, and in the city this rule is fairly strictly observed.

Show your soldier-friend around the city and don't forget to take him to the observatory on Mount Royal to show him the view of the entire city. And if, while walking, you happen to meet a rival accompanied by a serviceman of lower rank than your escort, be kind and quickly suppress the smile of victory which will rise to your lips.

La Presse, Montreal, 10 April 1942

CARRY THE BOTTLE

We used to go occasionally to the dance at the Nova Scotian Hotel, which was formal. The boys of course were always in formal dress anyway, because they were in uniform.

Liquor wasn't served in public, so you brought your own and put it under the table. The girls usually had to carry the bottle in their evening bags because the boys weren't allowed to have their uniforms bulging any place; they had to be as smooth as could be. You had to carry a fairly large evening purse.

Halifax

''Eat Right to Fight'' display at Woodward's, Vancouver.
PAC PA 803923

CONSTANTLY BEING PROPOSED TO
There were ten men to every girl in Halifax, and there were times when you'd end up with two or three dates on a Sunday. But it was a very frustrating experience because there was no way you could form a permanent attachment. If you met someone you did like, they were shipped out the next week.

You were constantly being proposed to. I think the boys felt that they were stepping off the end of the world when they sailed out of Halifax harbour. They wanted someone back home who was waiting for them. We used to say "Yes" to practically every proposal, knowing that when they got to England they'd meet another girl and know they hadn't stepped off the end of the world. You'd never hear from them again anyway.

Halifax

CONSCRIPTION
The conflagration which is now spreading the whole world over has assumed gigantic proportions. Our existence as a nation is threatened. There is no time now for recriminations over the past.

The French-Canadian people must realize that there may come a time when their sons may have to agree to a form of conscription, democratic enlistment, for the defence of Canada.

Are we going to wait until the shipyards, factories and railways of British Columbia are smashed and completely gone? Until the ancient and beautiful city of Quebec is a smouldering mass of ruins? It may be necessary for these French-Canadian sons, the same as Anglo-Saxon, Ukrainian and all other sons of Canada, to go outside the shores of this country to defend Canada. We may have to conscript them. . . .

Dorise Nielsen, M.P. (Unity Party) for
North Battleford, Sask., House of Commons,
10 February 1942

WHY DIVIDE CANADA?
People didn't object to doing their duty, but they didn't want to be pushed and just sent over like cattle, jamais de la vie!

Why divide Canada? Australia and South Africa had refused conscription, why put it on the head of Canada?

The Honourable Thérèse Casgrain, 1975

AN AFFIRMATIVE VOTE
Whether we approve or not of the action of the Dominion Government, the plebiscite has now been taken out of party politics with the leaders of all parties asking its support in the vote on April 27 [asking Canadians to release the government from its promise not to conscript men for overseas service].

We believe that an affirmative vote on the plebiscite will strengthen our war effort. No loyal Canadian can refuse to face his responsibility in the light of the present situation. The last war gave Canadian women the franchise. It behooves each of us now to exercise our prerogative. . . .

Mrs. Edgar D. Hardy, President,
National Council of Women, to the
Canadian Press, 10 April 1942

UNSCRUPULOUS POLITICAL TRICKERY
It [the plebiscite] is a completely unscrupulous piece of political trickery — Prime Minister King hopes for an indecisive result so he can continue his policy of doing nothing. . . .

Grace MacInnis, M.L.A.,
Vancouver-Burrard, B.C.

Thérèse Casgrain, Quebec suffragist and human rights activist, vigorously opposed the conscription of men for miliary service overseas. When she ran as an independent Liberal candidate in the November 1942 federal by-election in Charlevoix-Saguenay, Casgrain placed second among five candidates.

Casgrain did not oppose the war effort per se. She believed that war service should be voluntary. Earlier in 1942 she and Dr. Charlotte Whitton had successfully organized women's "watchdog" committees across Canada for the Wartime Prices and Trade Board. PAC PA 127290

UNNECESSARY EFFORT AND EXPENSE
At the annual meeting of Lord Nelson Chapter, I.O.D.E. (Toronto), it was passed by a unanimous vote that the chapter itself is opposed to the Government's forcing a plebiscite upon the people of Canada at this time. Members feel that the Government, having the mandate of the people, should shoulder its responsibilities, and not put the country to unnecessary effort and expense. A copy of the resolution will be sent to Right Hon. Mackenzie King.

Clipping from an unidentified
Toronto newspaper, 4 February 1942

JOY AND TENSION   I was three months pregnant when John went to sea, and he didn't see our son until he was a year and a half. Then he did get leave for three weeks.

Leaves were a funny experience in a way. Your expectations were so terribly high. But one life was so utterly, utterly different from the other life. Three weeks hardly gave time for two young people to pick up the threads that were so familiar a few years before.

The pressures were so great. It's hard to describe how much joy and tension were poured into those three weeks.

Winnipeg

When your husband's overseas, you're neither married nor single, are you?

Toronto

LOVE AT FIRST SIGHT   It was love at first sight for both of us.

He was a big, tall fellow. . . . He felt if my husband didn't make me happy, he'd like the chance.

I used to get letters when he went overseas, and I didn't know until the very last letter that this was the first one he'd actually written himself. I had to read it over several times to get the meaning of it. He wasn't very good at spelling or writing, so he said he used to get someone to write his other letters for him. He wrote to say that the parcel I'd sent had been divided among the men.

When he was killed they notified his mother and she wrote to me. When the letter came I was busy washing up the floor in the nurses' residence. I finished what I was doing; I felt it was going to be bad news, and it was. He'd been badly wounded and he died on August 5. He'd been shot in the head.

Toronto

THE CENSOR   Sometimes we didn't hear from my brother for a long time. It was eleven weeks, once. He wasn't allowed to tell us where he was — if he did, they cut it out with scissors. The censor didn't allow them to glue air letters down. If they cut something out, you lost the words on the other side of the page.

Toronto

BEING ALONE   This was my first experience of being alone, and I saw my house in a completely different way. Areas which had been completely male, like the furnace room, like the hot-water tank, like the garage, all became my domain, my responsibility. I didn't have any brothers or my father around to be supportive. And I had never carried on the day-to-day financing, paying the coal bills, the electric bills, the taxes.

It was a lonely life, in some ways. Radio took up a large part and I read a lot. There were some fun parts. I found out you could still go to symphony concerts, that a woman didn't need an escort to go out, that over five years you do build up a social life with friends in the same situation. It was the first sharing of my life with women, finding the depth of companionship that there is in a woman-to-woman relationship, and how supportive that relationship can be.

Winnipeg

A MAN AROUND THE HOUSE   My older son was six and a half, and very sensitive. He could read the newspapers, and he came to me one day and said, "If Daddy loses his legs, I'll be able to look after him." And then, "If Daddy's killed, they'll put it in the papers, won't they?"

Those of us who were busy were the lucky ones; we were too busy to think of ourselves. For women who sat at home during the war it was an unbelievably dreary existence.

I had two young sons at home and my parents came to live with me, because I was working. My mother was still active and she felt important helping out, doing something she knew how to do. And having my father there meant there was a man around the house, with masculine things lying about. That was very important for my sons.

Winnipeg

Peterborough, Ont. One of many wartime housing projects for industrial workers' families. PAC PA 116146

BLACKOUT   The blackout was announced in Victoria the day of Pearl Harbor, and that was on a Sunday. Early Monday morning I was on the doorstep of the department store, but there was not a yard of black material to be had. I guess some people had had access to the store before it opened. I ended up having to buy tarpaper to nail to the inside of my living-room window frames. It kept the room rather thoroughly blacked out during the day as well.

Our particular block was close to the sea, and very soon we each had a large pail of sand and a shovel on our front porch, to put out firebombs. They didn't materialize, but they could have. Our car headlamps had to be completely blacked out. We had a three-inch slit, half an inch wide, to see by. That, combined with the winter fog, meant we tended to stay in at night.

Victoria

SHOULD AIR RAIDS COME!

What To Do in an Air Raid
. . . If you are caught in the open without shelter, lie face down on the ground and protect the back of your head with your handbag.

What To Wear in an Air Raid
If you can sew, make yourself a "siren suit" out of those old ski togs. Make some for the children. Add a few big patch pockets with odd bits of material and keep it handy. Dig up an old pair of strong, flat-heeled shoes and a beret. You will find that if you actually have to go into action or lend assistance elsewhere, this garb will be very practical. At home you will be well protected from bruises and scratches on arms and legs.

Principal Sources of Danger
Fire bombs, or incendiary bombs, are light and burn with intense heat. You can't smother them, since they contain their own oxygen, but you can make them burn out faster by training a stream of water on them from *behind* a protective barrier. You can reduce the effects of a fire bomb by pouring sand on it from a *safe distance*, BUT, if the bomb has started a fire in your house, tackle the fire first — forget the bomb until the fire is out. Do your best before calling the Fire Services — they'll have plenty of work elsewhere.

Blackouts
During the blackout, and especially during a raid, if the A.R.P. Warden rings your doorbell *do not turn on*

the light outside your front door. This point is emphasized here because it was found that during practice blackouts hundreds of housewives made this mistake and it takes only one electric light to tell an enemy airman where he is.

What To Do about Children if at Home
You might think that your self-control will be taxed when children are about; that you will have to struggle against showing nervousness. Actually you will find that taking care of the children and seeing them safely in the refuge room will take your mind off the air raid. In the refuge room, see that they keep themselves occupied with games and books, or, if they are young, tell them interesting stories.

From an *Emergency Handbook for Women*
published with the approval of the Director
of Civil Air Raid Precautions, Ottawa, 1942

A GESTURE IN HIS NAME   Perhaps you have never thought of renting out the room belonging to your son who is now serving in the Army. But in opening your home to a worker who is helping to manufacture the weapons which our soldiers need to defeat the enemy, you are actively contributing to our war effort and you will speed up your son's return.

Maybe it is a young housewife with a small child who needs the room which you have shut up since the departure of your beloved son. This room is full of memories for you, and you do not want it occupied by a stranger. But if your soldier-son was here he would say to you, ''Mother, open up our home to this compatriot, give him the peace of mind that he needs to do his daily task well, welcome his young wife and their small child into our home.'' Because he knows the tragedy of being without a home.

La Presse, Montreal, 23 January 1943

My Dearest:
This is an anniversary note — going from me to you on this special day. I had your flowers today. They are so beautiful — a note attached said that they had no lily of the valley and so sent extra yellow roses — oh darling, the dearness of you to remember — I am gloating over the lovely things . . . I miss you so much — I ache, and not being able to speak to you and hear your voice is having a worse effect each day.

I went to town today to get my flowers and had my hair dressed, came home and have dressed all in white and so here I sit — alone — and dressed for you — over my heart is the brave red patch which I wear so proudly. I can feel you thinking of me tonight — so strongly — your wonderful letters are the only thing happening in my life at the moment — but next to the author, they are the best in the world. With this I send to my beloved all the love in my heart.

Your J.

PS. I still feel that I should address all letters Dear N and censor, and perhaps enclose a word of cheer for the latter.

Letter from a serviceman's wife,
Red Deer, Alta., 25 June 1942

Crowded living conditions in Kingston, Ont. The influx of war workers created acute housing shortages in many urban centres across Canada. PAC PA 142398

GIFT OF PYJAMAS TO
MY LOVE OVERSEAS

I fear you may lie cold in bed
As you from me do bide
Such fears would be superfluous
If I thee lay beside.

An English lass is comfortless
In bed, I have heard tell
And should you this report deny
I'll damn thee, dear, to hell.

Gwen Pharis Ringwood,
"War Time Rhymes to the Man of My Choice"
(unpublished), Edmonton

A TELEGRAM   That afternoon a friend came by the farm to say there was a telegram waiting for us. We didn't have a telephone, and the nearest neighbour with a phone was one and a half miles away.

Dad was sick in bed, and I had trouble getting the stallion harnessed, getting the bit in his mouth, so I walked to the neighbour's to use their phone. The telegram was to say our son Winston was missing through enemy action.

I walked back home to tell Dad. That evening our neighbour drove me over to his place to phone Jessie, my daughter. She was working in Calgary. Jessie came out to the farm right away, but when she got there I couldn't speak. It was too much of a shock. I couldn't get my voice to work.

Then the good news came: Winston was a prisoner of war.

Alberta

BEAUTY — BRIGHT BANNER OF VALOR

How fragile is the beauty of woman, yet it inspires the strength of man. Cheer the way to Victory by looking your loveliest — skin petal-soft and fresh, chin lifted, lips bright, hands caressingly smooth. Care for your beauty for the morale of your country . . . your soldier . . . yourself.

PAC PA 118189

HELLO SOLDIER:

If you'd like to know what the woman in your life is wearing this spring, whether she be your Mom, your Sister, Sweetheart or Wife, you may be sure that something in her wardrobe is in a shade of violet, ranging from deep purple to pale mauve. This year the hats are more frivolous and decorative than ever. Imagine her in a bit of straw with flowers nestling on both sides of her pompadour and soft veiling falling over her face or worn thrown back in a halo effect; or in a smart Breton sailor tilted provocatively over her eyes; or looking cute in a Dutch hat with matching Hobo bag.

Most of us are wearing last year's basic clothes, but we're going berserk over accessories. Did you know, Soldier, that a brand new, becoming hat can do heaps for a gal's morale? Sometimes it can be a badge of courage. . . . [10 April 1944]

HELLO SOLDIER:

. . . In Winnipeg these days people are talking about the Victory Loan, Blood Banks, the war news, mail from overseas, Christmas parcels for the boys, "The White Cliffs of Dover", college rugby games, remodelling and repairing last winter's wardrobe, Teachers' Conventions, putting on storm windows and the lovely October weather we're having with anxiety in their hearts and a smile on their lips, wishing, waiting, hoping and praying that this blankety blank war will be over SOON! SOON! SOON! [25 October 1944]

Letters from Aileen Small to servicemen
from Lac du Bonnet, Man.

CANADA KEEPS FAITH WITH OUR PRISONERS OF WAR

THE RED CROSS HAS PACKED & SHIPPED OVERSEAS 700,000 BOXES LIKE THESE

Do the PRISONERS Receive the PARCELS ? 100,000 RETURN CARDS HAVE BEEN RECEIVED Say YES! they do.

TO PRESERVE HEALTH + There is enough Food in one Parcel along with German Rations to provide an Adequate Diet for one Week

CRCS

ONLY TWENTY-FIVE WORDS   It was eighteen months after Hong Kong surrendered that I got the first letter from my husband, and it had been written a year before. At first I was told he was missing, and it was many months before I knew he was a prisoner of war.

We wrote through the Red Cross, and we could only write twenty-five words. We were asked to be extremely careful what we said. It was very hard to convey reassuring messages like we weren't really short of money, even if we were. I'd write, "We are

well, am not working," or "Children at same school," and hope he'd understand we hadn't run out of money, and hadn't had to move.

He didn't get all the mail I sent, but he got one parcel from me. It went out on the *Gripsholm*; the Red Cross told us what we could send. I sent clothing, but unfortunately I never thought it could get so cold in Hong Kong, so I sent warm-weather clothes and only one sweater — and it didn't have sleeves.

Victoria

2

Ready for Active Service: The Paramilitary

Well before the armed forces began recruiting women in mid-1941, dozens of unofficial women's auxiliary groups had sprung up in cities and towns across the country. Altogether, they boasted 6,700 members. Individual groups created their own command structures and designed their own badges and uniforms. They drilled and paraded publicly, provoking widely varying reactions, as well as some consternation in official military circles. Several unofficial commandants and colonels lobbied the government vigorously, first for official recognition and later for the right to serve as members of a national armed-forces auxiliary.

Many paramilitary women's groups were formed when the war reached a critical stage in 1940, after the collapse of France and the defeat of the British at Dunkirk. In British Columbia, however, some women had begun to organize several years before the actual outbreak of war. Their inspiration came from Britain, where, in September 1938, the Auxiliary Territorial Service was created as the official women's auxiliary of the British Army. Three weeks later, just after the Munich Crisis, ten Victoria women founded the first, unofficial auxiliary-service group in Canada. Originally called the Women's Auxiliary Drivers' Club, it evolved into the British Columbia Women's Service Corps, a province-wide organization with cross-Canada affiliations. Joan B. Kennedy of Victoria,

Controller of the B.C.W.S.C., was one of the original charter members.

In British Columbia other paramilitary groups quickly followed. Elsewhere in Canada, women were slower to organize, but in July 1940 several paramilitary groups sprang up, apparently spontaneously, in different cities across Canada. After Dunkirk, the groups offered many Canadian women a means of responding to the war, and of becoming personally involved.

In several provinces various groups competed for members. To some degree, they also competed with the newly formed Canadian Red Cross Corps, a smartly uniformed all-women's organization launched by the National Council of the Canadian Red Cross Society in June 1940. As part of an international voluntary organization, however, the C.R.C.C. did not seek admission to any possible Army auxiliary corps.

Uniforms of these different auxiliary groups varied from simple armbands and berets to professionally designed outfits made of serge or barathea, and were a matter of pride. On several occasions the Department of National Defence considered issuing warnings that women wearing unauthorized uniforms and badges were in violation of the Criminal Code as well as of the Defence of Canada Regulations.

By late 1940 some paramilitary groups had developed branches outside their province of origin. The

Members of the Red Cross Transport Service, Toronto, begin their daily five-mile march. The intensive six-week course for drivers included map- and compass-reading, Air Raid Precautions, advanced mechanics, blackout driving, and driving with gas masks. Many went overseas as ambulance drivers. CRCS

Women's Volunteer Reserve Corps—"the Beavers"—had units in the Maritime provinces and in Ontario, as well as in Quebec. The Canadian Auxiliary Territorial Service, which began in Toronto, acquired affiliates as far away as Saskatoon and Vancouver. The British Columbia Women's Service Corps was affiliated with groups in Alberta, Ontario, and Nova Scotia. None, however, was given official recognition, despite much lobbying by Joan Kennedy and her supporters.

The various unofficial auxiliaries did not disappear immediately after recruiting began for the Canadian Women's Auxiliary Corps (later the Canadian Women's Army Corps) and the Canadian Women's Auxiliary Air Force (later the R.C.A.F., Women's Division) in the summer of 1941. But many of the self-appointed officers were quick to join the services. Joan Kennedy became the first Officer Administering, C.W.A.C., in 1942, and in 1943 General Staff Officer, with responsibility for advising on training. Madeline Nation of Vancouver, Ethel English of Calgary, and M.E. Mumford of Halifax also joined the C.W.A.C. Evelyn Mills of Montreal became an officer in the Women's Royal Canadian Naval Service, created in 1942. For many Service Corps members, the recruitment of women into the armed forces finally gave them the opportunity they had wanted from the beginning.

WOMEN VOLUNTEER FOR RED CROSS

Montreal women and girls by the hundreds crowded the Red Cross volunteer office in the Drummond Building all day Saturday to offer their services in case Canada is at war. From 8:00 am in the morning until 5:00 pm, there was a steady stream of volunteers offering to serve as nurses, ambulance drivers and in dozens of other capacities.

Montreal *Gazette*, 4 September 1939

Canadian Red Cross Corps transport drivers in Air Raid Precautions (A.R.P.) demonstration, Toronto, 1941. TT 100-677

PEAKED CAPS AND TRENCH COATS   I got into the Red Cross Corps in Brockville, in the Nursing Section. We learned about bandages and making beds, how to read a thermometer, what to do in case of shock.

We wore grey dresses, shirt-waister type, with different-coloured ties for different units. Mine was blue. We had grey peaked caps and trench coats. We went to the Armouries every week. We formed up into platoons and we drilled and paraded about.

The Army asked the Red Cross for volunteers at the Officers' Training Centre, and I worked at night as a secretary to the Chief Medical Officer.

Brockville, Ont.

THEY'RE TRAINED AND READY FOR SERVICE OVERSEAS

Women to Drive Ambulances and Do V.A.D. Work

Trained and led by veterans, 150 Montreal women who have given up their spare time since last September to fit themselves for war work are now ready for service overseas as ambulance drivers or Voluntary Aid Detachment duties whenever such units are authorized by the Department of National Defence.

Completing their refresher course in various military subjects today, the company of four platoons, which is commanded by Mrs. W. D. Chambers, who won a Military Medal in the last war for heroic work during a German bombing raid, was inspected by Lt.-Col. K. M. Perry, D.S.O., president of the Quebec Division of the Canadian Red Cross Society, organizer of the course.

Montreal First

Montreal is believed to have been the first Canadian city to have organized such a unit, and the 150 members include 120 prospective motor ambulance drivers and 30 who have trained for nursing services.

The course included training in first aid by the St. John Ambulance Association, physical culture, lectures on sanitation and hygiene and cooking. Mechanical training for the ambulance drivers was given through the co-operation of General Motors and the

In April 1940, 150 Montreal women completed a Red Cross training course for ambulance drivers and Voluntary Aid Detachment workers overseas. Courtesy K. Catterill

Ford Motor Company, while the military training included map-reading, military discipline and duties, rank badges and road signals.

The second-in-command of the unit is Mrs. Dudley Ross, while the adjutant, Mrs. Lennox Black, is also a World War veteran who wears the Victory and General Service medals earned as a V.A.D. in France in the last war.

There are approximately 40 French-Canadian women in the company.

Montreal Star, 30 April 1940

ARP WORKERS STAGE STRIKING DEMONSTRATION

NORTH VANCOUVER, May 19—"Bombs" burst and "spot-fires" burned to the heavy roar of a low-flying RCAF bomber, and nurses, first aid men and ARP [Air Raid Precautions] wardens worked for nearly an hour Sunday afternoon, in a vivid, realistic demonstration of actual air raid conditions in Mahon Park.

An estimated 5,000 persons, who crowded the grandstand and lined the field, thrilled at the precision of the carefully-worked-out plans to combat conditions that would exist should a night air raid ever strike the North Shore.

The demonstration had all the drama of an actual raid.

There was the scream of sirens to herald the air raid warning and the "all clear"; there was an electric tenseness in the air, the roar of the bombers, the boom of exploding bombs and the acrid smell of burned gunpowder.

There were the frantically working volunteer fire fighters; engineers maintaining vital services like telephone and water supply; first aiders and nurses treating injured; scouts relaying messages that play a vital part in the work; central ARP posts, and ARP wardens constantly patrolling their districts.

Members of the Canadian Women's Training Corps took messages from ARP posts, located at strategic positions on the field.

For an hour previous to the actual demonstration a parade, a drumhead service and drills entertained the crowds. Drills were provided by members of the Canadian Women's Training Corps and the High School Cadets.

From a Vancouver newspaper, 1940 or 1941

St. John Ambulance Brigade members participate in provincial A.R.P. demonstration in Varsity Arena, Toronto, 1940. TT 100-676.
"The demonstration was presented before a huge backdrop representing a section of street, accompanied by screams of sirens and noise of bombs. Firefighting, demolition casualty and other work was demonstrated by groups of men and women." *The Evening Telegram*, Toronto, Wednesday, 6 November 1940.

SPRAY WATER ALL OVER A BOMB   I made St. John Ambulance training compulsory for all women students. They did first aid in the first term and home nursing in the second term. O.T.C. [Officers' Training Corps] was compulsory for the men. We had special lectures from the fire department. At the time we thought incendiary bombs might be dropped, we trained the students to spray water all over a bomb. A direct, strong hose on them would have caused them to explode. The head of the Phys. Ed. department organized drill and preliminary basic training in preparation for women going into the services. Some of them took motor mechanics at K.C.V.I. [Kingston Collegiate Vocational Institute].

Dean of Women, Queen's University, Kingston, Ont.

One hundred and fifty McGill University co-eds practise fire-fighting under the direction of the Montreal Fire Department, January 1942. PAC 108236

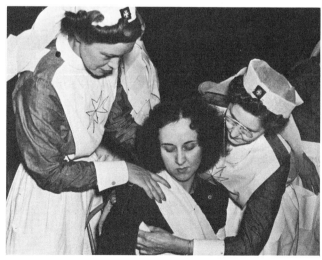

UNIVERSITY WOMEN'S TRAINING DETACHMENT SWINGS INTO ACTION

The University Women's Service Training Detachment turned out enthusiastically yesterday afternoon on the Trinity College Campus for their first organization drill. They marched in mufti, for their uniforms are still in the process of selection and manufacture. Both the uniform and the drill are required to give them army discipline for their more unromantic Red Cross work.

Evening Telegram, Toronto, 1 November 1940

The Hon. J. T. Thorson,
Minister of National War Services,
Ottawa, Canada

Dear Sir:

   The women of the Faculty of Arts at the University of Western Ontario are exploring the possibility of organizing certain training courses for women students desirous of preparing themselves for some kind of National Defence.

At a meeting held this week, the following courses were discussed:

Emergency Bacteriology
Hospital Laboratory Technique
   Water Sterilization
   Inoculation
A.R.P.
   Gas
   Decontamination
   Incendiary Bombs
Airplane Recognition
Home Nursing
First Aid
Occupational Therapy
Map Reading
Coding
Elementary Radio & Electricity
Nutrition
Group Feeding

   Would you be good enough to give us the advantage of your advice in this matter as to whether any of these, or other, courses would be of value?

Letter signed Jean T. Neville, chairman of the women's committee, Faculty of Arts, University of Western Ontario, London, 8 November 1941

Toronto, November 1940. University Women's Service Training Detachment hold their first organizational drill on Trinity campus.
TT100-676

Canadian Women's Training Corps members on duty in the A.R.P. Control Room, Vancouver, December 1941. PAC PA 112709

DEFINITELY A LEADER   Joan Kennedy was the prime mover in starting the British Columbia Women's Service Club—later known as the Corps. Its object was to train women to serve in the armed forces in the same manner as the Auxiliary Territorial Service in Britain, which was formed in 1938. It was hoped that the Corps would be recognized by National Defence Headquarters as a Corps of the Militia. Joan and nine others were the charter members.

By the time I joined in September 1939 I believe there were over one hundred members in Victoria, and other detachments had been formed on the Island and the mainland. Victoria detachment was organized as a battalion with four companies—clerical, motor transport, catering, and first aid. Each was trained in its own field, plus basic infantry drill. We paraded one or two evenings a week.

In the spring of 1940 we had a large influx of recruits—more than 150. I was by this time Regimental Sergeant-Major, and this group was handed over to me to train. I had to give lectures on various subjects about which I knew little, so had to do quite a bit of studying in between parades! Joan was very good at getting instructors from the Army, and the training I got was better than any I personally had in the Army later on.

At the time I first knew her, Joan was in her early thirties. She was most definitely a leader. She was rather like a terrier—bright-eyed, alert, intelligent, scrappy, and persistent.

Victoria

EVERYONE CHIPPED IN   Early in the war I remember that everyone chipped in a couple of dollars to send our leader, Joan Kennedy, to Ottawa. The trip was to persuade the powers in Ottawa that women in the armed services were a good idea.

Victoria

SEVERAL HUNDRED TURNED UP   In February 1939 there was a big ad in the paper for the B.C. Women's Service Corps, about a meeting in the Marine Building. Several hundred of us turned up.

There were some women in uniform, and one of them was Joan Kennedy, from Victoria. They passed out papers for people to sign up, and one of them said, "Hey! Don't you want to read what it says before you put your name on it?" But we were so keen, we just signed anyway.

We drilled regularly, I remember, in our uniforms. We wore navy-blue skirts, white shirts, and royal blue tams with a maple leaf on them. We had armbands made of felt, with a maple leaf on them, too.

When war broke out I used to go down to the Beatty Street drill hall and type out the applications for the men joining up.

Vancouver

"FALL IN! 'TEN-SHUN!"   As we sit in the Officers' gallery of Vancouver's military drill hall an unusual scene is being enacted on the grey asphalt floor below. The utmost feminine martial activity prevails. British Columbia's women have mobilized for "National Emergency".

Military drill sergeants are putting them through their paces—these purposeful women of the Second Detachment, Women's Service Corps of British Columbia. The rafters ring with the echoes of crisp army commands: "Fall in! 'ten-shun! Right dress! Eyes right! Mark time. Forward march!" Commands are repeated in the ringing treble voices of feminine officers. Companies wheel, form fours, about-turn, move with smooth precision as the intricacies of army foot drill are mastered with surprising acumen.

A trim band of women, they are wearing spotless white shirtwaists, trim blue skirts and stout British brogues. They expect to don a uniform (utilitarian) some day—if Ottawa can see its way to bestow official recognition and a Government grant.

Yvonne H. Stevenson, *Saturday Night*, 5 August 1939

Founding members of the British Columbia Women's Service Corps, Victoria, 1938. Joan Kennedy is at the far left. Mrs. C. H. Rayment, the first president, is in the front row centre.
BCA 96262 neg. G-3021

FINER STUFF THAN MEN

If anyone had wanted proof of the fitness and readiness to serve of British Columbia's women, he had only to attend their church parade Sunday.

Estimated at 800 strong, they won admiration on all sides as they swung smartly along Georgia Street to Christ Church Cathedral.

Young and not so young, big and small, blonde, brunette, redhead and grey-head, they all bore that trained, confident air of soldiers.

In the van was the Argyll and Sutherland Pipe Band, followed by a detachment of Edmonton Fusiliers — soldiers who were proud to escort such fair company.

In High Praise
Leading the women were the B.C. Women's Service Corps, in their blue berets and skirts and white blouses. Behind them the Canadian Women's Training Corps, smart in their navy blue uniforms and forage caps.

Third in line was the B.C. Women's Ambulance Corps, in lighter blue. Two detachments of teenage girl cadets brought up the rear.

Stating that he felt a deep sense of honour in addressing such a gathering, Dean Cecil Swanson told them ''I think women are made of finer stuff than men.

''I think the fact that they are mothers or potential mothers gives them a fierceness in the defence of their homes.''

From a Vancouver newspaper, 1940 or 1941

ARMY OF 1,000 WOMEN   Mrs. Winnifred Richards who has the rank of Lieutenant Colonel in the Canadian Women's Service Force said today (Toronto, CP) 500 Toronto women are under military training. She said the organization had been recognized by the federal government and that approval to recruit an army of 1,000 for home defence and replacement, if required, of men now enlisted for active service has been granted. The Force was organized five weeks ago. Drills are held in city parks and school grounds.

Mrs. Richards served during the first Great War as a delegate member of the Canadian Imperial Women's Veterans' Corps.

Victoria Times, 28 August 1940

VICTORIA B C 28 AUGUST 1940

COL J L RALSTON

MINISTER OF NATIONAL DEFENCE OTTAWA ONT

CANADIAN PRESS CARRIES REPORT TONIGHT THAT MRS WINNIFRED RICHARDS OF TORONTO HAS PERMISSION OF GOVERNMENT TO RECRUIT ONE THOUSAND WOMEN FOR HOME DEFENCE AND THE UNIT ORGANIZED FIVE WEEKS AGO HAS BEEN RECOGNIZED BY THE FEDERAL GOVERNMENT STOP THE BC WOMENS SERVICE CORPS REPRESENTING ELEVEN UNITS IN THIS PROVINCE AND COMPRISING TWELVE HUNDRED ACTIVE MEMBERS WANT TO KNOW WHAT FORM THIS RECOGNITION TAKES AND WHAT IS THE POSITION OF THE BC WOMENS SERVICE CORPS IN RELATION TO THE NEW TORONTO UNIT INSOFAR AS OUR REQUEST FOR RECOGNITION AND OFFICIAL STATUS FOR THE SAME PURPOSE STILL REMAIN UNDECIDED BY YOUR DEPARTMENT PLEASE REPLY BY RETURN

MRS NORMAN R KENNEDY CONTROLLER BC WOMENS
SERVICE CORPS
CANADIAN PACIFIC TELEGRAPHS

29TH AUGUST, 1940

MRS NORMAN R KENNEDY

VICTORIA, BC

DEPARTMENT OF NATIONAL DEFENCE HAS NO KNOWLEDGE OF THE MATTER MENTIONED IN YOUR TELEGRAM

J. L. RALSTON, MINISTER OF NATIONAL DEFENCE
CANADIAN PACIFIC TELEGRAPHS

Joan B. Kennedy (*left*), Controller-in-Chief, British Columbia Women's Service Corps, and A. Jean MacLennan, Commandant, HQ Division, inspect the Victoria detachment. By January 1940 the B.C.W.S.C. had detachments in seven centres in the province. A tally in the fall of that year identified fourteen units with a total membership of 2,500. BCA cat. 96263 neg. G-3002

Hon. J. R. Thorsen [*sic*]
Minister of Auxiliary War Services
Ottawa, Ontario, Canada.

Honorable Sir:
. . . The Alberta Women's Service Corps operates under its own Charter and is run on military lines.

This corps was formed in July 1940:
a) for the purpose of fostering, encouraging and developing the spirit of voluntary service amongst women.
b) for the purpose of training women in every form of service that could be useful in case of National Emergency, or that may be required by the Dominion of Canada or the Province of Alberta.

The corps is uniformed very smartly and neatly, the uniform consisting of a blue-grey tunic and skirt, with maple leaf badges in gold, black beret, grey hose and black brogues; each member pays for her own uniform.

The income of the corps is derived from the women themselves, each member paying dues which cover expenses of maintaining a building for drill and instructional purposes and all operating expenses. . . .

Letter from the Deputy Controller,
Alberta Women's Service Corps, Edmonton,
19 November 1941

SNIDE LAUGHTER   I belonged to the Alberta Women's Service Corps for nearly a year, drilling and training. There were many smiles, and snide laughter. People thought we were mad, that there would never be any call for women. We met at Western Canada High School in Calgary once a week, and we spent half an hour marching and drilling . . . the parade-square thing. Then we broke up into occupational groups, to wit mechanics, ambulance driving, first aid, and related things.

Alberta Women's Service Corps banquet, Edmonton. Ethel English of Calgary was Chief Commandant of the A.W.S.C., a provincial organization with branches in Edmonton and other centres. AA BL67511

We wore a uniform: a blue gabardine skirt and jacket, with a pale-blue shirt and a black tie and a black tam. My relatives viewed it with absolute horror —my parents were dead, but I had uncles and aunts. And old family friends—you can put a question mark after friends—actually crossed the street rather than meet me in uniform. That was a very great hurt.

Calgary

I PLAYED THE BASS DRUM   We wore blue-grey uniforms. Training offered was drilling and marching, motor mechanics, first aid, Morse code, and map-reading. The band was a pipe-and-drum band and I played the bass drum. We took part in Armistice Day services for the First War; I remember marching in the parade.

We were a service club and we raised money for the war effort by ushering and canvassing for funds. We packed parcels for soldiers too.

Regina

FIGHTING FEMALES

Plans for a Regiment of Women

Winnipeg may yet have Canada's first all-women fighting regiment. Such a unit became a possibility Friday with the announcement by Mrs. Gloria Queen-Hughes that registration of women interested would begin at

Band members, Saskatchewan Auxiliary Territorial Service, May 1942. S.A.T.S. emphasized community service, as well as military drill. Courtesy Ruth Williams

the Commercial Girls' Club, 309 Power Building, at 10 o'clock Monday morning.

While the amount of training that will be undertaken by the unit would depend largely on the number joining, present plans included training in the use of firearms, rifle drill, signalling and general military discipline, Mrs. Queen-Hughes said.

"We are trying to look ahead," she said.

Mrs. Queen-Hughes pointed out that the time might yet come when the need for men overseas might leave it up to the women of Canada to guard their nation. The reserve would be for that purpose. No sanction for the force had been received from M.D.

10, she added. Male instructors would be used in the preliminary stages.

Official comment on the reserve was not available at headquarters at Fort Osborne Barracks, Friday.

Undated clipping, *Winnipeg Free Press*,
July or August 1940

I WASN'T GOING TO SIT AND KNIT!   Other girls in the Manitoba government office knitted socks for soldiers at lunchtime, but I wasn't going to sit and knit! I joined the Women's Auxiliary Corps after Gloria [Queen-Hughes] advertised in the press, and I was in the Corps for two years before I joined the Army.

There must have been five hundred or even eight hundred girls in the Corps. We thought we could make a contribution to the war effort. Gloria said, "In war, women have the most to lose. We should do what we can to protect our way of life. Or our families, our children, will suffer."

We had to have an occupation which the Army could use — stenos, or filing clerks, or drivers, etc. I was a steno. We took classes in telegraphy, map-reading, and gas drills. People thought us a bit wacky when we put on drills in public parks. Our battalion drilled in Assiniboia Park.

Winnipeg

A VERY CONTROVERSIAL PERSON   Gloria Queen-Hughes was a very outspoken, controversial person. She got people's backs up. When she recruited us for the Women's Auxiliary Corps a lot of men snickered behind their hands, and a lot of mothers said it was degrading.

We met in the evenings to drill. I didn't have a uniform, I couldn't afford one, so I wore a navy-blue suit and a white blouse, and oxfords. We all wore little wedge caps.

Winnipeg

Hon. Joe Thorson
Minister of Auxiliary Services
Ottawa, Ontario.

Dear Mr. Thorson:
I am writing to you in the hope that you may have some information regarding Lord Beaverbrook's [Canadian-born Minister of Aircraft Production in the British government] appeal for at least 5,000 women who will be trained as radio technicians. Apparently they would be used to help operate Britain's new defence against night bombings.

Gloria Queen-Hughes founded the Women's Auxiliary Corps in Winnipeg in July 1940. Seen here in her uniform as a captain in the Canadian Women's Army Corps, Queen-Hughes went overseas in December 1942 with her company. WCPI 169-05293

I have been organizing classes and drill for girls for the past eleven months with the result that we have many girls who could fill the requirements of the above call. We are set up on a military basis, for the express purpose of assisting the armed forces as the women of Britain are.

I would be proud to recruit Canadian women to fill the appeal.

You may remember my husband — he was a member of the Institute of International Affairs. He is now out of the country on Active Service, and since we have no children, I am quite free to give my time to war work. I am also willing and anxious to go overseas if I can help there.

Letter from Gloria Queen-Hughes, Officer
Commanding, Women's Auxiliary Corps,
Winnipeg, 19 June 1941

30 Back the Attack!

"CATS" PEPPER TARGETS   The trail of "CATS" led out the Lakeshore Road to the Long Branch Rifle Ranges Saturday afternoon.

The "CATS", by now an established term for the Canadian Auxiliary Territorial Service, had decided it would be an ideal day for them to prove to the Veterans' Home Guard that they could hit targets in a way to make experts take a few pointers.

And prove it they did.

Sprawled on the long blanket-covered mound in varying positions so they wouldn't get cramped while shooting, the women were garbed in a weird assortment of roomy slacks and skirts topped with shirts, sweaters and jackets. Sporty hats of the type bowlers wear, handkerchiefs and wrap-around kerchiefs served to keep the hair out of their eyes as they took careful aim at targets 25 yards away.

The instructor, Lieut. Tommy Vamplew, R.O., said the association was the only civilian one that boasted full cooperation of the government. Before allowing the girls to use rifles, Mr. Vamplew had instructed them in safety-first precautions. In a preliminary lesson he had thoroughly taught them the three most important things to remember — good aim, steady trigger release and a comfortable shooting position.

More than a hundred girls and women turned out during the day for practice and others had to be turned away. The recently-formed organization grew to 500 members in the past week, according to Miss Ivy Maison, originator of the plan.

"All of them are prepared to leave everything and go wherever needed in any emergency," she said. The group has become so large it is necessary for the women now registering to wait until their turn comes for training. All the members are from 20 to 45 years of age and in good health.

A number of women officers are being taught to take charge of sections so the group can expand and take in everyone who wants to learn first aid, motor mechanics, army cooking and marching.

Margaret Wheeler, *Evening Telegram*,
Toronto, 15 July 1941

Members of the Canadian Auxiliary Territorial Service are instructed in the proper way to fire a rifle, Toronto, July 1940. Ivy Maison organized the program. TT 100-677

HUNDREDS OF WOMEN ANSWER CALL TO WAR SERVICE

Registration for the Women's Volunteer Reserve Corps sponsored by the Westmount Women's Club got off to a rousing start yesterday afternoon when in the first few hours more than 1,000 women thronged the doors to register at the Y.W.C.A., 4548 Sherbrooke St. W. The Corps is being organized on the lines of the Women's Auxiliary Force in England and its members are to be known as the Canadian Beavers. The emblem will be a maple leaf with a beaver in the centre, the motto ''Unity of Purpose''.

The Corps will be open for all sorts of war services, to stand behind the government in any way that may be required during times of emergency. The first physical drill will be held tonight in Trinity Memorial Church Hall. Arrangements are being made for rifle practice in clubs. Home nursing, invalid cooking and handicraft courses are to be given. The salvage corps will beg dresses worth recutting for clothes for refugee children and children of men overseas. . . .

Among those registering were women from across the country, including some who wanted to leave their homes in the west and come and work in the Corps. These were advised to stay at home and start corps in their own provinces and cities. The majority who volunteered were college women with qualifications for many different and important types of work: linguists, chemists, nurses. . . .

Montreal *Gazette*, 28 June 1940

Unidentified paramilitary group on parade, Toronto. TT 100-676

MY LIEUTENANT'S BADGE   I was on a teacher-exchange program in Montreal when I joined the Women's Volunteer Reserve. This was in 1940, before the government decided to admit women to the armed forces.

We marched and drilled and did all the same things that I did a few months later in the Air Force. I took the course for officers, and I got my lieutenant's badge and then my captain's in the Women's Volunteer Reserve Corps. I got my uniform too, although I never wore it, of course, because I joined the W.D.s.

We wore little bags over our shoulders, about ten inches by eight inches, and we called them ''Puddicombes'', after the officer who trained us.

Saskatoon

WOMEN'S CORPS STARTS RIFLE TRAINING

Mrs. A. Rubens, commander of the company, explained training in use of the rifle is in no way intended to equip women for combat duty, but to develop ''nerve control, steadiness, a spirit to succeed, concentration and a working acquaintance with a rifle that will ensure safety in its possible use''. In this particular instance, the women are using .22 calibre rifles and during the course of the evening many proved to be capable shots.

Montreal *Gazette*, 19 July 1940

''The Flying Seven'' women's aeronautical club, Vancouver, trained women in parachute-packing and wireless radio operation to prepare for work as ground-crew assistants with the R.C.A.F. In 1940 the club showered Vancouver with 100,000 pamphlets from the air appealing for ''dimes or dollars to buy our boys more planes''. VSWG

ALL CONDITIONS AND EMERGENCIES

. . . I know the problem you are faced with in regard to the employment of women in military capacity. Hence this suggestion that the Government should finance this as an experiment. I am sure that $200 would be ample to cover this.

I would advertise for experienced waitresses and cooks willing to put in hard work. I would interview them personally as I would not want any except willing, clean women of good moral standards of behaviour. These women would be given lectures on economy, rationing, diet, planning of meals and cooking with military rations and then, when other funds are available, the purchasing and cooking under all conditions and emergencies.

I would suggest the military then place at our disposal a small cook house and mess for a week's tryout and I know that given a fair chance this will be a great success.

Letter to the Minister of National Defence,
Montreal, 22 March, 1941

DRILLING, SIGNALLING, SHOOTING

Week after week the Halifax Women's Canadian Service Corps carries on its training in all branches of army work, drilling, signalling, shooting, transport truck driving, convoy driving and now a new course in motorcycle riding has been started.

These women, now numbering more than 250, are working entirely on a voluntary basis, supplying their own uniforms, giving freely of their time several nights a week, preparing to take men's jobs in the army should an emergency arise.

Undated clipping, Halifax newspaper, c. 1940

CONVINCE THE SENIOR MILITARY   When I
decided to start an Auxiliary Service in Halifax I wrote a letter to the C.O. of Military District No.6, who at that time was [Major-]General Constantine. I knew I would require experienced military personnel to train the girls, not having the experience myself. And, of course, we required space to do it. It was not an easy task at that time to convince the senior military that women would be required to serve.

Weeks went by and then I got a letter from the C.O. He gave me his blessing and arranged military personnel to help me. I decided the women would all be single and ready to join the regular force when they were required. The girls in my Corps paid for their own uniforms and I decided they would be like

Lieut.-Col. Evelyn Mills, Commanding Officer, and Major Sophy Elliott, second-in-command, Women's Volunteer Reserve Corps, Montreal, August 1940. PAC PA 140754

C.A.T.S. signaller practising. TT 100-677

A.T.S. [Auxiliary Territorial Service, in Britain] uniforms.

With the help of my officers I organized similar Corps throughout Nova Scotia, only on a smaller basis. Then I discussed affiliation with Mrs. N. R. Kennedy's Corps in British Columbia [the B.C. Women's Service Corps], which we did.

Letter from M. E. Mumford, Victoria

MAP-READING AND FIRST AID   Our uniform was very much in the A.T.S. style — khaki, with a belted jacket which wasn't too complimentary to some of our figures. We bought our own uniforms but the military trained us. These men taught us map-reading and first aid, motor mechanics, drill — it was all very useful when we went into the C.W.A.C. [Canadian Women's Army Corps].

Halifax

FOUND WOMEN EAGER TO SERVE

Tremendously encouraged by the sympathetic interest in and the growth of the movement all across Canada, Mrs. Norman Kennedy, controller-in-chief of the B.C. Women's Service Club [*sic*], has returned to Victoria after a two months' absence.

Accompanied by Mrs. A. F. Nation, Vancouver commandant of the Club, Mrs. Kennedy went to Ottawa to interview the authorities with a view to obtaining official recognition of the Club. They met with a most sympathetic hearing and Mrs. Kennedy was assured that the matter of the women's organizations is under serious consideration but it is unlikely any decision will be reached until the return of the Minister of Defence, Col. the Hon. J. L. Ralston, from England.

Visited Many Groups
Before presenting their brief at Ottawa, Mrs. Kennedy and Mrs. Nation visited cities between Winnipeg and Halifax to ascertain the extent of the movement to train women to complement the work of the forces, along such lines as motor mechanics, truck and ambulance drivers, clerical and commissariat duties.

They found everywhere signs of the growing desire of the women of Canada to lend every practical support to the war effort and on their mission to Ottawa were empowered to represent, not only the B.C. Women's Service Club, but also the Alberta Women's Service Corps, the Winnipeg Women's Volunteer Corps, the Canadian Auxiliary Territorial Service (C.A.T.S.) of Toronto, the Canadian Women's Service Corps, Toronto, the Women's Volunteer Reserve Corps of Montreal, known as the Beavers, the Halifax Women's Service Corps and the Peterborough Service Corps and all their affiliated branches.

Met Princess Alice
While in Ottawa, Mrs. Kennedy and Mrs. Nation were privileged to have a private audience with the Princess Alice. As commander-in-chief of the Wom-en's Transport Service in Great Britain before coming to Canada to take over her new duties as chatelaine of Rideau Hall, Her Royal Highness was intensely interested in the magnificent war work being done by the women of Canada. . . .

Clipping, *Victoria Times*, December 1940

WOMEN MUST BE RECOGNIZED   . . . Women should be doing more than merely knitting socks and packing parcels for the soldiers. . . . in every Province of the Dominion there are companies of women studying motor mechanics, cooking, nursing, clerical work and many other lines of national service. In British Columbia alone there are 1700 women who have trained themselves at their own expense and are now ready to relieve men for active service. . . . we have come to the place where women must be recognized and allowed to do everything in their power to assist Canada's war effort.

I hope there will not be any tedious delay.

Letter from Nellie McClung to Prime Minister
Mackenzie King, 14 December 1940

EQUALITY OF SACRIFICE   . . . Many Canadian women feel today that they are being denied that equality of sacrifice for which opportunity is accorded the women of the mother country.

They have had no opportunity as yet to serve in any public organization, nor have the auxiliary organizations which they have set up been given that recognition to which I believe they are entitled. I would ask the Minister of National War Services what use is being made of the training which these women are voluntarily undertaking. In the old country, women are organized into what one might call military corps: the Women's Royal Naval Service, in which they are enlisted as cooks, bookkeepers and the like; the Women's Auxiliary Territorial Service, where they are enlisted as clerks, stenographers and the like; the Women's Auxiliary Air Force, where they are organized under supervision to do work which is ordinarily done by men. . . . What is the government doing towards organizing the women of Canada along similar lines? . . . It has been estimated that women could take over 10 per cent of the positions now occupied by men in the armed forces of Canada.

John George Diefenbaker, House of
Commons, 19 March 1941

Recruits from western Canada, bound for the Canadian Women's Army Corps training centre at Vermilion, Alta., 1942. When the C.W.A.C. was formed in 1941, many self-appointed paramilitary officers were quick to join the new service. MA 198

REALLY, MR. RALSTON! The speech delivered by Defence Minister Ralston recently in the House of Commons on the employment of women in war work is one which must have place among the great addresses of all time — in the poppycock division.

The honorable gentleman explained . . . that in Canada there appeared to be only room in the forces for 1,500 women. Mr. Ralston acknowledged that 1,500 was an infinitesimal number compared with the number of women offering their services. Just how did Mr. Ralston and his staff arrive at this figure?

Women, conceded Mr. Ralston, might be used to a limited extent as drivers and as cooks in permanent camps. Why limited? As for stenographers, difficulties would occur, opines the Minister, in perhaps his best effort of the day:

> Clerical work in connection with field formations could not be performed by women, as the clerical staff of such formations had to go into the field and endure the conditions to which the units would be subject.

Prunes and prisms!

Kennethe M. Haig, editorial page,
Winnipeg Free Press, 2 April 1941

JOINING UP When the government announced there was going to be an Army Corps, our Commanding Officer, Mrs. English, phoned us individually at work, saying, "If you'd like to enlist, go down to the Post Office building to register." I had to do it in my lunch hour, and I was so excited I ran all the way, seventeen blocks.

The Depression was barely over, and I had my first real job, as a comptometer operator for Model Dairies. But I left it without a thought. For me, joining up was sixty per cent patriotism and forty per cent adventure.

Alberta Women's Service Corps, Calgary

3
Shoulder to Shoulder: The Canadian Women's Army Corps

MA 162

On 17 July 1941, newspapers across Canada carried a Canadian Press story datelined Ottawa which began: "The Canadian (Active) Army will issue a call very shortly for 1500 women for the new auxiliary corps, Defence Minister Ralston said today." Colonel Ralston also announced that Matron-in-Chief Elizabeth Smellie of the Royal Canadian Army Medical Corps had been asked to supervise the organization of the Corps.

The Canadian Women's Auxiliary Corps, established by Order-in-Council on 13 August 1941, was organized on a military basis but not subject to military law. Women would take over such jobs as drivers of light vehicles; cooks in hospitals and messes; clerks, typists, and stenographers at camps and training centres; telephone operators and messengers; canteen helpers and mess women. Between 2,000 and 3,000 women would eventually be absorbed into the Army, the Department of National Defence estimated.

Unlike the Air Force, which had begun to recruit six weeks earlier, the Army did not bring in officers from Britain to help organize the Corps. Matron-in-Chief Smellie set out immediately on a cross-Canada tour to organize a nucleus of women staff officers from each of Canada's eleven military districts. There was no large pool of professional Canadian women to draw upon, and few among those she

chose had had any experience with voluntary organizations. Those accepted were required to be women of good character, from families of good standing, with names that would be recognized. Smellie recommended that Joan B. Kennedy of Victoria should become the Officer Administering, C.W.A.C. Kennedy did not have the social standing of some of the other women named, but she had relevant experience. As Controller of the British Columbia Women's Service Corps, she had fought hard for the establishment of an Army auxiliary corps.

C.W.A.C. Staff Officers from each military district joined the new service as Junior Commanders. Their ranks were copied from the British Auxiliary Territorial Service, but their badges were Canadian: Junior Commanders wore three maple leaves upon their shoulders until March 1942, when the ranks and badges changed.

That month the C.W.A.C. had ceased to be an auxiliary corps and became an integral part of the Canadian Army. Although the initials remained the same, they now stood for the Canadian Women's Army Corps. Ranks and badges were quickly altered to correspond with those of the regular Army. Corps members were, however, designated as volunteers, and not soldiers, and it was clearly stated that they would replace men only in non-combat activities.

After their basic training at Kitchener, Ontario, or Vermilion, Alberta, selected servicewomen were sent to trade schools, depending on aptitude and previous experience. Courses ran from two weeks to six months in the initial thirty occupations that were open to women. These were primarily in the areas of food preparation and office work. By March 1945 opportunities for CWACs had expanded to encompass a total of fifty-five trades. The majority of trainees went into occupations that paralleled women's work in civilian life.

The first CWACs to serve abroad were sent to Washington, D.C., to the Canadian Joint Service Mission. By November 1942 the first overseas draft was on its way to Britain. In all, approximately 3,000 CWACs served in Britain and in Europe.

With the end of the war foreseen in 1944, plans were made to demobilize all three women's services. A survey made by Lieutenant-Colonel Mary Dover early in 1945 showed that many CWACs were interested in remaining in the service, should it continue. That possibility was never seriously considered by the Department of National Defence. By the time the Corps was disbanded in 1946, well over 20,000 women had served in the C.W.A.C., approximately 3,000 of them in Britain, Europe, and the United States.

I DIDN'T TELL MY PARENTS   It was one hundred per cent adventure for me. I wanted something new. I'd had a fight with my boyfriend, and I went and joined the Army. I didn't tell my parents until I was shipped to Calgary for my basic training.

Alberta

BREAKING THE NEWS   When I went back to the farm to tell my parents I'd joined the Army, my mother was alone in the kitchen, and she broke down in tears. "Wait till your father gets home!" she said. "Whatever is he going to say?" When he did come in, he said: "You may be twenty-one but I can still give you a thrashing!" I was twenty-four years old.

Alberta

IF I WERE YOUR AGE . . .   There was just my mother, my brother, and I, and my brother had joined up. I showed my mother the ad in the paper and I said, "I'm going to do it." She said, "You go ahead. If I were your age I'd join up myself."

There was no basic training at that time. I worked in ordnance, on Catherine St. [Ottawa]. We supplied gun parts to other districts.

Ontario

THREE REFERENCES   In 1941 you had to be above average to qualify. You needed three references, from a clergyman, from a businessman, and from one other person not related to you. Your background was very closely investigated. Later on in the war they weren't so particular.

Toronto

C.W.A.C. recruiting poster. NMC S83-19

WHAT TO DO WITH US   I got a slip of paper telling me to report to Stanley Barracks on September 1, 1941. Nine of us turned up.

When we got there nobody knew what to do with us! It was a public holiday. Eventually we were sent to Chorley Park military hospital, because there were nursing sisters there — other women! That's why they sent us there.

I worked in the Quartermaster's Stores at Chorley Park for a month before Junior Commander Eaton asked me to be her secretary. She was staff officer for the Toronto area, M.D.2.

I got my basic training after hours, in the evenings.

Toronto

Joan Kennedy, first C.W.A.C. Staff Officer for Military District No. 11, became the first Officer Administering, C.W.A.C. In 1943 Kennedy was made General Staff Officer with responsibility for advising on training. PAC PA 128245

BLACK ARMBANDS   For three months the first CWACs to enlist in Calgary wore black armbands bearing the initials CWAC in red. [Recuits in other areas wore red armbands with gold initials.] There were no uniforms ready in time for the first parade. We did our basic training at the Mewata barracks. The Army provided us with drill sergeants.

Calgary

SWAMPED WITH APPLICATIONS   There were, of course, a few C.O.s who said they would have no women in their camps, but they were soon forced to change their minds as men were withdrawn for active services overseas, and we were swamped with applications for personnel.

We had no accommodation to live in barracks. All personnel had to find their own quarters, so that it was difficult to start a true unit spirit.

Uniforms did not appear for some time, and we were a motley group in voluntary corps uniforms or civilian clothes. Officers were to receive a grant of $150 to fit themselves out. For the other ranks, Ottawa had thought up a very odd arrangement. We were told to recruit a seamstress in rank of Company Quartermaster Sergeant. She was to measure every other rank for caps, greatcoats, jackets, skirts, stockings and shoes. These were then sent to the unit packed in cartons — one per individual. When the cartons were opened, there was a good deal of swapping of things that did not fit! Later, of course, we had Quartermaster Stores like any other unit of the Army.

Sidney, B.C.

BEAVERS AND MAPLE LEAVES   Collar badges and buttons bore the helmeted head of Athene; the cap badge was a brass lozenge with three silver maple leaves on a single stem and the words "Canadian Women's Auxiliary Corps" inscribed within a beaded edge. Senior Commander Kennedy wore a beaver in each epaulette; Junior Commanders wore three maple leaves and subalterns two. Other ranks wore brass CWAC badges on their shoulders.

CWAC Newsletter, October 1945, recalling early ranks, uniforms, and badges

THE CURÉ WASN'T TOO FRIENDLY   We drove around Quebec recruiting in a fifteen-hundred-weight truck, a square metal box, no cushions. We bounced all the way down those country roads. We'd stop in a village to see the mayor and the curé and the President of Les Filles d'Isabelle. It would be announced over the radio that we were there, at a certain hotel.

Girls were supposed to have Grade 8, but it depended how badly they were needed. If they were healthy, we'd take them — we could always find a place. Their parents would rather have them enlist than go into town and work in the factories. We looked after them in the Army; they got medical treatment, dental treatment, and there were educational opportunities. I remember one girl from Sept-Îles, she hadn't got Grade 8 but she left the Army with senior matric.

Sometimes the curé wasn't too friendly. I remember one Sunday going to church and hearing him say these "whores" weren't welcome in his church. But they weren't all like that.

Quebec City

CANADA CALLS HER WOMANHOOD FOR SERVICE ANYWHERE IN THE CANADIAN WOMEN'S ARMY CORPS
"The Women's Smartest Service"

. . . A candidate for enlistment in the CWAC must be either "A" or "B" medical category; minimum height five feet; weight not less than 105 pounds or 10 pounds above or below the standard of weight laid down in the table for her height; no dependents; must have Grade VIII or equivalent education; must be between the ages of 18 and 45 and be a British Subject.

Advertisement in the *Edmonton Journal*, 13 February 1943

NO SHOWER CURTAINS I went to Kitchener for basic training, and that winter, 1943, was unbelievable. We just about froze to death. They had pot-bellied stoves to heat the huts, and the pipes would get red-hot, up to six inches from the ceiling — you had to watch them constantly. They had to take girls off clerical duties to go on fire duty. No fires broke out. I think the good Lord protected us.

We couldn't take a shower for days, it was so cold. And when we did, there were no shower curtains, and no doors in front of the johns. I'd been brought up with a silver spoon in my mouth — I was never allowed in the kitchen at home. But at Kitchener, on my first Saturday, I washed 750 plates and three floors.

Quebec City

Major Mary Dover, Officer Commanding the C.W.A.C. training centre at Ste. Anne de Bellevue, Que., and Lieutenant Natalie Platner, Officer Commanding Glebe Barracks, Ottawa, 1942. Platner, who was English-born, was sent to London as a captain, to organize a training school for Canadians who enlisted there. Dover began her army career as Staff Officer, C.W.A.C., for M.D. 13 (Calgary). As Lieut.-Col. Dover, she later commanded Eastern Basic Training Centre in Kitchener, Ontario. Eventually she became chief recruiting officer for the C.W.A.C. TT 100-679

PAID LESS THAN MEN We got ninety cents a day when we went in. It was raised later. The amount didn't bother me. You didn't think about it. You got your room and board and your clothes — look, the ninety cents was your fun money.

Nova Scotia

We got paid less than men, and our generation accepted it without even thinking about it, because we'd been brought up to expect less than a man.

Ontario

It didn't rankle, because men were expected to kill and we weren't. That satisfied me perfectly.

Alberta

We got two-thirds of what men were paid to start with, but we got it up to four-fifths in 1943. I didn't think it was fair to ask for five-fifths unless you required women to do guard duty, go on patrols, etc.

Women didn't stand up to pressure as men did. In Britain, on Air Force stations, they found that men could last a lot longer under pressure.

Women are in the world to give life not to take it — unless your country is invaded.

Col. Margaret Eaton, Director General, C.W.A.C.

I fail to see what logic is behind the position where women receive only two-thirds of the basic pay which men receive, when the women do the same job.

I believe it is a hang-over, a relic of the past, of the dark ages, which has hung on to us, relegating women to a position of inferiority. When we women have discarded the old Victorian red flannel petticoats to do the job, it is time the men discarded the red flannel petticoats around their minds and gave us equality.

Dorise Nielsen, M.P., House of Commons, 25 May 1943

HARDLY ANY MEN   There was a beautiful dance floor at Kitchener, but there were hardly any men to dance with. And there were 1,200 women! One night, though, I was asked to dance by a handsome young sailor, and I was so pleased with myself. After the dance he asked if he could walk me home. I thought I'd landed myself a man.

On the way out I asked him where he was posted, thinking he must be home on leave. But he said, "Oh, I live here. I'm in the Sea Cadets." What a letdown! Was I ever disappointed! He was about seventeen.

Ottawa

"WHERE'S THE DRIVER?"   There were seven of us, and we drove staff officers to work every morning. One day General Griesbach arrived from Winnipeg, and I was told to pick him up from the Palliser Hotel. When I opened the car door he said, "Where's the driver?" He wouldn't listen to me and he wouldn't let me drive him. He got a soldier to take over my car.

But Brigadier Harvey stood up for his CWACs. We had his support from the beginning, and the Army got used to us after a while.

Calgary

CWACs sort mail, Base Post Office, Ottawa. PAC PA 128222.

Servicing tank at the Longue Pointe Ordnance Depot, Quebec, April 1944. PAC PA 128260

Members of the Kine-Theodolite Detachment, Royal Canadian Artillery, recorded the accuracy of fire against "enemy" aircraft. The Kine CWACs worked on army firing-ranges on the Nova Scotia coast. TT 101-680

ACK-ACK GUNS   When I finished my basic training at the old Harbord Collegiate [Toronto] I was put right into the kine-theodolite detachment, to work with the artillery. I was only eighteen. You needed geometry and trigonometry to qualify. You had to have senior matric in maths.

When we got to Halifax we stayed in barracks for a while, then we were sent to A 23 Training Centre in Dartmouth. Each morning we'd drive out in our jeeps to where the guns were stationed, about half an hour's drive from Dartmouth. There were the ack-ack guns, the 4.4s, and the big coastal guns. There'd be a plane with a drogue behind it, and they aimed at the drogue. I was there until 1944 and there were never any accidents.

All the people who lived on this part of the coast had been moved out. The authorities were afraid of subs and we'd get a "yellow alert" when one was spotted. We were out in all weathers, and we wore battledress—lined trousers and tops, and a sheep-skin coat. We had boots with gaiters for heavy snow, and mitts of course. The uniform was more or less the same as the men's, but it was made to fit.

At any one time there'd be two thousand men and eighteen girls. I never felt uncomfortable. There were no snide remarks—well, they called me "Shorty", but then I'm shorter than most. That didn't bother me. You had a job to do and you did it. There was no time to sit around and suck your thumb. In the evenings there'd be a dance or we'd play cards.

In our unit there was a sergeant, a lance-corporal, and a corporal. I was the corporal. I had to look after the orderly room, and the records, and I had to parade the girls over to the mess. One morning I got told by the orderly officer that I was to eat all my meals in the bombardiers' mess. After dinner the first night I was told to go into the lounge. Such beautiful furniture, all red-leather chairs. I sat down at a table and all around me there were men having a drink. Suddenly a beer appeared on my table. Where did it come from? Well, a bombardier got up and bowed, and I stood up and curtsied. I drank it, and then another beer appeared. Where did it come from? A second bombardier bowed, and I curtsied to him.

After that I bought my own drinks. They accepted me.

Ottawa

LADIES   I find it difficult to make the Army appreciate that the women selected are ladies from good homes who desire to serve their country, and are not sailors or lumberjacks picked off the street. They are not successors to the "camp followers" of the armies of the previous age. All ranks must be made to realize that they are young women of good character who are making a sacrifice to serve their country.

Edgar W. Mingo, Registrar, Administrative
Division G, Army H.Q., 7 October 1941

LOOK AT THAT CHEAP CWAC   If people saw a boy and a girl walking hand-in-hand down by the Rideau Canal together, they'd say, "Oh, look at that nice young couple." But if the girl was in Army uniform, they'd say, "Oh, look at that cheap CWAC."

Toronto

TREATED LIKE DIRT   After officers' training I was sent to Saint John, New Brunswick, and there we were the lowest of the low. The T. Eaton Company put an honour roll in the window, with every CWAC recruit's name in gold paint — and it turned out that the entire red-light district had enrolled! From then on, any CWAC was by definition a streetwalker.

There was a Joint Service Centre in Saint John, operated by volunteers, where the local women would bring their daughters to dance with the boys. The Legion and the Y.W.C.A. didn't want armed-forces women there — just nice civilian girls. There was a big row, and eventually servicewomen were let in, but we were treated like dirt. Civilian women would pull away as you went by so they wouldn't brush against you.

It wasn't any better at work. The men regarded CWACs as girls to be exploited, and many of them were ripe for exploitation. They were straight off the farm. There was one handsome officer with a limp who got several girls pregnant. The Medical Officer knew, but he did nothing about it. In fact, he laughed. These characters were older men, permanent-force men; they were too old to fight.

If you were an officer, you had to go to parties in the mess. You could be ordered to go. But a party meant getting drunk, and I'd been brought up in a house where no liquor was served. I didn't know how to behave, so I played the kid who had to be protected. There was an older man who protected me, and I suppose I protected him. He was fifteen years older than me, and married.

Toronto

BEER-DRINKING   There was a terrific amount of beer-drinking once working hours were over. That's one reason why I didn't drink, so there was at least one person in the mess who didn't. I had junior officers serving with me, and I didn't want them saying, "I had to drink because everyone else was doing it."

Training Officer, Halifax

The school of cookery at the Ste. Anne de Bellevue advanced training centre gave courses to prepare servicewomen for field work in battalion kitchens, officers' messes, and casualty clearing stations in the rear of advancing troops. TT 100-679

Graduation parade, No. 3 C.W.A.C. basic training centre, Kitchener, Ont., August 1944. PAC PA 128257

Dear M:

. . . Have you ever heard a serviceman speak well of the girls in the Army, Air Force, or Navy? Nine out of every ten resent having girls in uniform, and my brothers, Stirling included, said they would disown me if I ever join such scruff.

If you are happy in the service, very well. But it isn't everyone who can put up with that kind of life. As for my being at home, that concerns only Mother, Dad, and myself.

Letter from Edmonton to a CWAC
from that city, 8 August 1944

Colonel Margaret Eaton, Director General, C.W.A.C., with Defence Minister J. L. Ralston (*left*) and Major-General H. F. G. Letson, Ottawa, 1944. One of the first staff officers appointed in 1941, Eaton had worked in the Canadian Red Cross Corps, Administration section, before enlisting in the C.W.A.C. Her father was president of the T. Eaton Company. TT 108-709

WOMEN ARE DIFFERENT

In our society we recognize that women are physiologically and temperamentally different from men — they are feminine.

1. They do not possess the same strength and endurance.
2. Our society has encouraged them to have more delicate feelings, more spiritual values and more romantic attitudes.
3. Their natural role is in marriage and that of home maker. No social pressure is brought to bear on their enlistment. They are volunteers without compulsion.
4. Their role in business and industry is temporary. They may leave when they choose. Employment is usually a preliminary step to marriage.

Though relegated to more static jobs in the Army, women have been made to perform these duties under the imposition of the traditional Army system, evolved for totally different purposes: i.e. the need of the fighting soldier. This indiscriminate application of masculine standards has created conflict. Current high CWAC rejection and discharge rates on grounds of emotional instability are indicative of the difficulty of adjustment to the Army which women are experiencing. Women are resisting submergence of their own individuality to the Army system. *They still remain women first and soldiers second. . . .*

Future Recruiting Policy

There seems to be general agreement that a policy of selective recruiting for CWAC should be adopted. It is felt that such a policy would:

1. Raise the general standard of enlistment.
2. Improve the prestige of the Corps.
3. Ensure a greater percentage of personnel suitable for trades training.
4. Remove discipline problems which frequently arise in low category personnel incapable of trades training yet unwilling to do general duties.

Internal Memorandum from the Director
of Army Recruiting, 28 September 1943

Inspection, 1944. A disturbing "whispering campaign" against servicewomen in the Army and the Air Force hampered recruiting in 1942 and led National Defence to commission a study of public attitudes to the recruitment of women. It appeared that women and French Canadians generally were the most hostile to servicewomen. MA 143

The Officers' Mess, Lansdowne Park, Ottawa. PAC PA 128217

MAINSTREETING   I lied about my age, and I wasn't the only one. I was sixteen, close to my seventeenth birthday. I was in Grade 11 at high school and it was June 1943.

I knew that a pipe band was being formed by the C.W.A.C., and I belonged to the Vancouver Ladies' Pipe Band. I had this feeling of adventure — a military band — a flag — a parade. I loved parades!

My name was MacDonald, and the majority of us had a Scottish background, although there were some Irish, and one French-Canadian girl. She first heard the pipes at the training centre at Kitchener and she pleaded to join. Her name was Framboise, and we called her MacFramboise.

We were the only active-service women's military pipe band in the Commonwealth. Officially we were pipers, or drummers, but we were privates, really. The Pipe Major was a sergeant.

We made two complete tours of Canada, coast to coast. Our main objective was recruiting, but we played at Bond Drives, at Army camps, at military parades. We met hospital ships and planes, and we'd be piping as families came to meet the walking wounded, and as the men on stretchers were carried off. Sometimes we were so choked up we could hardly play.

Wherever we went, we were treated royally. We had our own cars on the trains, and in summer we had our own trucks — army transports, as rough as could be, but we loved to be out in the fresh air, and out of the public eye for a while. The truck would stop at the outskirts of a town to let us off, and we'd parade through the streets. We were mainstreeting. Sometimes an officer would make a speech. It was our job to persuade the women of the town that joining the Army was a respectable and an honourable occupation. It was, too.

There'd be luncheon or tea put on for us by the ladies, and I ate so much ham and potato salad I couldn't touch it for years after. And I drank enough tea to sink a battleship.

One time we played at a prisoner-of-war camp, somewhere between Calgary and the Rockies. We went to entertain the Veterans' Guard, men who worked there because they were too old for active service.

We saw the prisoners, of course — all these gorgeous, handsome young fellows, just like ours. To see men like that behind barbed wire — it seemed so wrong. Some of them worked in the mess hall, and they were so anxious to talk to us. We weren't supposed to, but we did. And when we played retreat, the prisoners stood to attention. They didn't salute, but they treated the flag and the marchpast with respect.

At Army camps they would put on dances for us, all over Canada. We would march all day and dance half the night. In Quebec it was different. Part of our job there was to persuade conscriptees to go active. Zombies — have you come across that word? They were men who'd been conscripted and then wouldn't go active. We had very strong prejudices about them, and we wouldn't be caught dead dancing with them. We knew who they were because they wore the same uniform, but with different flashes.

Piper from British Columbia

KILT RULED OUT FOR ARMY GIRLS, KNEES EXPOSED

OTTAWA, June 8, 1944 (CP) — The CWAC pipe band is going to stay in khaki — they aren't going to get their kilts after all and it's because they would have to show their knees. Army officials decided that CWAC knees, however shapely, must remain hidden under regulation-length skirts and no kilt appears smart when draped to mid-calf. . . .

CWAC SONGSHEET

Tune: "Colonel Bogey"
Here come the khaki skirts,
The women volunteers.
Britain, you've got us on our way,
Britain, expect us any day.
Good girls, we've cut off our curls,
And the Nazis, the blighters, will pay.
Boy, but we'll get even.
Churchill, you said you wanted tools.
Watch us, we'll follow all the rules.
Chins up, we'll never give up,
And soon the skirts will be flirts once again.

Tune: "Mademoiselle from Armentieres"
We're the girls who joined the CWACs to beat the Huns,
We're the girls behind the boys behind the guns,
We're the girls who help the men,
We teach them all the tricks but then
We're the CWACs from Al-berta.

Alberta

AN ARMED GUARD   I was sent to England for three months on officers' training with the A.T.S. [Auxiliary Territorial Service]. We went over on the *Queen Elizabeth*, twenty thousand men and eighteen girls. We had an armed guard on our cabin door with a bayonet. I guess they were afraid we would be assaulted. There was a little area on the deck roped off where we were allowed to walk, at certain times.

Quebec City

The C.W.A.C. brass band and the C.W.A.C. pipe band, formed in 1943, were used extensively in recruitment campaigns across Canada. The bands were intended to help upgrade the C.W.A.C.'s public image. PAC PA 128246 and PA 128223

"Gas drill" by Molly Lamb, who was appointed official C.W.A.C. war artist after officer training at Ste. Anne de Bellevue in March 1945. Lamb became the first woman war artist in the Allied nations to be sent overseas. CWM 12059

GAS

On command "Gas" hold breath and open haversack flap.

Seize facepiece with right hand at valveholder and withdraw from haversack.

Hold facepiece in front of face with thumbs inside and either side of headgear straps — palms facing inward. Dig chin into facepiece and adjust headgear.

Run fingers around facepiece and headgear to see no folding over.

Breathe out hard to clear facepiece of any gas.

Army Instructions

PEE PARADE   We had to be as sure as humanly possible that the draft going overseas was not pregnant. Some girls got "caught", in the vernacular, and some had husbands. The Army didn't issue contraceptives to women.

I got an order from the Director General to conduct pregnancy tests, and that meant we needed experimental animals. The U.S. had a corner on all the rabbits used for these tests, so we looked around for possible substitutes. We heard about a type of South African frog which could serve the purpose, and we ordered five hundred of them. They came to our lab at Ste. Anne de Bellevue from South Africa, via Alexandria and London. Four hundred and ninety-nine arrived alive, and there was only one male among them! We called him Moses, and he was put to work. Somebody discovered a way of making frogs copulate, and it all began with Moses.

The girls going overseas were sent to a holding area, and a very careful eye was kept on them. There was a "pee parade" and they had to provide a specimen on the spot, and show their pay books, to stop anyone from substituting somebody else's urine for their own.

The frogs turned out to be very satisfactory. At the end of the war I read in *Time* magazine that the Canadian government sold the remaining frogs to the U.S. military for several thousand dollars.

C.W.A.C. Medical Officer

THE ENDLESS TRAMP OF FEET The *Queen Elizabeth* was a magnificent ship. It took two or three days to load her, and we were among the first on board. It was the strangest feeling, to lie in your bunk and hear the endless tramp, tramp, tramp of feet as thousands of men came on board, throughout the night.

There were so many men on board that we had no shipboard drill. And there was no room on deck to move around. But the ship went so very fast that we weren't part of a convoy. The R.C.A.F. came five hundred miles out to sea with us. Then they turned and flew low over the ship, dipping their wings before they turned back. It was a lonely feeling.

The voyage over took four and a half days.

Edmonton

MEN WERE WARY Most of us reduced to the ranks to go. We went to replace Army privates in the office in London, so I guess that was the reason why.

I was told later that the men felt great fear of the women coming, and they were certainly wary of us when we first arrived. The sergeant in my section at Canadian Military Headquarters said to me on day one: "If you think you are going to put me out of here, you have another think coming, girl." And he certainly managed to stay put. I went to Italy in 1944 and when I got back to London he was still there.

When we first arrived in London there was a dance given for us at Canadian Military Headquarters, and the men shunned us. But the attitude changed fairly rapidly. I think we were very good for the morale of our Canadian men over there.

Calgary

SEX One of the girls said there was an atmosphere of sex hanging over London like a pea-soup fog, and I know what she meant. Maybe it's always like that in wartime.

Saint John

Checking Bren guns, Central Ordnance Depot, Toronto, February 1944. PAC PA 128218

Lieutenant-Colonel Alice Sorby of Winnipeg was the administering officer responsible for all servicewomen overseas. Appointed Staff Officer to Canadian Military Headquarters in London in August 1942 with the rank of major, Sorby was made lieutenant-colonel in June 1944. In May 1945 she was reposted to Ottawa as Deputy Director General, C.W.A.C. Courtesy Isabel Macneill

"CWACs folding sheets", London, England, by Molly Lamb.
CWM12049

A THICK BLACK LINE   We were on British rations for the whole three months and the food was awful. I lost fifteen pounds while I was there. In London we were so hungry we went to a market and bought a live chicken. Then we drew lots on who would kill it!

In Pontefract our hut had a stove in it, and a little pail of coal. That was to last for the whole week. We were allowed a bath once a week, and there was a thick black line around the bathtub to limit the amount of water we used. It was hard, but I wouldn't have missed it for the world.

Quebec City

GO TO BED WITH THEM   Canadian servicemen found us very difficult at first, because we wouldn't just go to bed with them in London. They'd approach you because you were Canadian. They thought we were very stuck-up.

Toronto

MY KNEES WENT TO JELLY   My husband was wounded when I was at 40 Company. I had girls there who had lost their husbands, their boyfriends, their brothers, and their fathers. Everything. And I would sit down and talk to these girls and try to get them back on track. "Look, my dear," I'd say, "it's not going to do you any good to sit here and cry. Cry and get it over with and come back to work, because we need you. Don't let anything take you away from that."

I had all the girls in Signals, and they knew before I did that my husband had been wounded. I wondered why the hall was so full of girls that day, but they were there to see if I would do what I asked them to do. I'm telling you, my knees just went to jelly when I heard. I sat at my desk, thinking, "I've got to get myself under control. I'm going to show those girls that I can walk out of this office as their Commanding Officer and speak to them like I would any other time."

It was two doors down to the mess, so I didn't have far to walk. I got myself steeled up and I did it.

Officer, Ontario

BLOWN OUT OF BED   Jerry started bombing London again in 1943, and it was harrowing, nerve-wracking.

As soon as the alarm would go, everybody in the whole office would get down underneath our desks. They were just wooden desks, but they protected us from flying glass. The office had huge plate-glass windows. We took our telephones down under the desks with us, and we sat there carrying on with business. I had no injuries myself, but my room-mate was hurt. A skylight shattered in her office when there was a hit in the next street, and she had head injuries from flying glass.

One Sunday morning I was lying in bed on the top floor at South Street, because I didn't have to attend church parade, when a rocket landed on the corner of Marble Arch. I was blown out of bed and I ended up on the floor. The windows were casements; they were blown completely shut and then open again, and so was the door.

The day before, the Salvation Army hostel got a direct hit. It was full of servicemen on leave, and there was nothing left, just a great hole in the ground.

Manitoba

BUZZ BOMBS   I did fire-warden duty up on the roof of our house on South Street. Everyone took turns. You had to make sure that no fires started during an air raid.

It was rather frightening in a way, but when you're young you don't really see the danger. We found it rather exciting. From the roof you could see the V1's scoot across the sky. We called them buzz bombs. You'd see this flame spurting out the back and you'd think, "Ah, it's gone by," then it would circle, and sometimes it would come back.

Toronto

CUT DOWN ON PROMISCUITY   Near the end of 1944 we had a very good supply of personnel psychologists. This particular one wanted to talk to all the officers in the company. She said the Army was now ready to provide us with all kinds of sports facilities. They'd give us lessons in basketball, tennis, swimming, and skating and skiing in the winter. If we got all these things going in our units, we would cut down greatly on promiscuity.

Then this major spoke up. "Nothing will take the place of sexual intercourse!" she said.

London

CWACs learn fire-fighting techniques in blitzed buildings, London. CWACs serving in Britain were not sent to work with searchlight or anti-aircraft batteries, as were their counterparts in the British Auxiliary Territorial Service. TT 100-678

43 Company softball team, Hyde Park, London, May 1943. TT 101-680

My Dear Women Members of the Services:

It was not without trepidation that I saw your entrance into the Armed Forces to take your place beside your brothers on the field of battle. Misgivings assailed me. What precedent was there for such action? What equipment had Nature given you to withstand, not alone the physical dangers, but the emotional and moral impact of such association? Three years of war supplied the answer. Three glorious years unsurpassed in their record of achievement in the field of human fortitude.

What a privilege is yours! To hold aloft for men who live with Death the ideal of Christian Womanhood. To inspire them amidst the carnage and bestiality of battle to hold fast to virtues whose values neither time nor place can alter. To encourage, to comfort, to console. To be the link which binds them to home and decency. To bring them unscathed through the shadows of the Valley of Death to the life they must resume when Victory rests upon our banners. Or if, in His Wisdom, God accepts the sacrifice of their lives, to live forever in the knowledge that their glory in heaven is, in some measure, the result of your example and your association with them.

Do not think that I exaggerate your influence for good; neither forget that your power for evil is unlimited. It is almost a truism that no man ever made a great success of his life nor did any crash to collapse that a woman was not behind him. She may have been his mother, a sister or his wife but she was the ideal or the evil inspiration that moved him to action. Though Nature has formed you delicately she has compensated you spiritually in generous measure. Some day you must render an account to God of the use you have made of this great power. It is for you to decide whether you shall lead man to God or betray him to Satan. What an honour but, also, what a sobering responsibility. Pray earnestly, as I do for you, that you may be worthy of your high vocation. . . .

Charles Leo Nelligan, Ordinary to
the Canadian Forces, undated message
to Roman Catholic servicewomen

RUBBLE, WRECKAGE, SQUALOR   We were a tired and travel-weary looking group when we landed. We had more equipment than Dodd has pills. Hours to wait, heat, no food, ad infinitum! Too bad if the boys were looking for glamour girls. But they certainly concealed their disappointment under one of the biggest, best and most sincere welcomes that has ever been extended to CWACs.

What there was to see we saw in three brief days, and it can be summed up in a few cryptic words. Dust, filth, dirt, rubble, wreckage, squalor and disease. Starving, begging, ill-clad, vermin-infested natives. The whole place is a bomb-happy shambles where our boys dropped their calling cards on the departing Jerry.

But there were lights! Lights! Twinkling and sparkling in the rose-purple Italian night. Lights in the Bay lying like jewelled clips at the foot of the mountain. Lights! After nearly two years of groping and

Disembarking at Naples, Italy, June 1944. By early 1945 there were more than 1,200 CWACs serving in France, Belgium, Italy, and the Netherlands. PAC PA 108175

stumbling around in blackest blackness! And fruit! The one thing in plentiful evidence, but we were barred from eating anything save oranges with their protective coating, unless purchased by the Messing Officer and specially washed and treated.

Because of the badly torn-up roads and heavy military traffic passing to and from the front lines, our trip, a journey normally of only three or four hours, ran well over the twelve-hour mark, and we were dusty, hungry and tired. But this is the Army, Mrs. Jones, and for the first time in nearly three years of service we are just finding it out. No fancy uniforms here. We've put away our glamour suits — battledress and bush shirts are the order of the day. We are treated exactly on a par with the men. One difference only — the girls get sheets for their beds. That's all, though. No other single concession. Discipline, rations, quarters, clothing, working hours are all for one and one for all.

Our trip was an education in itself. There was much that twisted the mouth, tore at the heart and seemed to blur the landscape a little. Not with womanish tears, but with tears of bitterness and anger.

Example: Cassino! There is only this left to tell about it. There was not a murmur as the truck pushed its way through the only narrow roadway cleared of mines and booby traps, and the shattered Hell that was the town. Not a solitary thing is left standing, nor any human living thing, and God alone knows how many of Canada's sons make fertile with their blood the valleys of Italy that lie beneath the mountain.

One old woman sat on the outskirts of the town, head bowed and gnarled hands folded in her lap. Whether there was life in the body or not it was hard to tell. When we observe these people sitting in the ruins of what was once their home, with their dazed faces and empty eyes, gazing helplessly at the never-ending stream of strange uniforms, listening to thousands of voices raised in a strange tongue, dodging under the very wheels of a ceaseless procession of military vehicles, even as they did the intruder before us — what can, what must their thoughts be?

I try to picture Canada this way. . . .

CWAC Newsletter, August 1944

Damage done by a V2 rocket, Antwerp, Belgium, 1944.
PAC PA 141884

Cdn. Sec. GHQ 2 Ech 21 Army Gp.
B.W.E.F.

Dear Col. Sorby:

This is real army life — under canvas. The boys are grand to us. There is lots of work, but we have lots of fun too. I share a tent with nine others. No more private life. No matter where we go, or what we do, the army looks on.

One morning last week we had to literally bail ourselves out of bed. It had teemed with rain all during the night and was still raining heavily when we got up. I had a small pond beside my head and another on my tummy. Fortunately I had thrown my raincoat on top of my bed. But, as some of the girls said, they did not need to go to the wash-house that morning.

I am liking my work. As you probably know, I am working for Pers[onnel] along with a male sergeant. Our buzzer system is really something. The clerk's office is a few yards down the hall from the Colonel's, and we have a string running from his office, passing through the transoms along the hallway. On our end of the line is a tin can with stones inside of it. When the Col. wants us he pulls the string and clatter go the stones in the tin can. Since it hangs over our heads (our office is only *four feet wide* by four yards long) you can imagine how it wakens us up when he yanks on it.

Last night the sergeants of 2nd Ech held a dance and we all had a grand time. We even had lunch — sandwiches (spam and cheese), cake with ICING, doughnuts covered with sugar and COFFEE. We had a very good orchestra.

Personally, I am very happy and feeling exceptionally well. I think the outdoor life agrees, although it is very cold sleeping in tents these nights. I honestly believe we wear more clothes when we go to bed than during the daytime. It is really funny to watch us preparing for bed. Thank heavens, Ma'am, for those woollies. They go under the pyjamas, and over the top we pile on sweaters, socks (sometimes two pairs) and even dressing gowns. Tweedy even wears her balaclava. Most of us have discarded our sheets, preferring to sleep between the blankets. To think that I could ever do that.

Letter from a C.W.A.C. sergeant to her
former Commanding Officer, 19 September 1944

PEOPLE SWARMED AROUND US   Brussels was reached in mid-afternoon of the third day of our 350-odd-mile trek from La Délivrande [France] to Belgium. Here there was little or no sign of the ravages of war, crowds of civilians, plentifully stocked stores, cars and mechanical equipment of recent make; the whole giving a welcome contrast especially to war-torn England.

As the miles flew by, the people grew more enthusiastic; men, women and children seemed to be trying to outdo each other in expressing their gratitude and appreciation of the Allies' arrival. Flags were flying everywhere, flags of all the Allied Nations. The people have a spontaneous sense of humour and in the windows of several stores were cartoons showing the Allied soldier being almost smothered with welcome, which is literally what happened to us.

The evening we arrived, immediately we jumped from the vehicle the people swarmed around us and commenced to hug us — a bit embarrassing. We could scarcely stir, but we tried to be as patient as possible under the circumstances. You will appreciate that we were dead tired, hungry and dirty beyond recognition.

A curfew is in force and there are black-out restrictions. Cigarettes and tobacco are scarce, as is meat. Clothes are plentiful though rationed, fruit and vegetables are abundant. Ice cream and candy proved to be a most welcome treat.

Account by C.W.A.C. Staff Sergeant,
Cdn. Sec. GHQ 2 Ech 21 Army Gp. B.W.E.F.

ARMY OF OCCUPATION   Third Division Headquarters was near Oldenburg. We flew there in September or October 1945. We were very much an army of occupation. You didn't see much of Germany; you didn't go outside the perimeter of the area you served. You didn't have much to do with Germans either, though there were German waiters working in the mess. This was pretty soon after the war, remember.

There were always parties. It was a very gay life; there was too much fun, too much to drink. And crazy things happened. We heard there was this fur farm in the British zone, so we went there, and I picked out a bunch of little blue foxes — still alive — for my coat. We didn't have to touch our pay. We made enough marks selling cigarettes and stuff we got sent from home to buy those damned furs. But I never got my blue fox. Shortly after we went there the military government took over the farm and I got dollars back in return for my marks. Then there was this bird in Oldenburg with boxes and boxes of silk stockings he'd got hidden away. We bought dozens of pairs: we hadn't seen any for years.

To get to the officers' club in Bremen you drove through all the devastation. It was terrible, unbelievable. And you'd go through little villages with all the shops boarded up, and the people on the street were such a bedraggled lot. I went to Amsterdam for a weekend and I remember feeling tremendous relief as I went over the border, as if a great load had been taken off my back.

Toronto

AROUND THE ARC DE TRIOMPHE   In Paris we played at the tomb of the Unknown Soldier. It was Sunday, November 3 [1945], and General Vanier, the Canadian ambassador, asked us to play. Vanier was showing off his Canadian girls.

We slow-marched around the Arc de Triomphe. It's so enormous, we had played "My Home" twenty-two times by the time we got around. Then we broke into the quick march, and started off down the Champs Élysées, the longest, grandest avenue in the world. The gendarmes couldn't hold the crowds back, they all rushed in and marched behind us.

Then General Vanier asked if we would oblige by playing a small concert in the Tuileries gardens, at the foot of the Champs Élysées. We played for an hour. Afterwards, Vanier got in the back of the Army truck with us, and there were tears running down his face. "My dear girls, there were upwards of 250,000 people there today," he said.

Pipe Major, C.W.A.C. Pipe Band

Rehearsing for the Army Show, which toured miliary camps in Britain and Europe. Molly Lamb (Bobak) helped design sets for the show. Four performers were the first CWACs to enter a war zone when they landed in Italy, May 1944. TT 100-679

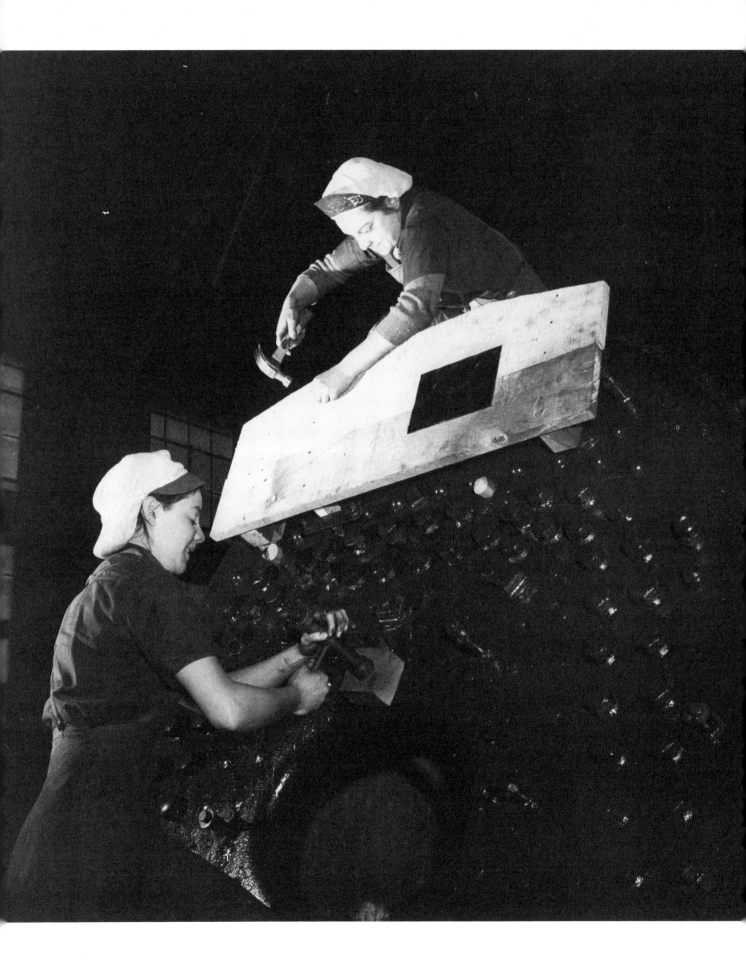

4

Roll Up Your Sleeves for Victory

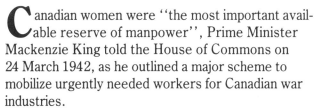

Canadian women were "the most important available reserve of manpower", Prime Minister Mackenzie King told the House of Commons on 24 March 1942, as he outlined a major scheme to mobilize urgently needed workers for Canadian war industries.

Newspapers, magazines, radio, films, billboards, and public speakers all carried the government's increasingly urgent message to women: "Roll up your sleeves for Victory!" To enter the labour force, on a temporary basis, became a woman's patriotic duty. And women responded to the call: by October 1943 an estimated 261,000 women were employed directly or indirectly in war production. Altogether, well over a million women were in the Canadian labour force, or in the armed forces, almost twice the number employed in 1939. By mid-1944 the Department of Labour estimated that one out of every four workers in war industry was a woman.

The National Selective Service campaigns to recruit women into the labour force had at least three objectives: to attract the necessary numbers of women into industry; to convince potential employers and male co-workers of the need for their services; and to reassure the general public that war work was a patriotic duty for women, on a temporary basis.

Left: PAC PA 116139 *Above:* TT 337-2257

Certainly the campaigns recruited large numbers of women, and numerous employers were convinced of their usefulness. Not all male co-workers were persuaded, however, and neither were all sectors of the Canadian public. In Quebec the employment of women in munitions plants was vigorously opposed by some Catholic clergy, by various concerned citizens' groups, and by some elements of the press, most notably *Le Devoir*.

To encourage married women to enter the labour force — and they were never compelled to do so — government-supported day nurseries were established in Ontario and Quebec under a Dominion-Provincial Wartime Day Nurseries Agreement. By September 1945 there were twenty-eight day nurseries in Ontario and forty-four day-care programs for school-age children; in Quebec there were only five day nurseries, all in Montreal, but no after-school programs. Another incentive to women workers was an amendment to the Income Tax Act which allowed a working woman's husband to claim the full married-status exemption, regardless of how much his wife earned.

As increasing numbers of women went into war work, the issue of equal pay for equal work was raised in various quarters, including Parliament. Dorise Nielsen, M.P. for North Battleford, was one of the only two women in the House of Commons at the time. (The other was Cora Casselman.) As far back as 1920 the National Council of Women had gone on record in favour of "equal pay for work of equal value in quantity and quality". In 1942 the Council became actively involved in the mobilization of women and in the National Selective Service; it also became increasingly vocal in support of equal pay for women in industry and in the armed forces. There were some wartime jobs for which women did receive equal pay during the Second World War: welders and riveters who belonged to the Boilermakers and Iron Shipbuilders Union in British Columbia; all delivery workers in that province; and streetcar drivers in Toronto, Winnipeg, and Vancouver. But these were isolated examples. It was impossible to get government information about wages paid to the vast majority of women workers, as Dorise Nielsen pointed out. One delegate to the Canadian Trades and Labor Congress convention in 1943 had called for the principle of equal pay for equal work to be embodied in Canada's labour code. The United States government had already accepted the principle. Why couldn't Canada follow suit, asked Nielsen, in September 1943.

"Girls! If you want to keep the big guns firing, see your Selective Service officer next door", Shells for Victory display, Ajax, Ontario, 1941. PAC PA 115550

THE WOMAN'S TOUCH   Canada's women have gone to war. By tens of thousands they're producing the actual sinews of war. By the thousands of thousands they're pursuing essential work on the home front.

Can you feel it, Johnny Canuck? As you blast your death-spitting tank across the desert? In the grim hardness of metal and the stern, implacable precision of guns?

Can you feel it in the skies? In the sure, steady purr of engines and the ghastly whine of bombs? On the sea? In the confident roll of a ship or the potent roar of its cannon?

Can you feel the woman's touch? Because it's there. A million touches imprinted by a million hands. Hands that have peeled potatoes and pounded typewriters and poured tea.

They're deft hands, strong and eager. They've seized the edges of a threatening breach and with their own power and will-to-do have pulled it together again. They've seized wheels and kept them turning. Machines and kept them humming. They've moulded bullets for Tunisia, filled bombs for Berlin.

They're quick hands and capable — young, old and in-between. And they're there with you as you fight. In the desert, in the skies, on the sea.

They're with you in the battle. Watch for it, Johnny Canuck, and you'll feel it as you fight. The woman's touch.

Women at War, J. H. Hodgins, David B. Crombie, Eric Crawford, and R. B. Huestis, Toronto, 1943

CANADA'S WOMEN REGISTER FOR SELECTIVE SERVICE

Canada's first women called under National Selective Service have just completed their registration as we go to press. They were promising looking workers — those 20- to 24-year-old women who responded to the registration order. They look as if they would fulfil easily the statistician's estimate that nearly 90 per cent of the operations in war plants could be done by women — and some of them more efficiently than by men.

Mrs. Rex Eaton, assistant director of National Selective Service, has explained that no compulsion will be used to force women to take war work but they will be interviewed and their duty put plainly before them. Married women will not be urged to go into industry while there are any other workers available but, Mrs. Eaton has declared, if the employment of married women means the difference between Victory and defeat, they will be directed to war work.

In Canada today only one out of every forty women is turning out the tools of war, but in Germany, our strong and most fearful foe, one out of every three women is working to defeat the United Nations, to build the weapons of war to take our homes from us, to make our children work for their children. Women of Canada will not be outdone, nor will our men be defeated by those who swear allegiance to Hitler simply because they lacked tools. Canada must supply them. Women must move up into the supply lines. As each group is ordered to report, they must go, as soon as possible, to register their willingness to work for victory whether in home, or farm, or field, or factory.

Kathleen Whitton Ryan, *Echoes*,
Autumn issue, 1942

HONEST-TO-GOODNESS EQUALITY You can tell your great granddaughter some day that this was the time and the place it really started; the honest-to-goodness equality of Canadian women and men in all the work of this country that is to be done; and the pay, and the kudos and the rights and the problems.

And you can say that it wasn't done by club women at luncheons; or orators on soap boxes; or legislators in parliaments.

It began to happen that hour when Canadian girls left desks and kitchens, elevators and switchboards, stepped into overalls and took their places in the lines of workers at lathes and drills, cranes and power machines, tables and benches in the munition plants of Canada.

Lotta Dempsey, *Women at War*,
J. H. Hodgins et al., Toronto, 1943

HOW FAR CAN WOMEN MEET THE MANPOWER CRISIS?

It is true that to employ a nation's womanhood on a large scale is more troublesome than employing men. It is true that you cannot uproot the wives and mothers of a community without providing a number of services and concessions which men do not need: nursery schools for young children; more complete provision of industrial hygiene measures as women are more susceptible to skin trouble caused by chemicals in the plants; convenient transportation facilities late at night; suitable housing; supervised nutrition;

more elaborate rest room facilities; time off for attention to grooming; maintenance of morals and morale.

There are admitted limitations. The average woman has only half a man's lifting power, two-thirds of his pulling strength; her endurance on night shifts particularly is rather less than that of men.

On the credit side of the balance sheet are these facts: of the 623 operations required in war plants, women can successfully perform all but 57. They have proved that their lighter touch means faster work on operations requiring manual dexterity; that they are sharper at inspection because all their lives they have been accustomed to pay more attention to detail; that generations spent at monotonous tasks of the housewife have given them more patience in handling repetitious machines. In addition to handling tools and machines they have shown great skill in production planning, in routing and control of operations connected with production, drafting, toolcrib and store tending, dispatching and timekeeping.

Women are considered exceptionally able inspectors and most plants have a number on their staff. On the Inspection Board of the United Kingdom and Canada there are more than 8,000 unskilled and 350 skilled inspectors, all women, and their work includes passing on munitions, inspecting gun barrels and gun-carriage parts, explosives, radio equipment and rejected materials.

Anne Fromer, *Saturday Night*, 17 October 1942

"Ronnie" Foster, the "Bren Gun Girl", was frequently pictured on the job at Defence Industries, Ajax, Ontario. PAC PA 117563

WAR, WOMEN AND LIPSTICK

Millions of you are fighting and working side by side with your men. Yet somehow, Canadian and American women are still the loveliest and most spirited in the world. The best dressed, the best informed, the best looking.

It's a reflection of the free democratic way of life that you have succeeded in keeping your femininity — even though you are doing man's work!

If a symbol were needed of this fine, independent spirit — of this courage and strength — I would choose a lipstick. It is one of those mysterious little essentials that have an importance far beyond their size or cost.

A woman's lipstick is an instrument of personal morale that helps her to conceal heartbreak or sorrow; gives her self-confidence when it's badly needed; heightens her loveliness when she wants to look her loveliest.

No lipstick will win the war. But it symbolizes one of the reasons why we are fighting . . . the precious right of women to be feminine and lovely — under any circumstances.

Lipstick advertisement, *Chatelaine* magazine, October 1942

SOFT, SMOOTH AND FEMININE

The hand that rocks the cradle can also do a mean job on a tracer bullet — if it's kept happy. If it's kept soft and smooth and feminine. If the nails are clean, bright and well-groomed; the skin white and supple through proper care.

Give your nails the victory cut. Keep them trim and neat at all times to avoid "breakage" and ragged edges. Keep your nails covered at all times with natural polish — for protection and a light, clean appearance. The polish cover gives them a smooth surface, precision-smooth edges. Both are important for finger dexterity.

Before you begin work, slather on a protective coat of hand cream. Cover your hands and forearms, and run your nail tips through the cream to keep them from dirt and grease. You'll find, if you do this, that the dirt rolls off arms and hands and out from under nail tips twice as easily at the day's end. If you do pick up stubborn grime spots, however, you'll find that cuticle remover is a most effective cleanser.

Nail polish advertisement, 1943

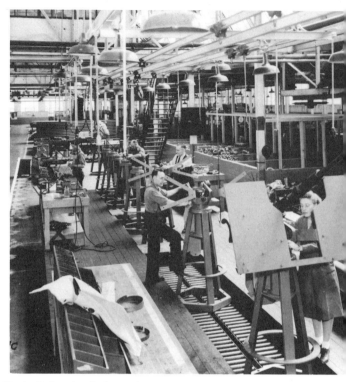

Regina Industries, Ltd., produced gun carriages for two-pounder guns. Under the Order-in-Council regulating government contracts, different wage rates applied to men and women. Men could be paid 35 cents an hour, but for women the minimum was 25 cents. The Wartime Wages Control Order of 1941 said wages were to be determined on the basis of the job performed rather than the sex of the worker, but later revisions to this Order rendered it meaningless. SAB R-B 9523

WOMEN ON LIFT TRUCKS   You had to be a heavy, healthy, strong person to work in the sheet metals. Where they put you depended on your body weight. If you were very slight, they would put you on light work.

You couldn't work in the same department your husband did. When my husband was sent to work in sheet metals, I had to go into tubing. You could be on the same shift, but you couldn't be in the same department. They felt that would cause problems. But you'd be jealous because your husband was working with other girls.

There were thousands of girls at Alcan [Aluminum Company of Canada] in the war. The men didn't mind us, they were glad to have the women there. I think it kept their morale up too. They had women on lift trucks, as well as men. It was sort of integrated. The only thing women complained of was the night shifts. They didn't like them. You worked Saturdays and Sundays, too, because of the war.

Kingston, Ont.

HIGHLY SECRET   I worked as a chemist for the British Inspection Board in a munitions plant, analysing a new form of explosive — it was highly secret — to see if it had the correct components.

I was paid less than the men. In fact, I was supervising young men who earned more than I did. I wrote to the Board to complain, and when the reply came back, eventually, it said this was a woman's burden!

I only stayed for seven months, but women finally did get equal pay.

Toronto

EQUAL PAY FOR EQUAL WORK   Not only do the women in our armed services not receive equal pay for equal work, but all women in employment have suffered this liability. In urging the government to make it the law of the land that there shall be equal pay for equal work, I would remind them that this principle has been acknowledged by the great trade union groups in this country.

Dorise Nielsen, M.P., House of Commons,
4 May 1944

COLD FACT   Here [said Colonel Ralston] was one person urging the employment of women, and another person protesting the dismissal of men employed as shell inspectors at Hamilton to make way for women "who would do the work at a lower price".

The cold fact is that the women at Hamilton are quite as good as the men. If the experience in Great Britain is any criterion, by and large, for this type of work women are better than men. Why, then, are they not being paid the same wages? If that wage was fair for the men, to pay the women less is for the Dominion of Canada to go into the sweated labor business.

Kennethe M. Haig, *Winnipeg Free Press*,
2 April 1941

If you've news of our munitions
  KEEP IT DARK
Ships or planes or troop positions
  KEEP IT DARK
Lives are lost through conversation
Here's a tip for the duration
When you've private information
  KEEP IT DARK!

Poster in munitions factory, Sorel, Quebec

DOUBLE STANDARD FALLS

— Canadian Institute of Public Opinion

Huge Majority of Canadians Favors Equal Pay For Women

The actual question put to representative Canadians from coast to coast was this: "If women take the place of men in industry, should they be paid the same wages as men?"

Results

Should get same pay	79%
Should *not* get same pay	16%
Undecided	5%

On most issues polled by the Institute, women are more inclined to be undecided in their answers than are men. On this issue, however, the situation is reversed, and women have a decided opinion:

	Men	*Women*
Same pay	73%	86½%
Less pay	20%	11%
Undecided	7%	3%

Colorful Arguments

What arguments are used, pro and con?

Said a manager of a finance company in the west: "Women have to be trained more slowly to do a specific job. They are usually not as interested in their work or as conscientious as men. They are frankly not worth the same pay."

But a girl munition worker in Toronto told the Gallup reporter: "Our foreman says that we are doing the job more accurately and faster than the men. Therefore we are entitled to the same pay."

In the main, arguments of those opposed to equal pay for women in industry maintain that a woman has usually not the same family responsibilities as a man; she is not burdened with ensuring the future of the family.

Another angle was advanced by a Quebec housewife who claimed that if women left their homes for work the family would deteriorate, and that giving them the same pay as men encouraged them to leave their homes.

A Gananoque dyemaker, in voting against equal pay, made a rather ambiguous reply: "After the war," he said, "it would be difficult to get women back to their proper level."

Machinist's View

The case for equal pay was eloquently put by a

Assembling radio equipment, RCA Victor, Montreal. PAC PA 116133

Montreal machinist who said: "An hour in a woman's life is as valuable to her as an hour in a man's life is to him. You cannot have a democracy by discriminating against 52% of the population."

Others thought that by demanding and receiving equal pay women were acting as guardians of the standard of living, pending the return of the menfolk after the war. They maintained that if employers could get women to work for them at lower wages it would threaten the post-war standard of living.

By far the most common argument from this side, however, was that each job was worth a certain amount, regardless of what the sex of the person doing the job was.

Vancouver *Province*, 18 November 1942

A LOT OF IMMORALITY   After I went to work at a war plant I saw a lot of immorality and it kind of shocked me. I saw a lot of affairs between the plant supervisors and the girls. These were guys who were exempt from the forces because they were too old, or they had health problems or something. They took advantage of those girls. Some of them had only been married a couple of weeks before their men went overseas.

It was kind of unfair. A lot of the married women stayed home while their husbands were running around in England, getting girls pregnant there.

Toronto

SHE MET THIS SOLDIER   One girl I knew at GECO [General Engineering Company] had two little children. Her husband was away in the Army. She met this soldier and he said, "I'm on a weekend leave. How about spending it with me?" And she said, "Oh, I can't, because of the children." So he said, "I'll pay your wages if you'll take a day off from work some time." And she did. She went with him to a hotel.

Toronto

YOU COULDN'T JUST QUIT   This ulcer on my leg, I got it from the magnesium powder. When we were on the night shift we used to lay down under these big ovens to have a rest; it was nice and warm there.

You needed a medical to get out of working, you couldn't just quit. The GECO doctor said I'd got a bug bite, but my own doctor said it was an ulcer, caused by a burn. It took three months to get rid of it.

Toronto

I WAS ALLERGIC   There were long cleanways between the shops, three miles of them, I believe, to keep down the gunpowder and the high-explosive powder. But they couldn't keep tiny particles from floating in the air, and I was allergic to it. I had a rash from the powder on my face, and it wouldn't go away.

Toronto

A BAD FIRE   We went into the change houses and stripped down to our underwear. Everything had to be made of cotton. Other fabrics had static [electricity] which caused friction, and that would have been dangerous.

We wore cotton brassieres, with all the hooks and eyes and fasteners removed. There was no metal allowed, so they were tied with tape. Our shoes were hand-made specially: they were stitched, there were no nails in them. Our uniform was heavy cotton, creamy-coloured pants and tops which buttoned down one side. We looked quite smart. And we wore turbans; you were supposed to cover every snitch of your hair, and every so often there was a crackdown.

We had quite a few blow-ups at the plant, but there was never a fatality. There was quite a bad fire in our shop once, but everybody got out. All the shops had exits along one side. We saw this big glare, and people running, and one end of the shop was fully alight. The fire department was there in no time flat. It was pure carelessness that caused the fire. We were making fuses, and you got to a point where you took a small mallet and tapped the end if it stuck in the mould. There was some loose explosive in one of the moulds, and the crash of the mallet set if off.

The majority of workers were women, although there were men to do the heavy work like heaving boxes around. We worked on the lines, and we had a heck of a lot of fun. We sang everything from the hit parade to hymns, lovely rollicking hymns. A lot of the women were married and they thoroughly enjoyed the companionship. Up to that time married women didn't go out to work.

Toronto

"MISS WAR WORKER"

"Miss War Worker" deserves more attention than the superficial sort that was given at the beauty contest. She is in fact a significant symbol, a person of importance now and for the future. The female war worker combines a double function: she is an industrial worker and a potential mother.

Thus the public's interest in this group of women must extend beyond that of pretty features and "hair-do". It needs very much to be centred on their working conditions. Large numbers of women are now laboring in heavy industries, doing unaccustomed work, lifting heavy weights and breathing poisonous chemical fumes. Unless protective measures are provided, the effects of these working conditions will be

Beauty contest for munitions workers. GECO

injurious to the women not only today, but especially in the future when the time comes for them to perform the function of motherhood.

Statistics show that almost twice as many women as men stay away from work due to sickness, that women are beginning to suffer from headaches, nervous strain, loss of appetite. Some are said to be showing the symptoms of chemical poisoning: gum and nose bleeding, corrosion of the teeth, chronic cough, yellow-stained face and hands.

Editorial, *Toronto Daily Star*, 25 July 1942

HEALTH OF WOMEN WORKERS MUST NOT BE HURT

There is still a difference of opinion as to the ideal length of the working shift to ensure maximum production, but Dr. Blackler [head of the federal Department of Industrial Hygiene] recommends a shift of 40–45 hours a week for women and 45–50 for men. One study disclosed that women working on fuse bodies on a 63½ hour week actually produced less than when they were placed on a 55½ hour shift. Of last year's 1,217 fatal industrial accidents, the department suggests as high as 25 per cent may be attributable to fatigue.

Constant din frazzles the nerves of workers, especially women, and tires them rapidly. Dr. Blackler is interested in experiments with music in factories, which is said to have the dual effect of overcoming fatigue, and speeding up production.

Anne Fromer, *Saturday Night*, 31 October 1942

In-house publication of General Engineering Company, Scarborough, Ontario. The National Selective Service paid workers' train fares and bought them return tickets if they stayed for six months or more. By 1942 large numbers of single women living in non-industrial areas of the Maritimes and the prairie provinces had gone to work in war industries in central Canada. GECO

BEETHOVEN, BACH AND BING HIT HITLER EIGHT TO THE BAR

A sample scientific program calls for:

First Hour—when workers are strong but distracted, strong rhythm is stressed: One Dozen Roses, Ain't Misbehavin', Margie, Good Morning.

Second Hour—workers settled down; quiet, in step, entertaining, bright music: Wedding of the Painted Doll, Kiss the Boys Goodbye, Elmer's Tune.

Third Hour—workers slightly fatigued; familiar, rhythmic tunes, sparklingly played: Noa, Dearly Beloved, Moonlight Masquerade.

Fourth Hour—workers fatigued, bored and hungry; relaxed, soothing music to ease tension: Tea for Two, Lovely to Look At, All the Things You Are.

Fifth Hour—workers have eaten, are refreshed, relaxed, interested; pleasant, non-rhythmic music: I've Told Every Little Star, Down by the Old Mill Stream, Yes, My Darling Daughter.

THE ROBERT MITCHELL CO. LIMITED
FACTORY AND FOUNDRY DIVISION
CASTINGS and PARTS for NAVY, ARMY and AIRFORCE

Sixth Hour—workers resigned, slightly bored, catching second wind; moderately rhythmic selections: The Very Thought of You, Parade of the Wooden Soldiers, Ciri-Biribin.
Seventh Hour—workers bored, fatigued; bright, effervescent "lift" music: Smiles, Anything Goes, Whistle While You Work.
Final Hour—workers impatient, clock-watching, tired; combination of relaxing and rhythmic selections: Shine on Harvest Moon, Among my Souvenirs, Marcheta.

Canada has more than 60 plants now using scientific music emanating from control rooms in Montreal and Toronto, with orders for many more not yet filled. The United States has 1,200.

National Film Board press release,
November 1943

C. D. Howe, Minister of Munitions and Supply, receives the 1,000,000th projectile produced in Canada by workers at Defence Industries Ltd., Montreal. PAC PA 116132

GULLIBLE GIRLS   There is a marriage that will never take place: that of the young lady who has ruined her health working in a munition plant in order to earn some money for the purchase of clothes with a view to getting married. After six months of slow poisoning, she is debilitated, sallow-complexioned, exhausted, underweight, incurable, and she has not one cent for medical treatment. She has been a habitual visitor at hospital dispensaries; her suitor no longer sees her, offended by her new manners that are too vulgar, and the parish priest has heeded her despairing cry which she would direct at all Canadian women for the charitable purpose of warning them.

Gullible girls will no longer believe the deceitful propaganda of newspapers which show smiling, well-dressed, elegant young ladies among shells, at work benches or tending greasy machines. Why, they dirty their faces like men, and it is uglier because least expected; that is not a proper environment for them. The gullible ones will learn that salaries are higher in Ontario than here for the same working hours and the same kind of labour; that the most dangerous work is done in Quebec; that the selective service which claims to offer a variety of jobs scarcely offers to our French-Canadian women anything but munition work, reserving for others the good office work at a high salary; that if the services of women are always needed, it is because the number of women workers who leave their jobs brings up quite a problem; a plant must replace on an average 1,200 women every month, and there is a reason for that: that

which has ruined the health of another woman in six weeks or six months will also ruin yours. . . .

To work at night, in violation of the law, for eleven hours and a half, in draughty rooms, to go from overheated places to damp and cold halls, to handle powder which gives off noxious fumes and explodes unexpectedly, to carry heavy burdens which cause a fall of the stomach, to breathe dust, the odour of rubber, of tobacco, of powder, of mercury, of banana oil paint, of chemicals that are a frequent cause of burns, that is all in the day's work. As regards explosions, fatal or otherwise, all are bound under oath to say absolutely nothing about them. . . .

Woman is neither the slave nor the queen of machinery; she is the queen of the home, the educator, the present or future governess of what is best and noblest in this world, of that for which we fight: the human brood.

Excerpts from an article by the Jesuit Father
Alexandre Dugré, quoted in the House of
Commons by Emmanuel d'Anjou, M.P. for
Rimouski, 23 March 1943

Parachutes were manufactured at a plant in Waterloo, Que.
PAC PA112907

BLOODY COMMUNISTS   This time-study man at RCA, he wanted us to go faster and faster. It was 1942, we didn't have the union then. I turned on this young mutt, this stupid man with a little brain, and I said, "Where is the time to go pee?" I guess he thought women didn't pee. "We're not machines!" I said.

I was in the middle of the assembly line, and I'd block it. These girls, they were exhausted. They were young, they were frightened, most of them were French Canadians, and they hadn't worked before. They were supposed to stay at home and make good babies. When I told them, "Take your time, take your time," the supervisor started pushing me and I called her a "maudite grande vache". She reported me, but the boss didn't speak French. "I just called her a 'dirty great wash'," I said.

Some of us started talking about the union and we brought in leaflets. At first we passed them around in the washrooms. "Bloody Communists" the management called us. It took a year, but we got a contract. When we had shop stewards and grievance committees that knew their business, we got better working conditions, and we got fifty cents an hour, not thirty-five.

Léa Roback, Montreal, organizer for the
International Brotherhood of Electrical Workers

HOMESICK AND LONELY   GECO was a high-explosives plant, making shells and naval torpedoes. It was at the corner of Coxwell and the Danforth [in Toronto]. When we had our full complement there were six thousand workers, and only about four hundred of them were men. I was hired as an employment interviewer. We took women up to sixty-five and sometimes over — we had many applicants in their sixties.

In 1942 and 1943 GECO sent representatives across Canada to recruit women. They put ads in the papers and went on the radio, and they brought trainloads of women to Toronto. Most trains arrived early from the west and the company laid on a beautiful breakfast. We took them from the station to the East End Y [W.C.A.] for their first meal. We used the Y housing service, but it was a real headache finding rooms.

Management gave them an orientation course, but many of those girls were homesick and lonely. Many of them were sixteen or seventeen and they'd never been away from home before. Some were running away from home situations and we had to counsel them. Sometimes mothers and daughters came together.

Toronto

"Ronnie" Foster, "the Bren Gun Girl". PAC PA 116067

WOMEN WORKERS TO BE ENGAGED FOR WAR PLANT

"Keep 'em firing" will shortly become the motto of 500 Saskatchewan women. C. H. Robinson, employment representative for an eastern munitions plant, is in Regina to hire hundreds of local girls for work in the plant.

The offer he makes to Regina girls is attractive:

Qualifications are not high. Girls must be between 18 and 35 years of age, have an ordinary education and be found in good health by a free medical examination arranged by the National Selective Service office at Regina.

Take Unskilled Girls

"The kind of girl we want," Mr. Robinson said in Regina Monday, "is the girl with a good head on her shoulders. We take girls absolutely unskilled in war industries and train them right at the plant. A Saskatchewan girl—whether a farmer's daughter, domestic servant, waitress, clerk, stenographer, college graduate or debutante—if she is willing to learn—has the qualities of a good war worker."

The scale of wages to be paid to the women workers in the plant is 35 cents per hour for a 48-hour week, as a starting wage, plus cost-of-living bonus of $2.85 per week. Time and a half is paid for overtime work. At the end of four to six weeks the rate of pay will be increased according to the ability of the individual.

Transportation from their Saskatchewan homes to the east is advanced to the girls by the company.

Uniforms Supplied

The girls work in three eight-hour shifts, and are supplied with natty white uniforms and shoes, and the uniforms are laundered for them without charge.

Furthermore, Mr. Robinson stressed, there are no housing problems near the plant. Women workers are given board at $7. per week and are housed in dormitories, 100 girls to each. Each dormitory has its own laundry, washrooms (tub and showers both) and hot and cold running water at all times.

Bedrooms accommodate two girls each, and are equipped with twin beds, twin dressers and a large closet. Each dormitory is under the supervision of a qualified matron, and under her are two housemaids who do the actual cleaning of the rooms.

Spacious Lounges

There is a spacious lounge in each building, attractive with Canadian rock maple furniture, green and red leather cushions, writing desks and all other things that make it look like a women's club room.

Meals are served in large cafeterias throughout the plant and are planned by trained dietitians.

For entertainment there is amateur night once a week at the recreation hall, dancing twice a week, badminton or bowling, fireside program on Sunday evenings and 15-cent-admission movies every Thursday night.

The plant has its own modern and fully-equipped hospital staffed with seven doctors and 27 nurses, its own bank, post office, large recreation hall and hairdressing parlor.

Maritimers Hired

Several hundreds of girls have been hired at the plant from the Maritime provinces, and because southern Ontario is practically drained of female labor, Mr. Robinson agreed to draw on the labor supplies of Saskatchewan.

Regina *Leader-Post*, 5 October 1942

Regular social activities such as fitness classes and dances for workers were a side benefit for women working at larger, well-organized plants. Courtesy Hilda Ricketts

UPWARDS OF 5,000 CHILDREN HERE LEFT DAILY TO INADEQUATE CARE

More than 125,000 women today stand shoulder to shoulder with men along the production lines of Canadian war industry. They are needed there. The Government has welcomed them, and may yet need to draft more of them. But in Montreal alone, upwards of 5,000 children of women war workers are left to care for themselves, or to the uncertain care of older brothers and sisters, grandparents or even neighbours. None of those 5,000-odd children is very old. Most plants will not engage women over 35 years of age.

The obvious solution to this problem is the day nursery, but the three in Montreal — and these in unstrategic positions — can handle a total of only 250 to 300 children daily: a mere one-twentieth of the number requiring care. . . .

Montreal *Gazette*, 1 June 1942

A PROBLEM OF GREAT IMPORTANCE: PRESERVING THE INTEGRITY OF THE FAMILY

A Catholic activist met a friend whose wife had just gone to work in a munitions factory. "Why did you allow that?" he said to his friend. "You're quite able to provide for your wife and child."

"Oh, it's a chance to make a little money."

"Are you sure? You've had to hire a babysitter to look after the child. When you've deducted the babysitter's pay from your wife's earnings, when you've taken account of the effects of your wife's absence (because you can be sure that the babysitter won't look after things as well as your wife does), how much money will you have left? And, as for your child, do you think it's fair for him not to have his mother's care and caresses, to make him put up with tired parents, too tired to make a fuss over him, too tired even to play with him at night? And the babysitter, to whom you've entrusted your child, who's the mistress of your household, what do you know about her? You have to give her some time off. Do you know who she spends it with, and what she could bring into the house and give to your little one?"

"Oh, I hadn't thought of all that!"

Next day, the Catholic heard from his friend that his wife was back at home.

Editorial by Omer Héroux, *Le Devoir*, Montreal, 28 August 1942 (translated)

Toronto day nursery for the children of female war workers. Open from 7.00 a.m. to 6.30 p.m., nurseries cost 35 cents daily for one child and 50 cents for two children. There were not enough nurseries to cope with the demand for places, although Ontario boasted twenty-eight by the end of the war. GECO

BEING A MOTHER   Being a mother is a 24-hours-a-day job. Right now I'm itching to go out and work and I flatter myself that I could be used very advantageously in several branches of business, old as I am, but I can't bring myself to leave the youngest, who is 11. How these young women can leave two or three of pre-school age and not much more is beyond me. That is where the Government should step in and forbid these weak-minded or avaricious girls to work unless competent care is provided and paid for by the mother first. We don't need the Government to provide shelter and care for these poor little waifs. Let the mother pay for them out of her fat cheque....

Letter to the editor, Toronto Globe and Mail,
12 August 1942

NEED FOR DAY NURSERIES

In Britain, where there are now hundreds of thousands of married women working in war industries, there is hardly a single industrial centre which is not equipped with a well-staffed day nursery, where any woman worker can place her child, and be sure that it is well looked after during her working hours. It has also been found that, since these day nurseries were established on a widespread scale, there has been a remarkable improvement in the health and general wellbeing of the children cared for.

Naturally a nation-wide system of day nurseries will involve considerable expenditures in capital outlay and for annual maintenance. But the main thing is to get some scheme of day nurseries in operation before children who are temporarily bereft of their mother's care through the exigencies of the war suffer further neglect.

Editorial, Toronto Globe and Mail,
16 July 1942

NEARLY FRANTIC   There was the snowstorm of the century in 1943, and when we came off the night shift at 7 a.m. we found that no one could get in or out, there was so much snow. There were all these crying, worried women around, whose children were at home alone.

A lot of women would put their children to bed at night before they went to work, and they'd ask a neighbour to listen. But that morning, when they found they couldn't get home, they nearly went frantic.

We stayed at the plant all day, in the cafeteria. The first ones got out at 6.30 that night.

Toronto

Cartridges were produced at the Dominion Arsenal Plant, St. Malo, Que. PAC PA 116093

Dearest N:

... You must be very curious about my venture into factory life. The work *is* hard and the shop I'm in is the most strenuous in the plant. Hopping in and out of the ships — generally speaking, I should be a walking shadow, but I am well and if not fat I at least look less scrawny than I have for years. I shouldn't be surprised if I didn't weigh almost 105. There are shorter girls in the plant but I am by far the tiniest. Most of them are grade school Prairie girls with bad grammar and, I should think, good morals. There are, of course, many exceptions, and I like most of them and get along nicely with all. The girl in the little tool room in our shop is the daughter of a Vancouver soldier recently elevated to the rank of Lt.Col. ... We share an appreciation of fine music and we exchange books — she is about eighteen, a jolly forthright girl.

Here I am sitting up in bed determined to write this letter and mother has just brought me a letter and an airgraph from you — they make me as happy and upset as they always do — you know — twittery. The letter was the one with the account of your New Year's week doings ... you seem to have had a hilarious if not a happy time and I'm glad to know at least you survived that date. As for advising me to do somewhat likewise — it's an impossibility. I do at least *see* people at work but the long hours make it impossible to tear around, and in any case no one ever asks me. I do think I told you somewhere in this letter than I am about the oldest girl in our shop.

Worker photographed at prayer in the chapel of the Cherrier and Bouchard Plant, Defence Industries Ltd., Montreal. The photograph emphasized that women did not leave their religion behind them when they went to work outside their homes. PAC PA 116135

Furthermore I let it be known that I am a married woman in love with my husband, and I am respected as such to the nth degree.

On the keel, I use a pneumatic drill, air drill, shears and, of course, pliers. The greatest work is in drilling from the inside out, and in hopping in and out of the ship about a dozen times an hour.

The old chap I was helping on the keel told the lead hand that, if I worked on a few more with him, I could take on the job myself. Much to my astonishment, this came about two weeks ago, and "Praise the Lord" I've not yet made an error.

As for wages, I get 40 cents an hour plus 8 cents cost of living bonus, minus all the minuses such as taxes, unemployment insurance, etc. It comes to about $77. a month, working six days a week. On the 15th of February I get an automatic increase to 50 cents plus 8 cents cost of living bonus, which being more heavily taxed doesn't come to so much more. . . .

Letter from Vancouver, 20 January 1942

Mrs. Florence McCracken, an inspector with Marelco Company, Toronto, was elected president of Local 3171, United Steelworkers of America, in 1945. PAC PA 120658

WOMAN WELDER SAYS UNION DEMANDS SHE QUIT JOB

Vancouver Labor Men Indignant at Report

Have Canadian women the right to work side by side with men on such war production jobs as they can competently undertake?

This question came to a head in Victoria Tuesday night when Mrs. Ethel Harvey, 28, only woman welder in B.C., charged that a union business agent had threatened male welders would walk out in protest if she did not quit her shipyard job.

Mrs. Harvey's charge was met with surprise and indignation by Vancouver labor leaders today. The alleged action, they declared, is contrary to trade union principles and, if carried out, might strike a damaging blow at the war effort.

Mrs. Harvey stated she would quit "as soon as my employers ask me", but in the meantime would ignore the asserted threat.

"I'm not doing any man out of a job," said the welder who learned her trade in a training school in Victoria. "I am proving that women can do this type of work satisfactorily. So far as I know, I am being paid the same scale as the men." She said she had not been asked to join the union, and believed such action would offer a solution to a problem which other women might face.

No Objection

Union welders in the yard are organized in Boiler-makers' Union Local No. 2, an affiliate of the Canadian Congress of Labour. Alex MacAuslane, regional director for the CCL, made it plain that the Congress is without prejudice in the matter of women workers. He agreed with Mrs. Harvey that joining the union might offer a solution. . . .

Vancouver Sun, 6 May 1942

GIRL WELDERS ACCEPTED BY BOILERMAKERS' UNION

Women who qualify for jobs as welders will be welcomed into the Boilermakers' and Iron Shipbuilders' Union as a result of a resolution passed by the Union Friday, accepting women into its membership.

The resolution stipulated that the union scale of wages must be paid to women workers.

Vancouver Sun, 22 August 1942

A REPETITION JOB   I had thirty-five or forty women working for me at the shipyard. I was a shop steward for the machinists' union, and the women all had to belong, because we were a closed shop. We didn't resent the women. Or I never heard any resentment. There was this understanding, it was a wartime job.

Material was scarce, so we took old bolts and nuts, used ones, to be rethreaded. In the bolt shop all the workers were women, because women are far better suited than what men are to do a repetition job, where there's not much variation all day.

Male shop steward, Vancouver

I DIDN'T MIND HOW DIRTY   It was a whole education for me, going into those shipyards. I was pretty left, and I mean left, left! As soon as we went there, we were accepted as pals.

It was a tremendous thing to earn your own money. We were buying back our self-respect. I didn't mind how dirty, how filthy it was, it was just great. It was a release from a marriage that was no good.

Child-care was a big problem, it was talked about all the time. I'd had three kids by the time I was twenty-one. I had a lady come in and live with us. She got twenty-five dollars a month and she kept house and looked after my kids. They were four, five, and six when I started to work.

Vancouver

A BOILER SUIT   I lied about my age. You were not supposed to be over thirty for the course they offered, how to put up electrical wiring in ships' hulls. I was thirty-two, and nervous, but I was good at the job. I had very strong hands. I was one of the first four women hired by the Victoria Machinery Depot. They were building Liberty Ships for the merchant navy.

I wore a boiler suit, like Winston Churchill, and a few women wore old-fashioned bib overalls with straps

Above: Women hired as shipyard workers in Pictou, N.S., included this sixteen-year-old girl. *Below*: A Micmac woman with her child worked in the same yard. PAC PA 116153 and PA 116154

over their shoulders. There were 2,000 men and eventually 225 women, and the women were not very welcome to start with. The men made it very hard. But eventually they realized we were there to work, and they were particularly helpful and kind to me when they realized my husband was a prisoner of war.

Victoria

RED-HOT RIVETS   I was on the riveting gang at the Pictou yard, and we wore coveralls like the men wore, with long-johns underneath. Standing up there on them decks in the winter, my God, you needed them.

I used to catch the rivets, the red-hot rivets, in a dipper like an ice-cream cone with a handle; then a guy would take them out right away with his big tongs and put them right in the girder, while they were hot.

When they threw those rivets down you had to watch out — if they hit you, you got burned, you'd get holes in your coveralls. For my hands I had special gloves, big gloves made of leather.

The reamers worked ahead of the riveters; they bored the holes for the rivets. There were women doing that job too. It was noisy, I can tell you, just like your ears would fall off.

They were getting desperate for workers at the yard, with all the men going overseas. They brought workers from everywhere, Antigonish, New Glasgow, Stellarton, that's where I lived. It was eighteen miles on the train each day, but it didn't seem far. It was fun and we earned good money. There were farmers and fishermen from Newfoundland, from Prince Edward Island, from Nova Scotia. All those men and I never heard a nasty word.

Stellarton, N.S.

SEW, WELD, OR RIVET   They trained pilots at Moose Jaw [under the British Commonwealth Air Training Plan], and the planes they used were brought into this shop for repairs. They ran big ads in the paper, saying they wanted women who could sew, weld, or rivet.

I was forty-two years old, and I had a ten-year-old son and a sixteen-year-old daughter. My husband thought it was all right for me to work during the war. So I applied for a sewing job. They employed a number of women as seamstresses, because part of the Cessna wing was covered with fabric. But there were no vacancies. The man I went to see about the job said, "Would you like to try welding?" And I thought, "Why not?"

I went to school for three months, to take a course in welding at the Technical School. There were eight

This "Flower" class corvette, built for the Royal Navy, was launched at Quebec City in August 1942. PAC PA 116156

THERE'LL ALWAYS BE AN ENGLAND

of us in my class. The others were in their teens or early twenties, but I was the only one who got my acceptance as a journeyman welder.

At first, all I did was burn off paint, and scrub the surface with a brush, but then I started welding. I worked as an aluminum welder, and I was the only woman in the shop.

The engines would come in for repairs, and you had to be very careful that all the gasoline had been drained before you started. If it hadn't been, the flame from a welding torch could make it explode. That never happened to me, but I caused a flash fire once when I dropped my welding torch. It took all the skin off my thumb.

Moose Jaw, Sask.

CONDITIONS WERE SHOCKING   We took a special train to Fairchild's [Fairchild Aviation] every morning from Windsor Station; we got on wearing our overalls. There was a real hodge-podge of people working at the factory, most with no experience. There were a lot of teachers, there was a clerk from Eaton's, one woman who was driven to work in a chauffeured limousine every day, and a lot of young French-Canadian women and men with very little education.

To begin with, I inspected small parts, to see that nuts and bolts were up to standard. The inspection department was a superior place to work, but I wanted more excitement. So I became a fitter, one of a group of five or six girls working on Bolingbrokes. We drilled holes in the bomb-bay doors before they were riveted. There were a lot of men around and they had trouble controlling their language. The foreman would make suggestive comments as he walked past.

We were told by our boss that there was a union in the factory but we didn't have to belong. I was curious and I found out it was the International Association of Machinists, quite left-wing, quite militant. I became a member.

The union wanted every department to elect a representative and I was chosen, to represent the fitters. I got to be a shop steward after a while, and I also became a member of the Communist Party. They seemed very good people, very earnest, and anxious to improve the lot of the working class.

Working conditions were shocking. You were at the mercy of the foreman, and he could fire you at an hour's notice. We worked ten-hour shifts, from seven in the morning to five at night, six days a week. We often stood at a bench for long hours, and we only got ten minutes' break in the morning. We had half an hour at lunchtime to go to the cafeteria, and another ten minutes in the afternoon. Wages were thirty-five cents an hour when I started, but I was earning sixty-five cents when I left: that's what the union did for us.

It was new for women to be active in the unions, and a lot of them did what men told them to do. I remember being furious when I was working on a particular case, and this man said he might support me if I went to bed with him.

There were guys at work who were out to pick up a sexual partner. I met my husband through my job, and when he went overseas I got a lot of propositions from men in the union. Some were my husband's friends. One said I owed it to him, for the war effort!

Montreal

Overhauling Trans-Canada Air Lines and R.C.A.F. aircraft, Winnipeg. ACA 09241

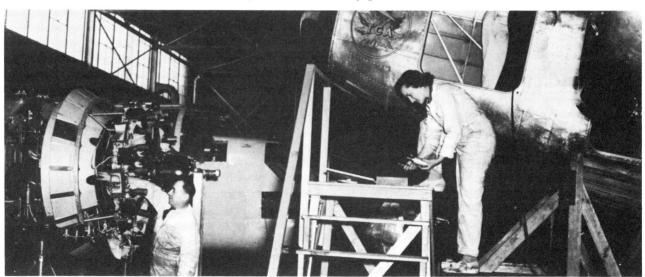

WOMEN GET THE BRUSH-OFF   It is true that women get the run-around. It is true that when post-war employment is discussed, women get the brush-off with the abrupt statement issuing from male throats like a mighty chorus: "Let them go back home."

Of course women are needed now; needed in ship-building, to help make planes and tanks and guns. They can do a hundred dangerous jobs. They can run the farm tractors, and feed the pigs, and milk cows, feed chickens; they can release men by the hundreds of thousands for active combat duty.

But let victory come and the need for womanpower disappear . . . what happens? Resentment, hostility, mounting sex antagonism, the most stupid, danger-ous and retrogressive trend of the times.

Dora Dibney, Saskatchewan journalist,
Canadian Women's Press Club *Newspacket*,
August 1944

Inset: Elsie Gregory MacGill was the chief aeronautical engineer with Canadian Car and Foundry in Fort William, Ont., during the early war years. She designed the precision tools needed to build the Hurricane Fighter aircraft, and directed construction of the plane. Hurricane Fighter, R.A.F. Fighter Station, England.
PAC PA 139429 and DND PL 3049

WHEN THE GIRLS TAKE OVER

1942

Jan. 7 — The blackout shutters were put on the school windows today. . . . Marks in my exam were 64. Just average. Did the best in manual work.
Jan. 8 — They're really rushing us at the school. Today we were divided into two classes. I'm in the advanced and we had fun taking an old plane apart. Some of us will be starting at Boeing's plant soon.
Jan. 17 — Finally worked today. Filed hinges. At 9.30 we were taken all through the plant in single file right through the offices to the "ladies", where we all took turns. There are no washrooms as yet.
Jan. 20 — I'm working the band-saw. At 10.30 we were all given ice cream to protect our tummys against all the sprays etc. I'm on night shift.
Jan. 23 — No wonder we don't turn out planes very fast. The boys sure don't strain themselves. It will be a good thing when the girls take over. They are more conscientious.
Feb. 2 — Riveted for the first time today.
Feb. 6 — This morning a girl in the machine shop had a big glob of hair pulled out when she got it caught in the drill press. Now we have to cover our hair

completely or else wear dust hats. Got first pay cheque, $48.53 for two weeks with deductions. We make 40 cents an hour.

Feb. 23 — After work went to town to buy a suitcase to carry my overalls in. It has no lock due to the shortage of metals.

Mar. 1 — Andy [the foreman] called me over today and told me I was to be in charge of the girls and the one boy on the job. There have been too many mistakes on the parts. It's a compliment. The Japanese are being evacuated from the coast.

Mar. 3 — Had most of the shop hammering on the D-brackets. Most of us felt light-headed. We think it's from the fumes from the paint shop. We were told to drink milk. They don't supply it anymore. Too many of us now.

Mar. 18 — Today I became butcher and took Joyce's fingernail off on the rivet squeezer. I felt awful and I guess she felt worse.

Apr. 27 — Today we're voting "Yes" or "No" for conscription. The answer will be "Yes".

Apr. 30 — Deburred Lucite for eight hours steady. Had a nose bleed, then my nose ran like a sieve. Every time I work on Lucite this happens. I must be allergic to it. If If feel like this tomorrow I'll have to stay home.

May 30 — Drove home on the bus and the driver said he didn't recognize me in my street clothes. He's so used to my overalls. We wear them so we don't have to change at work.

June 14 — Rained torrents but 969 turned up at the picnic and we had a wonderful time, dancing, drinking and running around in the rain, eating wet sandwiches, drinking sugarless coffee.

June 24 — Am now riding to work on my bike. Five miles. Buses don't stop in West Van any more.

July 11 — Congratulations Viv! Today Mr. Griffin told me I was to act as instructor and check all riveting done by the girls, also train the new ones. He says it's an honour as I'm the first girl to hold the position in the Boeing Plants. I also get a five cent raise.

July 27 — We listened to the launching of the first PBY at Plant 3 on Sea Island. It came over the PA system. Then it flew over our plant and we were all allowed to see it. A big day for us girls.

Sept. 24 — Pay day. $55.60. Not bad. We went to town to cash our cheques and there were literally thousands of girls in overalls doing the same thing. Four out of five girls work at Boeing's now.

Extracts, Vancouver war-worker's diary, 1942

A NICE JOB   Today women are performing over seventy percent of the operations necessary in the manufacture of machine guns. And more than eighty percent of those working in the instrument factories are women. They are wondering what their position will be when the war is over. This concerns not only industrial workers but professional women and women in other groupings. They want to know what attitude the government will take. Are the government and our employers going to say to those women, "Well, girls, you have done a nice job; you looked very cute in your overalls, and we appreciate what you have done for us; but just run along; go home; we can get along without you very nicely."

Women would like to have a definite understanding that this government recognizes they have a place to fill in the years of peace, just as they had in the years of war.

Dorise Nielsen, M.P.,
House of Commons, 4 May 1944

Dorise Nielsen, Member of Parliament (Unity Party) for North Battleford, Sask. PAC PA 47708

5

They Serve That Men May Fly: The Royal Canadian Air Force, Women's Division

"They serve that men may fly" said R.C.A.F. recruiting posters and advertisements. Or, more prosaically, the Canadian Women's Auxiliary Air Force will "release to heavier duties those members of the R.C.A.F. employed in administrative, clerical and other comparable types of service employment", according to the Order-in-Council of 2 July 1941.

The R.C.A.F. was the first of the armed forces to recruit women, six weeks ahead of the Army. Canada's commitment to train thousands of airmen as pilots, observers, and wireless air gunners under the British Commonwealth Air Training Plan put such a strain on R.C.A.F. resources that the employment of women became a necessity.

The British Women's Auxiliary Air Force provided the model for the new Canadian service. Two senior British W.A.A.F. officers arrived on 21 July 1941 to help organize the C.W.A.A.F. and to develop recruitment and training programs. Four others followed a few weeks later.

However, a Canadian woman had already been commissioned as policy officer for the C.W.A.A.F.: Kathleen O. Walker, head of the Ottawa Red Cross Motor Transport Corps. She later became the first Senior Officer in the Women's Division, R.C.A.F., as the service was renamed in February 1942 when its status as an integral part of the R.C.A.F. was confirmed.

The first 150 airwomen, very carefully selected as potential officers and N.C.O.s, reported to the Training Depot in Toronto. As in the other women's services, good family background and connections were important. By January 1942 the first group of officers had been trained, and the first squadrons of airwomen were ready to be posted. One group was sent to the Service Flying Training School at Uplands, near Ottawa; another went to No. 5 S.F.T.S. at Brantford; in March a squadron headed for Camp Borden. Soon W.D.s were serving at B.C.A.T.P. stations across Canada, and at Bombing and Gunnery Schools. It took some time for the new arrivals to be accepted.

In 1941 there were eight trades open to airwomen: clerks, cooks, equipment assistants, fabric workers, hospital assistants, motor transport drivers, telephone operators, and general duties. The number of trades grew to fifty in 1942 and reached sixty-five by the end of the war.

In January 1944, when Willa Walker (no relation), Kathleen Walker's successor, was Senior Staff Officer, the Women's Division numbered 15,147. Later that year, with the end of recruiting into the R.C.A.F. and the winding-down of the B.C.A.T.P., married members were released under a discharge plan announced in November. By the time the Women's Division was disbanded in 1946, 17,038 airwomen had served in Canada and abroad, in Britain, Newfoundland, and the United States.

SHE'S RIGHT IN THE MIDDLE OF THE BIGGEST JOB ON EARTH!

Just outside the window, aircraft are warming up, taking off, coming in. Those keen young airmen are tomorrow's fighting heroes. Wouldn't you like to be there to help them on their way?

As an airwoman in the RCAF you'll see them come in as students; you'll be there to applaud when they get their wings. A few months later you'll see their names in the headlines. Then you'll remember how you helped them on their way. You issued them their parachutes; recorded their flying time; prepared their meals; kept weather records for their safety; brought in their supplies in transports; carried on the stenographic work of the station; despatched secret teletype messages, worked at other interesting jobs . . .

The RCAF needs girls, ages 18 to 40, with at least High School Entrance. Apply at your nearest RCAF Recruiting Centre, bringing proof of education and birth certificate. NO WAITING! EXCELLENT OPPORTUNITIES FOR PROMOTION!

Recruiting pamphlet

CONNECTIONS   I saw an ad in the paper in June 1941, saying the R.C.A.F. would be interviewing women, so I applied. But getting into that first group for officer training was like getting into a convent. I remember I had a letter from Arthur Meighen and another from Canon Woodcock as references. You certainly needed your connections.

Toronto

JOINING UP   I came from Foam Lake, Saskatchewan, and I'd been raised on a farm, so joining up was quite an experience. I mean, I got on this train with a bunch of girls in Regina and none of us knew where we were heading. When we got to Winnipeg we had to change trains and none of us had ever done that before.

Saskatchewan

WHISTLES, BUGLES, BELLS   I was in my second year at university, in Toronto, and I joined up on a noon hour. They needed telegraph officers, and I had done that kind of work in my summer vacation. I didn't like to tell my family straight out what I'd done, so I called to say, "What would you think about me joining the Air Force?" My dad knew me pretty well, though. He said, "When were you sworn in?"

Capital Theatre, Ottawa. DND PL 12589

I was in the second batch of recruits, and we were called the CWAAF [Canadian Women's Auxiliary Air Force], a take-off of the British WAAF. We had British officers and N.C.O.s until there were enough Canadians trained. We took our basic training on Jarvis Street. The Air Force was a comparatively young service, and we didn't need to be told it was great to be in the R.C.A.F. — we knew that. We weren't told to scrub and polish the place like the girls in the Navy. Of course, there were whistles and bugles and bells to get used to. We had to learn to do what we were told, on the spot, to follow an order.

I remember the Flight Sergeant well. He was a tall, square redhead with lots of freckles, and he had all these women to teach. He was known as Flight Wright, and he was a real disciplinarian. He'd stand us out in the parade square in a puddle and he'd roar, "Get 'em up, get 'em up!" Of course we'd jump, and we'd end up soaked.

Toronto

I DIDN'T TELL THE TRUTH   I couldn't wait till the [Air Force] recruiting team came to New Glasgow. I didn't tell the truth about my age, not exactly. I was twenty when I came out, and I'd been in for three years!

My father wasn't going to stop me. He'd been in the Army all his life.

Nova Scotia

LOTS OF GOSSIP   There was a lot of excitement about the recruiting campaign. It said, ''Here's adventure!'' It appealed to our patriotism. The company I was working for in Ottawa told us they would guarantee our jobs on return.

I enlisted in September 1942, and within two weeks I was on a train to Toronto. My mother objected violently. I came from Schreiber—that's a railway town—and there was lots of gossip about the behaviour of military women. When I started my intensive training, Mother came to Toronto to try to get me out!

The lack of privacy at old Havergal College was a bit of a shock—forty of us to a dormitory, in double-decker bunks, and eight to a shower room, with no curtains.

Northern Ontario

A BOTTLE OF STOUT   I was teaching school in Montreal in 1943, and there was a rumour that the government was about to freeze teachers [in their jobs]. So a friend and I applied to the Air Force. We didn't feel tremendously patriotic, but this war was going on and we wanted to be part of it.

The Air Force wouldn't take me at first because I only weighed ninety pounds. But this officer said, ''Go home for two weeks and drink a bottle of stout before your evening meal. And eat oatmeal for breakfast. When you come back, drink as much water as you can before I weigh you.'' The second time I got in.

Montreal

Cooks enlisting at the R.C.A.F. Recruiting Centre, Bay Street, Toronto, November 1941. The initial age limit of 41 was later extended to 45 years. TT 98-670

YOU SHOULD SEE ME   Surprise, surprise— at last I'm not in Toronto! Yes, I actually have had a move. I'm opening up a new station to the WD. Mountain View is on the Bay of Quinte (more or less) about 10 miles east of Belleville.

I drove down with my senior officer, and believe me we created quite a sensation. Apart from a nursing sister, who is taken for granted, we are as yet the only women on the station of over 1500 men. The rest of the WD will arrive Saturday, we expect. There will be another officer and two corporals, but I am the only sergeant. You should see me eating in the sergeants' mess—so far I've been sitting in solitary splendour but the mess sergeant decided to change that, so I don't know what will happen tonight!

This morning one of the officers took us on a tour of the station—it is a very compact place and seems to be very well placed—the buildings are all temporary but painted greenish and blend with the terrain very well—I'd love to send you pictures but cameras are taboo on stations. Never have I been so close to so many aeroplanes—this is a bombing and gunnery school. A lot of the planes are outdated combat planes and you can see where bullets have gone in . . . they ship them here for training purposes. It was thrilling to get so close. We have to take one ''flip'' as they call it—it came out in orders that every WD must have a "formalization flight" as soon as possible after arrival.

The poor boys—I think they rather dread our coming in some ways because we rather cramp their style—but they like to have us come because they hear we do good work. Funny world. It's a funny thing to walk along the road and you can just feel the waves of curiosity following along. . . .

Letter, Mountain View, Ont., 16 June 1942

FRENCH SAFES We'd been promised that we'd live on an R.C.A.F. station under the same conditions as airmen, and we got proof of that at our first pay parade. We each received a packet of French safes! We took them out into the parade square later, and we blew them up like balloons!

Toronto

PEP TALK ABOUT MORALS After graduation I was posted to Rockcliffe, to the R.C.A.F. station, as steno to the base adjutant.

We lived in little houses on the rim of the hill, and we ate in the mess with the men. Many of the girls were away from their families for the first time, and we got pep talks about behaviour, about morals. We were told that the actions of one servicewoman could spoil it for many others.

Northern Ontario

Wing Officer L. M. Crowther and Squadron Officer E. C. Bather of the British Women's Auxiliary Air Force arrived in July 1941. In all, six senior WAAF officers came to train the first Canadian airwomen.
DND PL 5115

NICE LADS Funny how quickly you learn to be good friends casually. It's something you'd only learn in a set-up like this—but it's something you have to learn if you are not going to get hurt all the time.

They seem like nice lads—the nicest being married—they are so much easier to talk to—maybe they understand women better. . . .

Letter, Mountain View, Ont., 22 June 1942

WHAT TO CALL ME? My job was to organize the equipment store at No. 7 Manning Depot, Rockcliffe, all the flyers' gloves, helmets, goggles, and boots. The officer in charge never spoke to me. Not once! He communicated with me through the sergeant.

I discovered later that he couldn't figure out what to call me. "Miss" was reserved for officers, and he couldn't bring himself to use my surname. Suddenly he realized he could call me "AW 2 Carry."

Toronto

A NOVELTY NO LONGER The experiment is over. You are a novelty to the Service no longer, and soon we shall wonder how we got along without you.

Chief of the Air Staff, Air Marshal L. S. Breadner, October 1942

THE OFFICERS' MESS Some Commanding Officers on the stations wanted to put up barbed wire around the airwomen's barracks. They were horrified that women and men would mess together and—horror of horrors—women officers would be allowed in the Officers' Mess! In 1942 it took a great deal of patience and tact to stand up for our rights as planned and laid down by the Chief of the Air Staff.

I well remember those early visits to the air stations in cold winter weather. I was accompanied by a group of male officers, but women officers were not welcome in the Officers' Messes. I therefore always carried my own thermos and sandwiches with me, and when not welcome I cannily insisted on eating my lunch by myself either in a cold car or in the equally cold, unfinished airwomen's barracks. My officer friends from Headquarters were upset by this and gradually the C.O.s felt embarrassed too.

Flight Officer, later Wing Officer, Willa Walker, addressing the Royal Canadian Legion, Fundy Branch, New Brunswick, June 1979

Crokinole game, Prince Rupert, during A.R.P. alert. DND PL 23681

EVERY INCH IN TOP CONDITION   Performance is the thing that counts, as any airwoman in the tough wartime job of parachute rigger knows. Every inch of the RCAF's big silk umbrellas must be in top condition; every line, harness, strap and buckle.

Inside the Parachute Section, in a lofty maintenance hangar, the silks line racks running the length of a long, bright room. Below, airwomen fold inspected chutes. These are weighted during packing, not with the usual shot-filled bags, but with smooth hardwood chips designed by Flight-Sergeant R. G. M. Grubb of the Section.

Halfway down the room, the lines of packing tables are split by two power sewing machines. You might find Corporal Vera Groves of St. James, Manitoba, at one, stitching tricky new ripcord pockets on pack cases. Corporal Groves, whose father and two brothers are in the army, explains you don't have to make a jump to tear the pockets. They grow battered in the process of being carried flight after flight.

AW 1 Jean Hudson of London, Ontario, runs another machine, its long, wicked needle biting through thicknesses of new harness straps for chutes. Jean, like Vera, is one of a uniformed family, with a brother and sister in the Air Force.

Leading Airwoman Edith Edwards of Sarnia perches on a table beyond the machines, to sew a fine seam by hand. Some chutes are plain white, but she patches red on red and white on white of the two-toned canopies that do a double job of life-saving by being

easy to spot from the air when rescue planes fly in search of baled-out crews.

In the hangar proper is the Section's most spectacular gadget—another of Flight-Sergeant Grubb's inventions: a drop-tester for parachute harness. The chute may open, and the harness or its buckles break with the stress, so they, too, get expert attention.

The harness is hooked to a dummy which hangs on a gallows-like framework. One airwoman, turning a crank, hoists the dummy to a platform about 12 feet from the ground. There, another airwoman releases the figure and down it goes. If the harness hold firmly it is okayed.

CP item datelined Winnipeg,
5 January 1943

TO COUNTER THE CHEMICALS   The wings were covered with cotton. It was brought up to tension by dope. Before we applied it we had to drink a quart of milk—to counter the chemicals, I believe. Sometimes we went up on a flight to watch the tension on the wing, to see if the fabric ripped.

Ontario

"Parachute riggers", painting by Paraskeva Clark (1898–   ).
CWM 14086

IN THE CONTROL TOWER   I worked in the control tower for the chief flying instructor, where all the records and logs were kept for the training school. The control tower was at the hub of the base, and I was the N.C.O. in charge of the orderly room. I gave orders to men, because trainees got assigned to make entries in log books, or to clean windows, and I never ran into the feeling that women shouldn't be there.

I did quite a bit of flying. When the weather flight went up, they always wanted a weather observer, who could report any visual flight problems to the met. officer aboard. But this wasn't long-distance flying.

Saskatoon was one of the best cities for accepting the military, for caring for them. There were canteens run by volunteers, and the churches found ''adoptive'' parents for us. One family gave two of us the key to their house when they went away in the summer.

Northern Ontario

Squadron Officer, later Wing Officer, Kathleen O. Walker (*right*) was born in England and raised in Montreal. She was the widow of a former R.C.A.F. group captain. In 1943 she was posted to R.C.A.F. Headquarters, London, as Senior Officer, W.D. With her are three officers who graduated from the first class: (*from right*) Flight Officer Willa Walker (no relation), Kathleen O. Walker's successor as Senior Staff Officer; Squadron Officer Jean Davey, later Senior Medical Officer on the staff of the R.C.A.F. Director of Medical Services; and Flight Officer Winnifred Taylor, later Commanding Officer, No. 6 Manning Depot, Toronto. Another senior officer (not pictured) was chief Messing Officer Kathleen Jeffs. The first woman to head a deputy directorate at R.C.A.F. Headquarters, she supervised food preparation for the R.C.A.F. in Canada and Britain. TT 98-670

Recruits on weekly route march, Toronto, April 1942. TT 98-669

Stretching fabric over aircraft wing. DND PL 11317

IN THE BOMB BAY   I went on an aerial photographer's course at Rockcliffe for three months. We flew in the daytime and we studied at night. We were mostly young ones, straight out of high school. I was on the 33rd course, and there were approximately thirty on each course.

They used old Anson aircraft for training. They were slow and lumbering, but they were fine for photography. We went in pairs, and we'd set the camera up in the bomb bay — we used a K24, and it was quite heavy, and bulky — then we'd run a wire up to the nose of the aircraft. When we were up in the air one of us would crawl into the nose, which was Plexiglas, and if we wanted a particular line of photography we'd raise a foot. All the pilot could see was our feet, so that was the signal. Then we'd press a button which would set the camera rolling.

You took a series of photographs timed to overlap. Maybe you'd have ten miles to photograph. When you developed the prints, if you used special glasses, you could tell if the grass was broken in a field. You'd know how many people had walked across it — one, or a hundred, or a few hundred — or if a vehicle had been there: an ordinary car, or a tank, or several tanks. Women didn't fly in war areas, but in England there were W.D.s who developed pictures taken over Europe and they mounted them on linen, and rolled the prints up like a calendar. They would be dropped down to the troops in the line.

When we flew we wore "teddy bears", coveralls like mechanics wear, only softer material. In summer that's all we wore. But in winter we wore flying suits, furry-lined, and long flying boots which didn't fit. I used to wear shoes under the pair I had, though we weren't supposed to.

We wore parachutes on our chests, but that was darned awkward when you were handling a camera, and after we passed inspection on the ground we'd keep the harness on and toss the 'chutes in the back. The pilot would laugh, and I'd say, "Well, how can I crawl into the nose with that on my chest?"

There were occasional crashes at Rockcliffe. We'd be told to take photographs, sometimes so they could investigate the cause, sometimes just as a record. One day there were five men in a plane that crashed. Two got out and the others didn't. We were called out to photograph the plane as it burned. We were thinking about those three young men trapped in that plane. The night before they'd been joking and laughing in the dry canteen — if they were flying the next day they didn't drink — you didn't know their names, but you felt close to them. You lived with laughter, hilarity — you laughed at the world. And next day they might be gone — or they might be dead.

New Glasgow, N.S.

DRIVING A STAFF CAR   I was a time-keeper with the air training program. After a year I remustered and went in as a motor transport driver. You were assigned to a vehicle for a week at a time, and one week I might be driving a staff car, in full uniform, and another week I'd be on a garbage truck, or on the mail run, in coveralls. You wore coveralls if you drove trucks. Sometimes I was on the bank run, taking the adjutant into town, or in a station wagon, picking up men from the train.

I drove an ambulance, too, and I saw a few accidents. The worst was when I had to take a medical officer out to a plane crash, in a snowstorm. The pilot had crashed a mile from the end of the runway, and we found the plane, and we found his shoes, but we couldn't find him. It turned out a local farmer had found him and brought him into the hospital, but he died the next day.

Saskatchewan

BEER IN THE TOILET TANKS   A lot of the rules were utterly silly. Men could drink beer in their canteen. Women could not. Of course, women being pretty sharp, we managed to get around that rule quite often. We did it by being friends with the flight sergeant who was in charge of the men's canteen.

We would sneak out at night and get some beer bottles from him and hide them in the toilet tanks in our barracks. They kept beautifully cold there. The only trouble was that occasionally the labels would soak off and plug up a toilet.

Victoria

LET'S HAVE SOME RESPECT   No. 1 hangar and No. 4 hangar both had a coffee bar, and I worked behind the counter. The odd man wanted to talk dirty, but all you had to say was ''There's a smoking-room next door.'' I was doing my job, so let's have some respect, that's how I felt. And it was good for men to have girls working around them. It lifted their morale.

Some of the girls would go out and get real drunk, and they got bad names for the rest of us. But the officers were very strict about behaviour off duty. If you were going into town they insisted your hair was off your collar. Lipstick was another thing. They didn't like us all painted up.

When you got a leave pass you had to be on station by 11 [p.m.].

Saskatchewan

Aerial photographers prepare for a training flight at Rockcliffe Air Station, Ottawa. Despite the hopes and ambitions of many qualified recruits, servicewomen were never trained to fly or to be members of air crews. ''They serve that men may fly'' was an accurate description of women's work within the R.C.A.F., as it was within the W.A.A.F. DND PL 20836

THE NICEST CHAP   Last night was the usual Saturday night officers' dance. I was lucky to meet a "good type" (as we say) to begin with. A very nice Scotch lad. He is actually Army, but is Army Reconnaissance and is a pilot with RAF wings. He is the nicest chap I have met for some time. The majority of the nice ones are either married or already spoken for! Now don't get alarmed or excited. That is merely a statement of fact.

This station is amazing in one respect, you meet people from everywhere. Newfoundlanders, Dutch,

millions (more or less) of RAF, Australians, Americans, one lad from India, Free French, Polish, Norwegians, New Zealanders.

On the way down on the train I had a very good conversation with an Army captain. These conversations with people you'll never see again can be such fun — you meet such interesting people and, because you know you'll probably never see them again, you can say things you would say only to good friends.

Letter, Trenton, Ont., February 1943

COMPLETELY SNUBBED   After a hard day, to come in and be completely snubbed by some of the officers' wives is a bit much. I almost agree that "the female of the species is more deadly than the male." I can understand now why some girls "go wrong", as the saying is. After the way those women treated me tonight it almost makes one feel like going out and doing the things they seem to expect one to do.

Why women should completely snub us just because we're in uniform I don't know — no invitations to homes, and when we're introduced they quickly turn and talk to each other. And it's no imagination either. Even some of the men remarked on it. It is a bit hard — after all we don't want their men, if that's what they are worried about, and ten to one our morals are just as good or better than theirs — at least I don't sit around and drink!

Letter, 28 March 1943

A LETTER FROM HOME   If you people lived in uniform and on stations in the semi-artificial state we do, you would realize just what a letter from home means. It makes you realize that there is a world of homes and naturalness and being cultured and doing things one wants to do and should be able to do.

Letters from home give me a weekly renewal of determination to get this job over and done as quickly as possible — and you people talk of cutting your letters short to save paper and stamps!! That practically amounts to sabotage.

Letter, 19 March 1943

Checking for loose equipment on an amphibian plane, Jericho, B.C., and refuelling aircraft. Airwomen's pay was initially two-thirds of what airmen received, but in 1943, as part of a concerted effort to bring more female recruits into the forces, basic pay was raised to four-fifths of the men's, and trades pay became equal.
DND PL 23679 and DND PL 20440

VICIOUS AND MALICIOUS   In the summer of 1942 all the women's services were much harmed by a vicious and malicious whispering campaign. The gossip was that men and women were sharing barracks, that immorality was rife, and that the hospitals were full of illegitimate babies. Those of us in the services didn't think that the public would believe these things, but the rumours cut down our recruiting drastically. Women were needed desperately, particularly in the R.C.A.F. to keep the Commonwealth Air Training Plan going. The authorities felt that something must be done.

So we in the R.C.A.F. enlisted the support of that great woman Charlotte Whitton. She was president at that time of the Canadian Welfare Council. She arranged to contact all the large women's groups and clubs, right across the country: church groups, Girl Guides, V.O.N., Red Cross, Women's Institutes, the Y.W.C.A. She also called the press.

On certain days we had "open house" at every Air Force station where W.D.s were serving. All women's groups were invited. They were to observe the airwomen at work and inspect their barracks, mess halls, and hospitals. . . .

Wing Officer Willa Walker, addressing
the Royal Canadian Legion, Fundy Branch,
New Brunswick, June 1979

Dear Family:

The trains were all late and the wires were down so a good many signals didn't come through. So we met trains and picked up recruits mostly by guess and by gosh, but we got less than 100, which is not good.

Recruiting is definitely poor. And when I think of so many girls (and men) sitting at home doing little or nothing and people working in non-essential industries, it burns me up.

And the war is not as far away as they think. You realize that when some of your girls report back from leave in Newfoundland and tell about being four hours overdue because the boat was being chased by a sub — zigzagging her course and dropping depth charges all the time. If people would only wake up and join up. . . .

Letter, Ottawa, 3 January 1943

H.R.H. The Princess Alice chats with Wing Officer Willa Walker, Officer Commanding No. 7 Manning Depot, Rockcliffe, Ont., at Rideau Hall, 24 July 1943. The Rockcliffe depot turned out 1,000 airwomen a month at the peak of its operations.
Courtesy Mary Saunders

PRAYER OF A WD

Dear God, as I kneel down I have so much to ask:
My prayers are for the strength to serve a nation's
    mighty task.
I need the grace with which to wear in dignity and
    pride
My uniform and take with me its meaning in its
    stride.
Teach me, O Lord, obedience that I may do my best
Until our country once again is peaceful and at rest.
And, having these to guide me while our Air Force is
    in the war,
I have but then to thank You. I cannot ask for more.
Thank You for our country, brave and free
And make me ever worthy, Lord, to be a "WD".

Published in Crosswinds, R.C.A.F.
Station Rockcliffe, Ont., January 1944

IN THE OPS ROOM   The ops room in Victoria was big. Filter ops filtered the information we received and applied it as appropriate. We were connected to boys in radar posts out west. They gave their locations by letter and number, but the information wasn't coded. Sometimes we got to know the boys well enough they'd ask for a date! As the information came in we plotted it on the big board.

A lot of civilians looked down on us in Victoria. They thought we were having too good a time with the boys. And we did have a good time. If you wanted to live a wild life you could. But the majority of girls were good types. I loved associating with the other airwomen. There were upper class, middle class, all strata. But we were just like one big family.

I worked for two years in the ops room in Victoria, then I spent a year in Prince Rupert in a similar set-up. There'd be about fifteen of us on duty on each shift. It wasn't always hectic, but in the quiet times we weren't allowed to read: we had to keep our eyes peeled. Towards the end I had a responsible position: I sat up on a balcony with an officer and read information off the board as it was plotted to the Army, Navy, and some American stations. They were interested in the location of aircraft, ships, and the like off our coast.

I was chosen to go on officer training, and I was taking an advanced course in radar when VE Day took place.

Toronto

SCADS OF U-BOATS   Thirty of us went overseas with the first draft in August 1942. It was all done so secretly that we suspected later it was because there were scads of U-boats in the Atlantic at the time. Ottawa felt there would be criticism about sending women over at the height of U-boat activity.

It took ten days to cross, in a huge convoy. Vincent Massey [Canadian High Commissioner to Great Britain] came to Glasgow to meet the troops when we landed, and over the PA system he said, "I understand there are Air Force women on board. People in London are going to be very surprised." Well, everyone *was* very surprised, and they took pictures of us when we got there.

Calgary

CHASED ALL OVER THE ATLANTIC   We arrived in London on Halloween night, 1943. We went over on the *Aquitania*. There was no convoy, and we were chased all over the Atlantic, down to the Azores and practically to Iceland. I didn't really think of the danger. I was twenty-two at the time.

There were nine or ten of us in one cabin, quite a small one. We couldn't open the portholes because there were American soldiers sleeping in hammocks on the decks outside.

Toronto

W.D. precision squadrons took part in recuitment drives across Canada in 1943, when the need for airwomen was most acute. TT97-667

Staging a mock battle in the "Fighter Control" room, Rockcliffe, Ont. Bombing raids were planned and enemy movements charted in the ops room. Some airwomen were trained at Western Air Command Headquarters in Victoria, and some at Eastern Air Command Headquarters at Halifax. DND PL 21594

The first draft overseas in August 1942 included six Manitoba WDs. The caps they are wearing were replaced by a smarter model in 1943. Within a few months there were 1,500 WDs serving in Britain. Airwomen had to be twenty-one or older to serve abroad. DND PL 10676

I HEARD THIS DRONE   The R.A.F. had recently lost twenty-six of their top-notch women air controllers in a direct hit on their London barracks, so the R.C.A.F. were told, "Don't put your women all together, whatever you do. Have them live out, and see there are no more than four people in one place." So we were given a living allowance and told to find something not too close to the river or to a power plant.

A friend and I found a place through looking in the evening paper. You could get apartments on the top floor anywhere, and there were eighty-four steps up to our flat. It had two bedrooms overlooking Brompton Oratory. One night Irene went to bed but I couldn't settle. I was washing up in the kitchen about 11.30 when I heard this drone getting nearer and nearer, louder and louder. I opened the casement windows in the living room, just in time to see this V1, so close that I could have touched it. It dropped on an apartment block across the way and exploded. The blast sucked my windows shut.

There were three Americans living downstairs on the main floor, and they went over to the apartment building. There were many, many people killed, but they brought some of the injured back with them, and we helped treat them for glass cuts. Later on, when I went back upstairs and into my bedroom, I found a big nut and a bolt from the doodlebug lying on my pillow, right where my head would have been.

Calgary

CHOSEN TO BE COMMISSIONED   Ottawa said women going overseas were not to be commissioned immediately, but Air Marshal Breadner objected to that. He said, "Women overseas aren't going to be discriminated against."

A few months after we got to England, eight of us were chosen to be commissioned, and we went to Windermere, to a WAAF [Women's Auxiliary Air Force] school for two months. I came back to London as an administrative officer.

Calgary

OFFICER TRAINING

Wednesday, May 12 — Arrived at Innsworth Reception Wing 1930 hours. Issued with mug, knife, fork and spoon. Ground sheets are also issued at the same time, but as we had raincoats we did not take them.

Thursday, May 20 — Today's P.T. was followed by Air Raid Drill, finding our nearest shelter, the one assigned to our particular hut, and precautions to be observed. Section Officer Shemming gave us the History of the RAF, in fact, a resume of the history and advancement of flying generally. After lunch a lecture on types and recognition of gases and how to combat gas warfare. On the parade square five girls were chosen from each flight to march in a Wings for Victory Parade at Newent. Domestic evening, and those of us who did not report for parade rehearsal scrubbed and cleaned the hut thoroughly.

Friday, May 21 — A civilian, probably the local Member, gave us a long and meaty talk on Current Events, opening with the question "What are we fighting for?" Interesting to note how few people knew. He had lived in Germany for some years and painted the picture of Nazism and its efforts to engulf us in strong terms. After lunch paraded to a film and lecture on salvage.

Sunday, May 23 — Free all afternoon, after Church parade in the morning. Walked up a hill which forms the last part of the Cotswold ''Churchdown''. Lovely 12th century church on the very top, and glorious views on all sides of the surrounding counties.

Monday, May 24 — Reveille etc. Colour hoisting cancelled because of rain, which also made it necessary to have P.T. in one of the hangars. The M.O. gave us a talk on hygiene, the necessity for keeping our person and attire clean, etc. She touched but lightly on V.D. because, she said, ''it is such a repulsive subject'' and anyone that sets themselves a high standard of morals would have nothing to worry about. Second and last gas lecture followed break.

Thursday, May 27 — Our Wing Officer delivered an address on Discipline. She believed that a smart salute indicated a high or low degree of discipline, as the case might be. We then paraded to Church and had a last talk by the Padre, who made a simple and inspiring appeal to us to always keep our religion as the mainspring of our everyday life. Dinner was followed by a talk on Security, and the need for watching every word we spoke in public, and how important it was to keep faith with the men in the air by never divulging by gesture or word the slightest piece of service information that we might possess.

Report by a W.D. on an officers'
training program run by the W.A.A.F.
at Innsworth, Gloucestershire, May 1943

NO. 1 FIGHTER STATION   About a dozen of us were sent to No. 1 Fighter Station at Digby in Lincolnshire, and we were there until D-Day. It was a British station, and we were on shift with the WAAFs in the Ops Room.

We had head-sets and long rods with magnetic tips. Messages came in code over your head-set so we could identify aircraft as friendly or hostile, the speed and the range — it all came in a series of numbers — and we plotted it on a huge table, with an arrow in the direction indicated. When we were busy it was hectic, and we spelled each other out.

We worked shifts, 56-hour weeks, and after a total of six weeks we got off at 8.00 one morning and we were free until 5.00 the next day. We didn't go to bed after that last night-shift. We struck out for places such as York, to meet friends, have hot water, food, drink, exchange pieces of news. The 56-hour weeks

Airwomen helped to train wireless operator/air gunners. They also taught aircraft recognition at No. 1 School of Fighter Control, Rockcliffe, Ontario. DND PL 24469 and DND PL 21599

didn't include time spent on pay parades, kit inspections, billet inspections, dental inspections, or injections, or other kinds of parade.

We didn't grumble very much, but we loathed the W.A.A.F. officers, and our morale was bad. In the Ops Room the officers were almost all British, and they had a distinct class sense. They didn't mingle with the airwomen like Canadian officers did. There was some jealousy involved. We were paid more than the British were, we got food parcels from home, we brought silk stockings with us. They had reason to resent us.

We were expecting D-Day in 1944, but we had no idea when exactly it would come. On the evening of June 5th the sky was black with squadrons, American, British, Canadian, and we couldn't help but guess. I was on duty that night from midnight till 8.00, and I came off for a meal—not breakfast, but grey meat and gravy, dehydrated potatoes and bread pudding—and then I went back to bed in the Nissen hut, cranky and unwashed. Very soon some airwomen came running in, shouting "D-Day has started!"

After D-Day I was sent to Intelligence, to look after the maps used by the crews at No. 6 Bomber Group, Linton on Ouse. What a difference! This was a Canadian station, with Canadian officers including Canadian Messing Officers [dietitians]. Corn-on-the-cob appeared in season, and we were in heaven!

I recall, in 1945, a huge machine arriving at Linton which converted powdered milk and cooled it. The dietitians in Ottawa wanted to let their colleagues in England know that this machine and others like it were on their way, after all the planning. So they sent a cable saying "Greetings from the udder side".

We received an orange in rations once a month, and a fresh egg for breakfast about once every six weeks. But sometimes we could buy eggs from a farmer and cook them over the fire.

Letter from a former W.D., Brockville, 1984

WHERE THE ACTION WAS   We learned the basics of intelligence and photographic interpretation at Highgate. Then we were sent to No. 6 Bomber Group at Linton on Ouse, Yorkshire, just south of the Cheviot Hills.

Intelligence officers interrogated crews when they came back from a bombing mission. They usually went out at 2000 hours and returned at 0400. Sometimes they were scared sick; they had been through a terrible ordeal. The pilot would come over and say if it had been particularly bad. They had hot coffee or rum, if they wanted, and each crew would sit down with an intelligence officer and we would just let them talk.

It was very high-powered. You got raw answers to questions, exactly how they felt, and that's what you wanted. "Did you hit the primary target? The secondary target? Was the weather as briefed? Was there something you weren't prepared for?" You had to find out where the concentrations of power were, where the searchlights and the ack-ack guns were. It was fascinating. You were right where the action was. Later we examined the photographs they'd taken

Some airwomen posted to air bases in northern England lived in Nissen huts. TT 97-667

during a bombing raid. The cameras were automatic: they rolled when the bomb doors opened.

The crews were all British Commonwealth Air Training Plan, Australians, New Zealanders, Danes, Americans, you name it, as well as Canadians. They were all in Canadian units. They were very young men. Near the end of the war they got younger and younger. We were debriefing pilots of eighteen or nineteen. We got emotionally involved. The first squadron I went to was a Toronto squadron, and I knew a lot of the boys' sisters. We looked after each other. They were friends rather than boyfriends, a good gang.

One of my jobs was to issue the crews with emergency rations, in a khaki-coloured waterproof bag with a round tin in it, and a can opener. There'd be concentrated cheese and concentrated sweets, water-purifying tablets, a very small razor blade, and a fishing line and hook, in case they came down over enemy territory. We had to see they had all the help they could get, but you could only hope they would make it back. Not all of them did.

Toronto

Section Officer Ishbel Mutch of Regina was an operatic and concert singer who sang with the Metropolitan Opera Company in New York before she enlisted in the R.C.A.F. (W.D.). She went to England as Entertainment Officer with the Canadian Bomber Group commanded by Air Vice-Marshal G. M. McEwen. DND PL 29783

Wedding in Epsom, Surrey. DND PL 43374

DINNER AND DANCING   Nearly all of us had a network of men, and if anyone landed on the same Station, or was passing through, it was considered perfectly o.k. to meet for dinner and dancing. It might be someone's uncle, or the brother of a friend, or someone else's husband.

Likewise, we went to dances, evenings, on the Station. Many women were already attached: they were married or engaged or had "steadies". Many men had a girl or a wife elsewhere. Some of each sex were on the make, certainly, but most simply wanted company, to talk about "Back Home", and to exchange news of connections here and there. In a pub or café, it was normal for Canadian men of any rank to go by your table and strike up a conversation, starting with "It's great to see Canadian girls . . . where're you from?"

Letter from a former W.D., Brockville, 1984

REPORTED MISSING   My fiancé was in the Black Watch and after I arrived in England we were married in London in January 1944. He went to France in the Normandy landings, and he survived Caen. He was taken prisoner in Holland, but I didn't know that at the time, because he was reported missing.

I heard eventually through a network of Black Watch friends. Someone had seen two German stretcher-bearers carry him off the field. And in the New Year I finally got a letter from him. In the meantime, I was lucky to be somewhere where the action was, with crews coming and going, new squadrons arriving, and station dances to go to.

Letter from a former W.D., Brockville, 1984

ABOUT CONTRACEPTION   Soon after my arrival overseas, and in anticipation of marriage, I consulted a WAAF Medical Officer about contraception. As she pulled herself together (shock) she said that in THEIR Service they didn't give this kind of advice, and that she would make an appointment with a Specialist. The date, when I finally got it, was going to be too late for my purposes, so I didn't accept it. Instead, passing Boots the Chemists, whose windows were stacked with the product I wanted, I went in there.

Montreal

The "W Debs" played to Canadian military personnel at home and overseas. Some WDs were members of other R.C.A.F. entertainment troupes, such as the "All Clear" and the "Blackouts". TT 97-667

WE DID THE CAN-CAN   The "W Debs" were organized at Rockcliffe, eleven girls, the performers, and two men as pianists. We toured eastern Canada in 1944, then they shot us over to dear old Blighty.

We had a great time going over on the *Andes*, performing for the troops. They put two mess tables together and we danced on the table tops. We did the can-can as the boat rolled, until the pianist got sick and rushed away.

In England we had our own bus, and we played all the stations, Air Force, Army, and Navy, and the hospitals too, in northern England. The word would get around: "They're our girls from home!" We were morale-builders. We came down to London to make recordings with Robert Farnon and his orchestra, for Canadian troops on the continent.

Robert Coote was our C.O. in London and he sent us out three times to the continent in 1944 and '45. We really roughed it. Our crew built a stage for us in a field near an Army camp, and they dug holes for our "johns" there too. We'd do two shows a day, and then there'd be a meal at night in the mess, the sergeants' or the officers' mess. There'd be spam and chips, or spam and eggs, or eggs and chips.

When we played the hospitals in England the boys were usually so enthusiastic, and we'd knock ourselves out to be funny. But there was one hospital, in East Grinstead, where we couldn't understand why there was hardly any reaction to the show. There was a dance afterwards, and when we saw those boys we understood why. They were there for plastic surgery. Some had no legs, no eyelids, no noses. One boy I danced with had no hands. They couldn't clap, they couldn't whistle.

Ottawa

PARIS ON VE DAY   When we left for France in March 1945 we'd toured England, Scotland, Ireland, and Wales. The girls and I went to Normandy on an L.S.T. following a minesweeper — the war wasn't over then.

In Holland, at General Crerar's camp, you could hear the guns, they were that close. I spent one night at a staging point, and the moment the light went out the rats came out. It was terrifying. A couple of days later I was covered with lice, just crawling from head to toe. I was put in isolation for four or five days, and when we got to Paris I had to be treated for scabies. I went for oil treatments to Elizabeth Arden: Goering had kept Elizabeth Arden open for the German officers' wives during the occupation.

VE Day, Trafalgar Square, London. DND PL 33998

It was wonderful to be in Paris on VE Day. Nobody went to bed for three nights. Four of my friends were attached to a Mosquito squadron in Germany, and they simply took the rotors off their planes, commandeered a huge Opel, and drove to Paris. I had this American officer from Charleston with me, too. God, he was attractive!

Everybody in Paris was out on the streets and you couldn't move, but somehow we got down to the Arc de Triomphe. The Germans had lowered the flame over the grave of the Unknown Soldier, and on VE Day the French turned the flame up again. It was a very moving ceremony, with people weeping openly while they watched.

Entertainment officer from Toronto,
in charge of W.D.s
in the "Blackouts"
entertainment troupe

WHEN THE LIGHTS CAME ON AGAIN

We were in London on VE Day, when the lights came on again! We'd got so used to the blackout, when the streetlights just glimmered, like candles.

When the news came through that war had ceased, we went out into the streets, in the crowds. When we got to Piccadilly, the streetlights came on — and we were just in a daze!

Next day there was a Victory Parade through London. Buckingham Palace was floodlit, the King and Queen came out on the balcony, with the two princesses and Winston Churchill. It was just like a champagne cork had popped, there was such great jubilation.

We felt like we were part of a big, big family.

Calgary

6

You Too Can Free a Man to Serve at Sea: The Women's Royal Canadian Naval Service

Unlike the Army or the Air Force, the Royal Canadian Navy saw no need to establish a women's auxiliary service force in 1941. In the spring, when all three services were asked by National Defence Headquarters to estimate the number of jobs which women might usefully fill, the Navy's view was that only a handful of drivers — twenty women at the most — might be required. Certainly not enough to justify creating a service.

Twelve months later, the Navy's estimate had been revised significantly. As the Allied war effort expanded, and the Battle of the Atlantic intensified, the need to free shore-based sailors to serve at sea became apparent. The Army and the Air Force had both proved that women could replace men in an expanding number of trades. Early in 1942 the "senior service" began to plan for a Women's Royal Canadian Naval Service, established by Order-in-Council on 31 July.

The new service was modelled carefully on British lines, although there was an important difference from the beginning: the W.R.C.N.S. was an integral part of the Navy, not an auxiliary like the British W.R.N.S. The Canadian service was set up by British officers on loan from the W.R.N.S., but the first Director was a man: Captain Eustace A. Brock, R.C.N.V.R., who had been serving as Canadian liaison officer with the British Admiralty.

Shortly after they arrived the British Wren officers set off across Canada to promote the new service and to interview possible recruits. Fears that the best candidates had already joined the Army and the Air Force turned out to be groundless. Many able and qualified women had held back for various reasons, and serving with the Navy had a certain cachet. The number of applications grew steadily.

On 29 August the first sixty-seven recruits reported for basic training. Upon graduation they were sent across Canada as recruiting officers, or they were posted to Galt, Ontario, to help run the new basic training centre. About four hundred recruits could be accommodated at Galt, and new ones arrived each week in the "duty boat" which picked them up at the local station. From Galt, Wrens were posted to naval establishments, to ports in different parts of Canada, and to Naval Service Headquarters in Ottawa.

Eventually there were thirty-nine trades open to women in the W.R.C.N.S. The majority of Wrens served as general duty writers, supply assistants, messengers, cooks, messwomen, and wardroom attendants. Some had very interesting and responsible jobs. W.R.C.N.S. dietitians performed an important service to the Navy. Paymaster Lieutenant-Commander Doris Taylor became Chief Dietitian at Naval Service Headquarters in Ottawa, advising the Director of Victualling on food preparation on board all ships. Sub-Lieutenant Elspeth Middleton headed the R.C.N. school of cookery at H.M.C.S. *Cornwallis* which ran courses for seagoing cooks. Adelaide Macdonald Sinclair, an economist with the Wartime Prices and Trade Board, became Director, W.R.C.N.S., with the rank of Captain, a post she held until the service was disbanded in 1946.

The first Wrens to serve abroad were posted to Washington in April 1943, to work for the Canadian Joint Staff. Approximately fifty Wrens served with the Navy in the United States. Five hundred and eighty-six Wrens served in Newfoundland, which was considered an overseas posting in the war years. In September 1943, twelve Wren ratings and two officers were the first Wrens to be sent to Britain. By 1944 approximately three hundred Wrens were serving there, principally in London, Greenock, and Londonderry. At final count, more than one thousand Wrens had served abroad.

W.R.C.N.S. recruiting stopped early in 1945. In August 1946 when the service disbanded, nearly seven thousand women had seen service with the Royal Canadian Navy.

Recruiting officers, Vancouver, April 1943. Unlike the other services, the W.R.C.N.S. had no need to mount extensive advertising campaigns. With a limited target of 5,000 recruits, the W.R.C.N.S. found it could afford to be "choosy". PAC PA 128244

WOMEN OF CANADA

The opportunity to serve your country and your Navy is here — NOW CANADA IS AT WAR!

Her Navy is fighting the Battle of the Atlantic so that the Empire life-line may be preserved. Her men are continuously risking great hazards in small ships, and daily sacrificing their lives for freedom. You too must help. The rapidly expanding Canadian Navy requires trained men for duty at sea. Wrens are urgently needed to release these men for active service.

There is a job waiting for YOU at a shore establishment.

Don't delay.

Join the Wrens and hasten victory.

You too can free a man to serve at sea.

Wren recruiting literature, 1942

Shore-duty cooks were badly needed, but the Navy had difficulty finding enough recruits for this domestic work. R.C.N. sketch by Grant Macdonald, courtesy Adelaide Sinclair

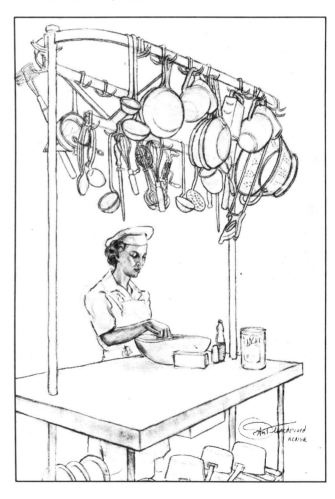

WHICH OF THESE DUTIES FITS YOU?

COOK — Should have had previous employment or professional experience as Cook; however, any woman who has an aptitude for cooking but whose previous experience is limited could be trained.

STEWARD — Previous employment as a waitress or in general domestic service preferred. Women who are used to housework and like it can be trained. Usually employed in W.R.C.N.S. Quarters.

WARDROOM ATTENDANT — Duties include cleaning officers' cabins, valeting and waiting at table. Women who enter as stewards can be trained as officers' stewards later if they show aptitude for this type of work.

QUARTERS ASSISTANT — Catering for numbers, bookkeeping, control of staffs, etc. Dietitians and housekeepers would qualify for these duties. A Quarters Assistant helps to run the W.R.C.N.S. quarters. She should not be under 25 years of age.

LAUNDRESS — Previous experience in laundry work useful but not essential as a thorough training is given in this category.

SUPPLY ASSISTANT — In general a supply assistant is responsible for the issuance of and the accounting for food, clothing, and other stores. Candidates should have neat handwriting and should be good at figures. Previous experience in bookkeeping and checking stock would be an advantage but any woman who has an aptitude for this type of work could be trained. Educational standard not less than Grade X.

GENERAL CLERK — Filing, indexing and general office work. Neat handwriting. Knowledge of typing a great advantage.

STENOGRAPHER — Minimum speeds: Typing 45 w.p.m. Shorthand 90 w.p.m.

CONFIDENTIAL BOOK CORRECTOR — Secondary school education. Fine neat writing. Accuracy and power of concentration, keen sense of responsibility.

POSTAL CLERK — Intelligent workers with good handwriting. Those accustomed to working with a large index have an advantage.

SECRETARY — Good stenographic qualifications combined with administrative ability. Experience as a Secretary is necessary.

PAY WRITER — In general a Pay Writer will be required to work on pay ledgers and general books of account. Candidates should have neat handwriting and should be good at figures. Previous experience in bookkeeping would be an advantage, but any woman who has an aptitude for this type of work could be trained. Educational standard not less than Grade X.

COMMUNICATIONS AND OPERATIONS — The decision as to the suitability of applicants for duty as plotters, coders, wireless telegraphists, etc., rests with the Commanding Officer at the Training Establishment. All recruits interested in this type of work must enter as general clerks and be willing to accept the decision of the Commanding Officer as to the category for which they are most suited.

TELEPHONIST — Experienced at answering the telephone and taking down messages correctly. Knowledge of typing is an advantage. May be required to do a certain amount of messenger work.

TELEPHONE SWITCHBOARD OPERATOR — Experience as a switchboard operator with outside lines and inside extensions would be an advantage, but any woman who has an aptitude for this type of work could be enrolled as a switchboard operator and trained.

TELETYPE OPERATOR — Women with previous experience most acceptable. Women to be trained for this work should be able to touch type at a minimum speed of 35 w.p.m.

M/T DRIVER — Experience in driving and knowledge of running repairs. Must be prepared to handle light truck, station-wagon, etc. Should be at least 5' 4" in height.

SAIL MAKER — Experience as a fabric worker of any kind desirable; strong fingers and manual dexterity essential.

MESSENGER — Young, alert, intelligent and observant. No previous experience necessary. Should be reliable.

SICK BERTH ATTENDANT — Good education, preferably two years or more of High School; should not be timid when exposed to sickness or disease or sight of blood.

REGULATING — Experience in handling personnel. Pleasant manner, capable and responsible, preferably over 23 years of age.

Newspaper advertisement, 1943

RECRUITS "CAME ON BOARD"

The "quarterdeck" (ground floor) at Kingsmill House was found to have a small "regulation office" where new recruits "came on board", a "fo'castle", a mess, a small washing-up pantry and the "galley". The "fo'castle" or ratings' sitting room is furnished with several deep chesterfields and numerous chairs of the soft comfortable variety and their coverings of pastel pinks, greens and blues contrast nicely with the green of the walls and the flowered chintz of the drapes. There are also several writing desks and smaller tables. Pastel shaded lamps add a pleasing note and many recreation hours are spent around the combination radio and gramophone. . . .

Ottawa newspaper clipping, 4 September 1942

"RED LEAD" FOR BREAKFAST

The gal in charge of victualling used Royal Navy recipes, and she was trying to feed us on forty-nine cents a day. She gave us "red lead" for breakfast — that's canned tomatoes thickened with cornstarch, and it's what used to be given to British sailors at sea. And we had bread, not toast, for breakfast, because that's what sailors used to get. We gained a little more sanity later on.

Officer in training from Montreal

H.M.C.S. *Conestoga*, Galt, Ontario. The W.R.C.N.S. training establishment was declared a full training "ship" in June 1943. Before the ceremony, *Conestoga* was known as H.M.C.S. *Bytown II*. Phyllis Sanderson was the Master-at-Arms. RCN photo, courtesy Isabel Macneill

JUST STUNNED

Those English officers came out with very English attitudes. When I was called for an interview for the first class of potential officers, one of them asked me if I could make beds! I was just stunned.

Toronto

WHEN A COMMAND IS GIVEN

In the Navy when a command is given it must be obeyed whether you know it is a mistake or not. The Army freezes and does not carry out a command which is obviously wrong, but the Navy carries out all orders.

Each rating is an integral part of a ship and each a cogwheel in a machine. The machine will then move so smoothly that the cogs will lose their identity. On duty you are part of a machine, on shore you are an integral person. Each Wren is just a part of a machine on the parade ground.

Lecture notes taken by a member of the first group of Wrens to enter officer training, Ottawa, September 1942

The first W.R.C.N.S. Director was Captain Eustace A. Brock, R.C.N., second from right. The women in the group are British Wrens, who helped set up the new service. *Left to right*: First Officer Doris Taylor; Captain Edmund Johnstone, Deputy Chief of Naval Personnel, R.C.N.; Superintendent Joan Carpenter; Commodore Howard E. Reid, Deputy Chief of Naval Staff, R.C.N.; Chief Officer Dorothy Isherwood; Captain Brock; and Second Officer Elizabeth Sturdee. PAC PA 142302

In 1943 Lieutenant-Commander Isabel Macneill became Commanding Officer of the "stone frigate", H.M.C.S. *Conestoga*, and the first woman in any Commonwealth country to command a ship. Born in Halifax, the daughter of a Dalhousie University professor, she had studied in England and later taught in a girls' school in Washington, D.C. On her return to Halifax at the beginning of the war, she did volunteer work for the Navy before enlisting in the W.R.C.N.S. in August 1942. Courtesy Isabel Macneill

THEY BLEW WHISTLES   The Dean of Women approved when I said I was leaving Queen's to join the Wrens. She came up one night in the residence and sat on my bed and told me how she had left McGill to do war work in England during the First World War.

I was sent to Galt for basic training. The "ship" was a former school for delinquent girls, up on a plateau, and you could see the mist rise up all around you in the morning. Basic training was exhausting. They blew whistles for everything. You'd march madly, until your heels were blistered, and you'd scrub and scrub — we scrubbed that "ship" from top to bottom. And we polished the brass, too. Then there were lectures, including all the terrible things that could happen to you, like venereal diseases.

They had nautical terms for everything: "quarter-deck" and "galley" and the "regulation office" where we came "on board" as new recruits. It was a lot of nonsense and a lot of fun. If you've seen *H.M.S. Pinafore* you'll know what I mean.

Ottawa

PRAIRIE SAILORS   At first I disapproved of women in the services. I thought women who joined up were doing it for notoriety. They were invading a man's area. But then the war effort became more urgent in 1942. I was teaching Grade 12 English in a high school near an Air Force training centre, and when the planes came over the boys couldn't concentrate on Keats and "Beauty is truth, truth beauty." It wasn't pertinent any more . . . for them or for me.

I thought I'd go east to make armaments, but then the British Wrens came across Canada recruiting for the new Canadian service. I'm one of those prairie sailors — we're so far away from the sea, it appeals to us.

Manitoba

ADVENTURE, EXCITEMENT   Patriotism? Well, I was very idealistic, but I didn't go for King and Country and duty. I went for the adventure. There was an excitement to it. You had a feeling that something great was going on, and you were part of it.

My father had a book on the First World War, and there was a picture in it that really took my fancy. It showed a seaswept deck and a sailor trying to load a shell into a naval gun, a handsome blond boy. So I really fancied the Navy.

I enlisted in Montreal and I went to Galt for basic training. Right from the start there was a wild mixture, and that suited me fine, all the way from schoolteachers to a girl who had her own night-club act in Montreal. She distinguished herself by flying the white ensign upside down at morning divisions.

Discipline was very tight. If you ran around, you did so at your peril. I was only eighteen, and I had to be in at 10 o'clock.

Montreal

MY BOYFRIEND   My boyfriend didn't say too much when I said I was joining the Wrens, just that he was not too happy. He was not as frank as some other people were at the Knights of Columbus, where I'd been working evenings at the drop-in centre. They seemed to think that all women in uniform were prostitutes, and I took exception to that.

Winnipeg

Wrens and ratings, Galt. TT 108-709

Dear Mother:

. . . After dinner, when I went back to the Duty Officer's cabin to get my hat and start on my rounds, here my bed was turned down, my housecoat (I think it is eight years old and cost 23 cents a yard — but I washed it recently, so it was nice and clean, and you shouldn't have gorgeous things in wartime anyway), my pyjamas (the ones with the blue top made from your dress, Mother), and my Chinese bedroom slippers — all laid out so nicely.

Well, I chuckled and chuckled. . . . It seems at first all Wren officers got this treatment, but now only the senior officers do — which certainly is sensible.

You have to be dressed, hat on, etc., by 7.30 to inspect the first group of messengers before they go to work. Then you have breakfast and inspect the next group at 8.00. All this service — your clothes all laid out, and coffee in your shirt-tail — is fun once in a while. I wouldn't want it as a steady diet. . . .

Letter from an officer in training,
Hardy House, Ottawa, 1943

Dear Mother:

. . . Will try to explain what I mean when I write about "aboard HMCS York", "going ashore", etc. You see, we have to act just as if we were sailors in a ship, and everything is referred to as such — the main floor is the Main or Lower Deck, and the second floor is Upper Deck, windows are portholes, stairways are gangways, and so on. Whenever we leave the ship we "go ashore", and if one of the trucks takes us home to Holwood House, the truck is called a "liberty boat" (or if a streetcar is chartered for anything special it's called a liberty boat too) — they would be the rowboats that take the sailors from the ship to shore.

Our kitchen is the galley; our reading room the fo'c'sle; our bathroom, the heads (because it's always at the head of the ship). Then there are no end of sayings that we find originated in the navy, like "pipe down" for keep quiet or shut up! Five minutes before lights out is pipes down, which means everybody puts his pipe out and goes to bed. So maybe you'll be able to figure out my letters now. . . .

We use the same time as the airforce — or rather the airforce uses the same time as we do — that is, the 24 hour watch going from 0100 hours to 2400 hours. Right now it's just 4 o'clock and time for "Tea Boat", which means we can have tea in the middle of the afternoon. Pip! Pip!

Letter from Holwood House, Toronto,
14 May 1943

Stewards serve R.C.N. officers, Halifax, October 1943.
PAC PA 128205

VITAL TO THE SERVICE
Many of these jobs are not spectacular, but they are vital to the service. They must be done and done well, or the service will suffer.

I know how important, for instance, the work of Wren laundresses is. Perhaps these girls are not aware that they have contributed greatly to the efficiency of the service, but I know they have.

Vice-Admiral G. C. Jones, C.B., R.C.N.,
Chief of Naval Staff, 26 August 1944,
after a visit to H.M.C.S. *Conestoga*,
Galt, Ont.

DULL AND DISTASTEFUL
Messwomen were the hardest category for which to recruit. The work was dull and distasteful. The civilian stigma on domestic work seemed to carry over into Service life and morale was difficult to maintain. . . .

*Reflections on the Service: Records of
W.R.C.N.S. Organization and Problems*, 1946

BACK TO FEMININITY
A Wren is a lady before she's in the navy, so she conducts herself like one, rather than like a sailor. That is the decree set down by officials of the Women's Royal Canadian Naval Service.

When a naval man goes into a building—café, church or mess—he takes off his hat, but when a Wren enters a building she leaves her little tricorne on, just as if she were a civilian.

The Wrens are pioneers in this particular back-to-femininity movement, and they believe it pays dividends. Women of the other services remove their hats.

Ottawa Journal, 18 January 1943

WE WERE LADIES
We kept ourselves aloof because we were always told that we were ladies. And we were so proud of our uniforms. When we went indoors we were told to keep our hats on. The CWACs took theirs off. A lot of them were tough. We had beds with nice bedspreads on them, but the CWACs had bedrolls.

Saskatchewan

DOING IT IN UNIFORM!
There was this Wren officer who was in love with a naval officer, and when he came into town she spent the night with him, at his hotel.

You should have heard what the senior officers had to say. There was great disapproval, not only because she was doing it, but because she was doing it in uniform! What I mean is, she went in and out of that hotel in uniform, and she could be seen. We were always told, *never* disgrace your uniform.

Vancouver

Chief of Naval Staff Vice-Admiral P. W. Nelles had a Wren driver at Naval Service Headquarters, Ottawa, November 1943.
PAC PA 128196

Wren signallers in Newfoundland, which was considered an overseas posting during the war. PAC PA 12841

THE WRENS' MARCH

Hark, do you hear
To the Wrens down the years
Comes the call of Drake's resounding drum.
Whatever the job to do, together we'll see it through.
Our marching feet
With steady beat
Tell all the world there's no retreat.
We're in the Navy with a will to win the war,
We'll keep the ensign flying
Nelson gave in days of yore.
Wrens, Ho!
Stand by to lend a hand.
Carry on! Carry on!
We'll never let the Navy down.

Music by Dorothy Madgwick; words by the
Wrens of H.M.C.S. *Bytown II*, as H.M.C.S.
Conestoga was originally known.

GOING OUT SALUTING!   We wore scratchy
navy-blue serge and black stockings, and a pork-pie
felt hat, like a nursing sister's hat, although they
changed that later. We also wore starched collars,
with collar studs, very uncomfortable. I got a rash on
my neck from it, and I was allowed to wear a white
silk scarf for a while.

You used to change your uniform a little bit, subtly,
to try and get a little bit of individuality into it. The
officers would have doeskin uniforms made, but we
had to wear issue.

I bought a silk knitted black tie, and stockings
which weren't issue. An officer would go by and
know something was not quite right, but what? She
hadn't time to catch on. And I had a shirt made, with
french cuffs, and I wore gold cufflinks, sometimes. Of
course, I'd be careful not to shoot my cuffs where
there was an officer around.

I used to like saluting. All the brass were in Ottawa,
and I rather liked giving smart salutes to all these
guys. I'd say, "I'm going out saluting along Sparks
Street!"

Montreal

MEN OF WAR AND MINESWEEPERS   Our
Yeoman was disgusted to be teaching women signalling. There were fourteen of us chosen, and there
were just girls on our course. We learned visual
signalling, semaphore, flag hoists, and Morse code.
It lasted about fourteen weeks, and the men were
very proud of us, in the end.

Captain Adelaide Sinclair was appointed Director of the W.R.C.N.S. in August 1943, succeeding British Chief Officer Dorothy Isherwood. As a professional woman, Sinclair was unique among the directors of the women's services. Educated at Havergal College, the University of Toronto, the London School of Economics, and the University of Berlin, she had taught economics at the University of Toronto before her marriage in 1930. Widowed eight years later, she resumed her career as an economist with the Wartime Prices and Trade Board in 1942. RCN photo, courtesy Adelaide Sinclair

We were drafted to the west coast in December 1943, and we were on our way when the signal came for some of us to go to Halifax instead. For me it was a dream come true. My father was a bluenose.

There were ten Wrens working in the signals station in the Dockyard tower, two in the office and eight as signallers. We thought we were the cat's pyjamas. Two of us would be on duty together, three when there was a man with us, on eight-hour watches. We worked on the roof; we had a little shack there. We signalled to the ships coming in and out of the harbour, to the men of war, and the minesweepers. They berthed right below the Dockyard signal tower.

We very seldom used semaphore. We had ten-inch lamps, with shutters and a handle on the side, to send out Morse signals. It's important never to send faster than you can receive, because if you send fast, to be smart, the operator comes back at the same speed. There was a certain speed we had to pass out at, at St. Hy.

Most of the messages would be routine, but sometimes a ship would need a doctor, and once or twice ships would signal they were bringing in survivors.

We worked outside in all weathers. At St. Hy we got issued with bell-bottoms, and in Halifax we had duffle coats, mittens and turtlenecks, and flight boots. It could be perfectly calm on the street, and really windy up above. In summer we wore coveralls, because it was a dirty, sooty job.

Manitoba

A CERTAIN EXCITEMENT   There was a certain excitement to life, but with absolute security. You were fed and clothed and looked after and paid. You moved around, you learned new things, you had male companionship and entertainment. But it was a very sheltered life in some ways.

For those who got overseas it was different, of course.

Montreal

Dear Mom:

Today an American ship called up and said, "Is it really true there are Wrens signalling there?" When I sent "You bet, I'm a Wren," the signaller sent back "Sure is nice to talk to a girl by light." He told us he was a Yeoman, Canadian Navy, aboard the American ship.

Dear Mom:

The ten of us here are adopting a ship in the New Year, probably a Fairmile [coastal patrol boat] because there are only about fifteen men aboard, which is just enough for our number. They sure take a beating. We'll knit for them, and have a fund on hand to buy them food, etc. I think it'll be fun and something to do that's useful in our spare time.

Excerpts from two letters, December 1943, from a Manitoba Wren serving in Halifax

WAITED ON HAND AND FOOT   Uniform does frightening things to people. It makes you feel special, important. In Halifax we were fed meals like you wouldn't believe. The chef had been assistant chef at Banff Springs.

We were waited on hand and foot by stewardesses. We had taper candles on the table, and a bar in our wardroom. All of us drank a lot more than we'd ever done before. In my generation women didn't drink like that.

W.R.C.N.S. public relations officer, Toronto

IN CHARGE OF CENSORSHIP   When the men wrote letters home, they were not supposed to give any details about where our ships were, or where they were going, because this information might be intercepted and passed on to the enemy. So we censored any references to ships in Halifax, or leaving Halifax. We snipped out any information, however slight. Even the weather was not supposed to be referred to.

We had to inspect parcels sent by ratings to their girlfriends, and there'd be ghastly satin cushion covers saying HMCS *Avalon*, which would show that the ship was in port at the time. We'd hold the parcels for two weeks, so the ship would be miles away before the parcel arrived.

Wrens were put in charge of censorship for the Navy, and there were offices in Halifax, Shelburne, and Newfiejohn [St. John's]. I worked in all three, and I was in charge of the Shelburne bureau. There was just a Wren rating and myself.

Shelburne was a refit base, mainly for destroyers, and there was a large officers group. I'd go into the wardroom before dinner, and how they'd stare! I felt very conspicuous. There were these old, retired engineering types who'd come back into service — and found there were SKIRTS in the Navy!

Ottawa

THE GUNNERY CENTRE   I went into Special Duties [miscellaneous]. We used to say that SD meant we were sub detectors. A lot of Special Duties girls had got a degree, or they had done two years at university, as I had.

When the call came to go to Halifax, I was sent to the Gunnery Training Centre, in the Halifax Dockyard. When the first two Wrens arrived, a few months before I did, the Gunnery Centre was so appalled, so horrified, that they ignored them. Gunnery was the backbone of the Navy, and these men were the policemen of the service. It was a male precinct. But by the time I arrived, in October 1944, they had got used to the idea of women working there.

We got men from destroyers and corvettes, and minesweepers and "dems" — that's what we called defensively equipped merchant shipping. The ships would be in port for three or four days, and their gun crews would come in for training. The Gunnery Centre operated six days a week, and we could do six "runs" a day. There was a gun battery in the centre, and of course the guns used varied from ship to ship. There were big naval cannon, 16-millimetre guns

with a long muzzle, and anti-aircraft guns, Oerlikons, they were called. For anti-aircraft practice, they projected an image onto the ceiling for the gunner to aim at. But I worked with the big naval guns.

We used a spotting table, which had been specially invented to train gun crews to bracket a target at sea. We could put up a fairly convincing mock battle for the gunnery officer, who would be forty feet away, down a dark passage. One Wren was in charge of radar, and put on fake pips, and I put up the splash, representing the fall of shot. You could tell if the target appeared behind the fall of shot, or in front, or whether the gunner scored a direct hit. If the target was always in front of the fall of shot, the gunner knew that the "enemy ship" was heading straight for him.

The Gunnery Centre was a segment of the Action Room, where mock battles were more elaborate. The Wrens there had battleship models which they moved around with sticks, and submarines which "fired" torpedoes.

Ottawa

Wrens in the operations plotting room, Naval Service Headquarters, Ottawa, and coders at work in Halifax.
PAC PA 108179 and PA 128194

CODING

1. In a code the letter A is represented by figure 1, B by 2, C by 3, etc.
   Write out the words: "King's Squad" in this code.
2. What is the meaning of the following in the same code:
   1 . 12 . 9 . 6 . 5 . 15 . 14 . , 20 . 8 . 5 . 15 . 3 . 5 .
   1 . 14 ., 23 . 1 . 22 . 5 . 19 .
3. In a code GOOD NIGHT is represented by FNNC MHFGS.
   Put TEST POINTS into the same code.
4. What is AKZBJ OZHMS in the same code?

From the Initial Test for Coders, prepared by the British Royal Marine Signal School

U-BOATS   Operational Intelligence had an incredible collection of "odd bods". There were scientists and geologists, professors of romance languages, a clergyman who was a Chinese scholar, a ham radio operator. I almost stumbled on it: I was brought in as a Wren because I had a scientific background, and there were various other Wrens there for the same reason.

The Navy had built up a network of stations to monitor U-boat signals in the Atlantic. Some of the sharpest Wrens took wireless telegraphy training, and they worked on monitoring stations on the east coast. The commanding officer was a Wren.

At Headquarters in Ottawa we plotted the information we got from the receiving stations. We were familiar with where the convoys were, and the Duty Officer's job was to signal a convoy about any U-boats in the vicinity. The job called for a certain amount of judgment, because you were alerting a ship's captain to possible danger.

We worked three watches over twenty-four hours, and sometimes at night there would be just myself, as Duty Officer, and four Wrens. The U-boats came up at night, and from eight o'clock on it could be exciting. Sometimes a "flap" would occur in the middle of the night, and speed was of the essence. The Canadian Navy trusted its women with a lot.

Twenty-four of us were all set to go to Australia after VE Day, to run a similar operation there for the Pacific war, but the section collapsed on VJ Day.

Ottawa

Helping to plot a ship's course in the Action Room, Halifax, where battles at sea were simulated for training purposes. This was the closest Wrens came to going to sea. Unlike their British counterparts, Canadian Wrens were never given responsibility for operating harbour craft or serving aboard certain ships as communications officers. TT 108-709

ENEMY TRANSMISSIONS   Coverdale was a direction-finding station. We didn't send much, but we received. We had radios with earphones and we listened for enemy transmissions. We knew the frequencies submarines transmitted on, and we knew the codes. The station was in the middle of a field, on a farm outside Moncton. It was a pig farm originally.

It was isolated, monotonous work and it required precision. Girls proved to be good at it. There were eighty Wren "tels", all high school graduates, several with university, and ten or twelve men, including a couple of technical officers, stokers, and the radio artificer — he was a real rough-cut diamond. The men reported to me as Commanding Officer, but in reality I had limited disciplinary authority. If a man was drunk and unable to perform his duty, for example, I had to report him to Halifax.

The farm and the river were all we could see. Moncton was four miles away, too far to walk. But there were ten thousand airmen in the Moncton area, on three different stations, so there were lots of dances to go to. I remember one when I was dancing with an Air Force sergeant and he asked, "Who's the old bag in charge of your outfit?" I was twenty-seven at the time!

On one occasion I had to officiate at a naval funeral, after a regular sailor had drowned at Lunenburg. His family wanted a naval funeral. So I found an Anglican minister, a chaplain in the reserve, and I organized a firing party with guns and blank cartridges. I got the seamen on the station lined up, all ten of them, and I rounded up another ten boys who were home on leave in Moncton. I found them through the Y.

I rode to the cemetery in a car with the minister, ahead of the funeral procession. The minister was in a hurry because he had a wedding to perform afterwards, so he asked the chauffeur to speed up. When I glanced out of the back window at the squad of seamen marching behind, the Petty Officer was shaking his fist at me, because we were going too fast for them.

I had to stand at the head of the grave and take the salute.

> Frieda Dougherty, Officer Commanding,
> Coverdale (Special Wireless
> Telegraphing Station)

Frances Mills, a Wren officer from Manitoba, commanded this Long Range Navigational Aid station at Lower Whitehead, Nova Scotia.
Courtesy Frances Mills

IN CASE WE WERE ATTACKED   I was doing decoding in Ottawa, and I got asked if I'd volunteer for related work. They didn't give me any details, but it turned out to be LORAN, Long Range Navigational Aid, a type of radar. It was designed to help convoys in the fog off Newfie, and it was very accurate. The range was about seven hundred miles. You'd get a fix from a couple of stations down the coast, and you'd send your signal out. You never knew who was using it.

The station was outside the village of Lower Whitehead, about thirty-five miles down the coast from Canso and two hundred miles up the coast from Halifax. There were a dozen fishermen's houses in the village, and the place was an island when the tide was in. It was very isolated.

Deming had been run by sailors before we got there, and some of them stayed on as technicians. They ran the diesel which generated our electricity. There was a Petty Officer too. Our Wren officer was in command, and that was a bit unusual.

We were armed in the early days, in case we were attacked by an enemy submarine. There was a rack of .303 rifles in the Quonset hut where we did the transmitting, and there was a Bren gun on a tripod. We worked in pairs, in a kind of cage, and there were .45 Colt revolvers inside, in case of trouble. But we had very little training in how to use them. The Petty Officer took us out and fired a few practice rounds.

> Montreal

Dear Mother:
. . . Two officers and eight sailors came out from Canso. They were a nice bunch of boys. During the afternoon they disposed of a depth charge which had been in the operational hut. It was there so that, had the place been attacked, the fuse could have been applied and the whole place disposed of in thirty seconds.

Letter from Frances Mills, Officer
Commanding, Lower Whitehead, 26 June 1945

BUZZ BOMBS   The picture of the procession up the gangway onto the ship was a memento for posterity. Wrens, groomed to an inch of their lives in pusser navy-blue with smart white shirts and collars on a steaming August day, rapidly assumed a melted look with even the hard collars wilting, forlornly, as the girls staggered up the too-narrow gang-

Embarking at Halifax for Britain, February 1944. About 300 Wrens served there, principally in London, Greenock, and Londonderry. In London during air raids, Wrens slept in the basement of the Canadian Naval Mission Overseas. PAC PA 108181 and PA 128191

way with greatcoats, Burberrys, glamour boots, and a few extra paper parcels in the left hand; a large, barely liftable suitcase, with interesting objects such as coat hangers, bell-bottom trousers, hot-water bottles tied on the outside, in the other hand; gas masks with, truth will out, a few chocolate bars, bobby pins, and cookies occupying the forbidden areas within the case, tin helmets and bursting pochettes over the shoulder.

The seven days passed very quickly without alarums or excursions, between the final fade-out of Halifax and the first strange sight of endless rows of chimney pots descending to the river Mersey.

A narrow lane bounded by buoys up a river; towering anti-aircraft gun platforms rising from the water; docks damaged beyond disguise; great yawning gaps between jagged walls talked of a country at war — a fact which the mind had failed to grasp during a peaceful summer crossing and the first lovely vision of green rolling hills. Suddenly it seemed more than a gay adventure coming to a land we wished to see.

London came upon us by way of Euston Station — dirty, bustling, porterless, and unaccountably thrilling with uniforms of every nation rushing madly back and forth and not a civilian to be seen — and a double-decker bus to take bags and baggage to South Kensington.

The British Wrens welcomed us in, fed us, chatted with us, and made us feel at home in the tall, narrow buildings with the high, dark rooms in the street just off Kensington Gardens. We were escorted up flights of stairs, past great mirrors, through corridors to the rooms where we might hang our hats, wash our hands, fling our clothes, but might not sleep. It was the basement for us as visitors and the nearest air-raid shelter for the permanent staff when night fell and the buzz bombs came over thick and fast.

What a horrible sensation to lie shivering in bed while monstrous weapons roared overhead, every nerve and muscle strained till, sharply, silence fell and seconds later a dull, distant thud and a vague shuddering came to us through the earth. Or sometimes the shudder became a great upheaval and everything around shook and swayed and creaked and glass fell with a tinkling crash. We felt abandoned and scared through the nights but came groggily up from our basement retreats each morning with a feeling of exaltation that again we had survived and really perhaps we were pretty good fellows after all.

From an unpublished article
by a Wren librarian

JUST BEFORE THEY DROPPED   I got married in England. He was with the R.C.A.F. overseas band; he played clarinet. My poor mother! When the telegraph office phoned her with our cable, to say we were engaged, and she heard the cable was from London, she didn't hear one other thing—she thought I must be dead! It was 1944, it was the time of the buzz bombs, and she was sure I'd been killed.

There were lots of times when I kissed my husband goodbye at the tube station when I wondered if we'd see each other again. When the V2s started coming over, they'd blow down a whole block, and you wouldn't even hear them coming. The V1s you could hear. There was this steady drone, and just before they dropped the motor cut out and you would hit the deck—you lay flat on the ground if there wasn't any place to shelter. It told on our nerves.

We lived from day to day. We went to concerts, to the Adelphi and the Albert Hall. We joined the Queensberry Club, our one extravagance. Glenn Miller played there every week. We heard his last concert before he flew to France to set up, ahead of the band. It was a terribly foggy night and he was never heard of again.

Brockville, Ont.

HAM, SPAM, AND JAM   The British Navy was short of motor transport drivers, so we were sent over on loan. We were based in Greenock on the Clyde.

There were ten of us, billeted in a beautiful house called Lindores. The British Wrens were next door, and at first they resented us. We were paid more than they were, and our food was better, too. They were the cream of the British crop: those drivers came from families with two or three cars. We came from different walks of life. But we all worked out of the same naval garage.

We did supply runs with flat Bedford trucks. We'd back those big Bedfords onto the dock, to stock up from Canadian ships in the harbour with canned goods, sugar, potatoes. ("Ham, spam, and jam" we called it.) We lifted and lugged, we pushed and pulled. Once I took a load of oil to Newcastle in a big Spitfire truck. A Spitfire was the size of a dump truck. There was no door on the driver's side and you had a grab handle to help you climb up. It was hard for short people like me.

We drove staff cars, Austins and Hillmans and the odd Vauxhall. They'd been camouflaged a dull greeny-brown; all the chrome had been painted over. We met naval personnel coming in; we loaded and unloaded their baggage. I drove officers up the coast to detonate bombs which had washed in, but I never saw a bomb: I was ordered to park the car a safe distance away. Nobody was ever hurt on one of those trips when I was the driver. I ended up with an engineering admiral; I drove him all over Scotland. If you got a puncture you had to get help, because we never carried a spare. There weren't any spares—they needed every available part.

Most of the ships coming into the Clyde were corvettes and minesweepers, to refuel and resupply, and troopships, there were always troopships: the *Queen Elizabeth*, the *Queen Mary*, the *Nieuw Amsterdam*, the *Île de France*. At night they were blacked right out, but on a moonlit night they stood out very clearly. There were no bombs dropped though, but several times submarines got into the Clyde anchorage.

Midland, Ont.

Drivers were issued with parkas and leather gauntlets for winter driving in Scotland. Courtesy Joan Boyd

TRANSATLANTIC LEGS   You don't have to visit the Hippodrome out of any sense of duty. The Canadian Navy has sailed up the Thames and London is its prisoner.

The show began with an effective opening of vigorous young men on the stage and attractive young Wrens with transatlantic legs and transatlantic teeth (than which there are no better in the world). By the time the curtain went up on the second half of the performance the audience was electrified. Applause grew to cheers and the whole thing proceeded to its climax in a gale of excitement. Now we have to hail Mr. and Mrs. Lund (they were married the other day), who are such an exciting pair of dancers that we should refuse them an exit visa and defy the Canadian government to do its worst.

Beverley Baxter, *Evening Standard*, London,
1 February 1945

Chorus line (*top*), Blanche Harris and Alan Lund (*bottom*), from the Navy Show. The professional dance team had joined the show at age eighteen, and married a few months before the highly successful show went overseas in 1944. PAC PA 128197 and PA 128209

PARIS, BRUSSELS, AMSTERDAM   "Meet the Navy", that was the big number, then there was "The Boy in the Bell Bottom Trousers", and "Beauty on Duty", all about the naval nurses. Alan and I danced to "Our Waltz" by Dave Rose, that was our special number, and an encore called "Bright and Breezy".

All the money the show made went to the Widows and Orphans Fund. And there was so much money — Captain Connolly went and presented it to the King in person.

The war ended in May, and in June we left for Paris, then Brussels, then Amsterdam. We were there for fourteen weeks, to play for the servicemen, to keep up morale, because they were so frustrated, they wanted to go home. We were there for the local people, too. We were the first show to play Amsterdam after the war ended, and this was the first time the Dutch people could stand up and sing their anthem in public since the war began. Everyone on the stage and everyone in the audience cried.

Blanche Lund, Toronto

HALIFAX RIOTS, VE DAY 1945   I think the riots happened because of bad management. These sailors had been drinking all morning, and there was nowhere to go, nothing to do in Halifax. There should have been entertainment planned, and celebrations to keep the men occupied. And the wet canteens should have stayed open, to keep the men on the base. There were thirty thousand servicemen in Halifax, and there were a lot of lonely sailors.

I saw the beginning of the trouble. I was going out of the Dockyard onto Barrington Street at midday, and I watched this group of sailors demolish a streetcar. It was old, made of wood, and they toppled it onto its side, off the tracks. It was extraordinary, and rather horrifying. It was the first time I'd ever seen mob violence.

I was supposed to be leaving Halifax with some friends that afternoon. We had two days free, and we planned to go to a nice place down the coast. But I was frightened by what I'd seen, and I turned back into the Dockyard, by the Gottingen Street gate. The sentinel said, "If you come in, you can't go out again." I went in anyway, and it was true. The Wrens inside were not allowed out again for forty-eight hours. And when I did go out again, to get my collars from the Chinese laundry on Barrington Street, I was escorted. Barrington Street was ankle-deep in glass from the store windows.

Law and order had broken down in Halifax. Some of the local population had really taken servicemen to the cleaners. They'd been overcharged for everything, and there was a tremendous build-up of resentment. On VE Day they'd been drinking, there was nothing to do, so they vented their rage against the local people who had abused them.

About two hundred naval personnel were the spearhead for the mob, but lots of local people joined in. They just surged into the shops, smashing and looting. A friend of mine was at the station, and she saw all these people, looters, pouring onto a train. One man had obviously come from a jewellery store; he had trays and trays of rings.

At *Stadacona*, the Navy went all through our lockers to see if we had taken anything during the looting.

Ottawa

Halifax riots, VE Day, 8 May 1945. PAC C 79586

Dear Mom and Family:

Just a short note for after VJ Day. . . . We were expecting the news at any moment and then we heard there would be a broadcast by the P[rime] M[inister] at 8 o'clock. So I came back to the dockyard tower in case the news should be good, which, of course, it was. We thought Big Ben would never stop striking but it finally did, and then all we heard was "Today Japan has surrendered", and with wild whoops we were up on the bridge laughing and yelling our heads off, hoisting "VJ" and flashing it on the lights. The ships immediately did the same thing and with their sirens in addition. It was really a wild place.

I stayed until nearly 10, and then went back to *Stad[acona]* to see what was going on there. Visited the Drill Shed first, where they were giving away free beer, but didn't care much for the smell or the crowd so left and meandered over to the Rec Hall, where there was dancing and free sandwiches and Cokes. Didn't stay there very long either.

I thought maybe Jimmy would phone, as he had tried to get me the night before. However, I found the phone out of order when I got back to the annex and anyway I can imagine how busy long-distance lines would be. Gosh, I wanted to talk to him! But I had a letter from Jimmy today, and he had to stand watch from 8.30 a.m. till 2 a.m. VJ night, so he didn't do much celebrating either at Shelburne.

Now everyone is back to normal routine — how dull. And the main topic is discharges, of course. However, there doesn't seem to be anything definite so far, but I don't think it should be very long. Jimmy should stand a pretty good chance for an early one. . . . So glad and happy it's all over.

Letter, Halifax, 16 August 1945

7

Woman's Place Is Everywhere

The opportunity to earn what seemed like "immense sums" — in reality anywhere between twenty cents and ninety cents an hour — seemed like a miracle to many Canadian women after the long Depression years. The government recognized the strong financial incentive, but the major emphasis was always on patriotic service; on the importance of women's work to the war effort and to life on the home front; and on loyalty to Canadian men fighting overseas. Young girls and middle-aged women, single women and mothers of small children, were all eventually urged to do their duty by joining the labour force on a regular basis, part-time or for a three-month period.

A few had very unusual jobs, like Ethel Dickson Dingwall, who was the Assistant Harbour Master at Sydney, Nova Scotia, where large convoys of merchant ships assembled for the Atlantic run. Several other women also worked as skippers for coastal freighters. But the majority of women in civilian occupations worked in the service sector, where they had been traditionally employed, or in the textile industry. Wages were often low and working conditions poor, and many women left for higher-paying jobs in war industry. Some employers were left scrambling for workers, but no one could advertise jobs or fill them without permission from the National Selective Service.

In the federal civil service, the number of women employed rose sharply. Most of the new jobs were clerical, but some were at senior levels. Outstanding examples were Mrs. Rex (Fraudena) Eaton, Associate Director of the National Selective Service, and Mrs. W. E. (Nell) West, Director of Women's Voluntary Services for the Ministry of National War Services. Byrne Hope Sanders was Director, Consumer Branch, of the Wartime Prices and Trade Board, and Phyllis Turner, economist, was W.P.T.B. Administrator of Fats and Oils.

Job opportunities were available in most fields, including the media. In the newspaper business, some women journalists got off the women's pages and into general or specialized reporting. Margaret Ecker Francis, a Canadian Press correspondent, was sent to Britain and Europe, where she covered the surrender of the German armed forces to General Eisenhower in May 1945.

At the Canadian Broadcasting Corporation and the newly created National Film Board a number of talented women were hired as producers, directors, and technicians. Former Winnipeger Elizabeth Long was responsible for setting up a national network of CBC women commentators, who broadcast daily to listeners in their particular regions, keeping women at home in touch with their community's war effort on the home front.

GREASE AND GRIME FAIL TO DISMAY WOMEN

It isn't traditional. It might make Casey Jones turn in his grave. But for the first time in the history of the company's roundhouse at Alyth yards, Calgary, nine grimy women in traditional blue overalls have taken their places beside the men, and spend their working hours clambering over snorting, dirty locomotives.

Their Work Regarded as "Tops"

The feminine "railroaders" claim that "Getting up in the morning" and "Getting the dirt off" are the toughest parts of their jobs. But they like the work and the chief clerk at the yards uses the superlatives "tops" and "one hundred per cent" to describe their efforts.

The nine women, who range in age from the teens to the forties, just got tired of their other jobs. They had heard that a number of Calgary women were working as laborers, pushing wheel-barrows, heaving shovels and driving trucks, so they asked the [Employment Insurance] Commission for employment of that type. They got it. They admit they were scared stiff when they first reported at Alyth, but hastily add, "Not any more worried than you would be about an ordinary job."

The women have a private rest-room where they go for lunch. In the lounge there are no frilly curtains, no blue powder room, but plain benches, somewhat greasy, and a table where they spread out the contents of their black tin lunch boxes, the same kind as those taken to work by the men.

Cleaning-up Is Problem

Getting clean — that's one of the hardest by-products of the jobs. Using wiping rags and cans of solvent, these women get right next to the shiny black monsters. The work is wearing when it comes to clothes, but these women are sensible enough to dress properly — heavy blue jeans, caps, thick gloves are in the fashion parade at Alyth, and still the dust sifts through.

Audrey Reid had an unusual idea. "I wear nail polish," she said, displaying pink-tipped, grime-covered hands. "It seems to keep the dirt from getting into your nails too hopelessly."

The ambitions of Chris Prowse go beyond wiping the mammoth engine. "I'd like to learn to run an engine. If women can ferry planes, why couldn't we be at the throttles of engines, at least in the yards here?"

Several others indicated they were anxious to learn more about the machinery because in that case they would be more valuable as workers.

Although the work takes more energy than most employment the women were enthusiastic and they plan to stick. When the war is over and the need for women in men's jobs no longer exists, "We'll fight that problem when we come to it," they said.

The men seem to enjoy working with the lady railroaders and in deference to them have tamed their language to the point of calling an engine a plain "hog" instead of a so-and-so kind of "hog".

Undated copy of Canadian Pacific
Staff Bulletin, c. 1942–43

Engine wipers. CN 4413

I BELONGED TO THE UNION   I was a widow and I'd never worked before I went to the C.N.R. I had four children, three in high school, and my son was nine. I went in at eight and I had one hour for dinner. I went running home to get meals at noon like a streak of lightning in my coveralls.

I was a seamstress in the upholstery department. I sewed curtains for sleepers in the Pullman cars, and I sewed the blinds and repaired old ones.

Some of the men resented me, because it had been a man's job all those years, but I let it go in one ear and out the other. I made the same money as the men, and I belonged to the union.

Toronto

WE MADE THE SAME MONEY Doris and I went to the T.T.C. [Toronto Transportation Commission] in September 1942. We had an eye test and a medical and an IQ test—I was kind of surprised, I got eighty. We had to go to school for a week or ten days, and then we got a cap with a badge on it. I was a conductor, and there were six of us in the first class.

We were stationed at the Eglinton barns. I went northbound and Doris went southbound, to begin with. We gave out tickets and transfers. I was so seasick the first three days. On my first day this guy got on, his language was something else, and he gave me this funny look. He said to the motorman, ''I don't think I'll take this car.'' And the motorman said, ''Well, then you'll have a seven-minute wait.'' After that he said he'd stay, but he sat right up behind the motorman.

I don't know how long it was before girls started to drive, but after a time there were all-girl teams. There were about 250 girls at our barns alone. The men accepted us very well. I never had any problem. We made the same [money] as the men, the conductors, and so did the girls who drove.

They had a bungalow for us, we called it the white house, with housekeeping and a bedroom, so that if you came in at 2.45 [a.m.] you could hop into bed and sleep until they called you on the intercom. There

was a shift that started at 4.30 a.m. You had to be available for thirteen hours a day, but there could be a four-hour layover. My youngest was three years old in 1942, but I could manage because my mother was at home.

If the pole came off the wires you had to get off and put it on again. And I worked the bell to help the motorman back up. In the winter I had to look after the stove. It was at the rear and it burned coal. Happy Hannah! That crazy fire! They were always supposed to have it ready for you, in the yards, but I remember one morning going out at nine below zero and that fire hadn't been stoked up. I was wearing gloves with the fingers out of them—one of the passengers knitted them for me—and the ends of my fingers stuck to the metal when I touched it. But I got that stove going.

I was so withdrawn before I went to work. After I got that job I was just a babbling brook. It gave me all the confidence in the world. There's no job in the world that can compare with it. I was able to cope with everything, even drunks. One time a postman got on when I had a standing load. He'd had too much to drink and he wouldn't let this heavy lady pass. I did the wrong thing, I gave him a push. I had just about had the bun with him; he was getting disgusting. You can take just so much. I was lucky an inspector hopped on the car behind us. Our inspectors were very, very kind to us.

Toronto Transportation Commission ad, 1944. TTC 14906

Toronto

Auto mechanic, Vancouver, 1943. VPL 33328

TRULY FEMININE   I want to see young girls from the country, now working in big cities, return to their homes. . . . I hope that young girls living in the cities will understand that it is in their best interests to do work that is truly feminine, such as domestic service.

> Cardinal Rodrigue Villeneuve, Primate of
> the Roman Catholic Church in Canada,
> 11 October 1941

SELF-CONSCIOUSNESS, TIMIDITY   Woman's greatest fault is self-consciousness and timidity. When a woman loses herself in the vastness of the need [war effort] she will cease to be a "lady" in hat, scarf and gloves, speaking very correctly and self-consciously. She will be a woman doing a good job of work.

> Agnes Macphail, former M.P. (and the first
> woman to sit in the House of Commons),
> speaking on behalf of the C.C.F. party,
> 5 December 1942

DON'T WORK FOR PIN MONEY   If you are doing a good job of work, it is only self-respecting to ask that you be paid properly for what you do. If you do not show that you expect this, you are suggesting both to your employer and to yourself that your work is not of much account.

There are more far-reaching reasons than this, however, why women must demand standard rates of pay during the war. If women persist in working at low rates, they will help in establishing low rates for everybody, and depressed wages would be a pretty present for the men coming home! We have an obligation to them to keep up standards of pay. If we don't, we are doing direct and definite harm *right now* to the men who are so anxiously in our thoughts.

Not only that: we are also doing definite, direct harm to women, too. Before the war there were about 600,000 women in paid jobs in Canada. Now there are twice as many. After the war one cannot say how many of them there will be, but certainly a great many more than before. And remember that many of them will be women who have lost husbands or sweethearts overseas, and therefore deserve our best consideration.

Women must see that rates of pay are maintained both for their own sake and for the sake of the men coming back and their families. *Every woman now working should demand a rate of pay which would maintain her fully if she were working full time at it to earn her living.*

> Dorise Nielsen, M.P., *New Worlds
> for Women*, Toronto, 1944

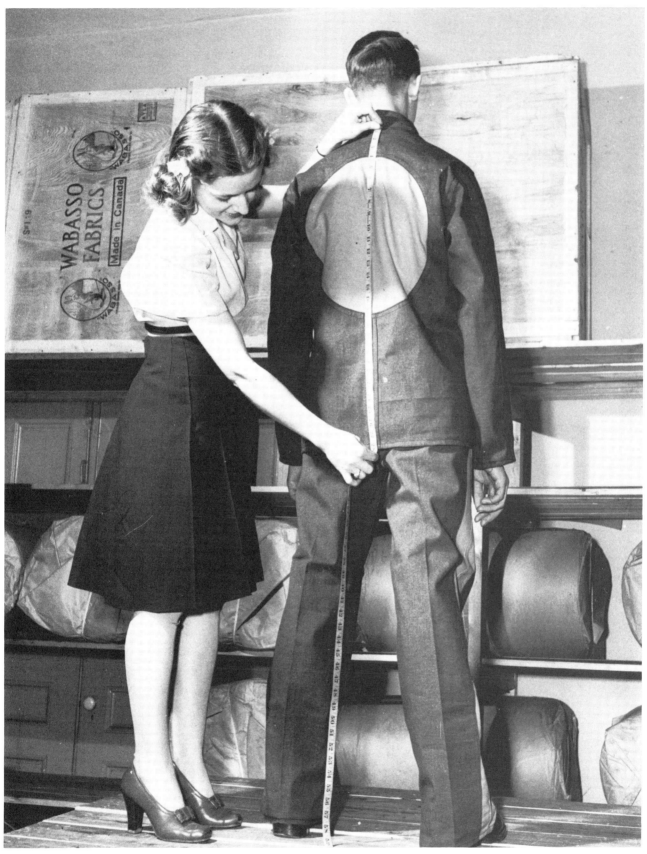

Measuring prisoner-of-war uniforms, Montreal, 1943.
PAC PA 116152

Madeleine Parent, Montreal, became Office Secretary for the American Federation of Labor's War Labor Organizing Committee in 1942. The next year she took charge of organizing the workers of Dominion Textile cotton mills in the St. Henri district of Montreal for the United Textile Workers of America (AFL). PAC PA 120397.

Military hats in production, Hamilton, Ont., 1942. The National Selective Service assigned women to civilian jobs according to their importance to the war effort or to essential civilian services. PAC PA116094

TEN HOURS A DAY   It wasn't new for women to be in the work force in Quebec, but in the war they quickly became much more needed. Certain traditional elements, elitist elements around the Church and certain groups of professionals, they criticized women for taking jobs. But they were less influential than they said they were.

True, there were many jobs, but in the textile industry wages were still very low, twenty or twenty-five cents an hour and no paid holidays or sick leave. Women worked ten hours a day, five days a week, and often they had to work five hours on Saturday. They worked on shifts, and the night shift was ten hours too, although the men worked twelve.

I went to help organize workers in the cotton mills in 1942. We fought for an eight-hour day, for sick pay, for maternity pay. We won our first big contracts in 1946, but the workers in war industries, they got their contracts earlier, during the war.

Madeleine Parent, United Textile
Workers of America, Montreal

ARE WOMEN A BARGAIN?

Being comparatively new in the business world, women are inclined to underestimate their own value. They're willing to work hard for so little.

Now, when women's work is needed, is the time to have our labour taken off the bargain counter.

Commentator Mattie Rotenberg, Toronto,
CBC, 1 May 1941

THE NIGHT SHIFT

It was a strange thing how that very, very strong anti-war pacifist sentiment was turned around so quickly into patriotism and pro-war sentiment by the jobs that came along, and the opportunities to earn what seemed like such immense sums — seventy-five cents an hour, when people had been getting twenty-five cents a day.

I went to work in the local canning factory, canning green beans. I went on the second shift, the night shift, because I could leave my daughter with my husband at night. I could keep an eye open on her in the day — well, one eye, at least.

We graded the beans, sorted them on the long belts. We took out the small, tender ones to be canned whole for the officers. All the big, coarse ones were chopped up for the infantry. Nothing was wasted.

I'd read about speed-up, and I saw it there myself. At nights the boss would step over and twist the machine so the belt lines would go just a little faster and then a little bit faster again. And I experienced the way the grapevine went through. The word would go from one belt line to the next, "Let them go, let them go." That meant, refuse to sort at this speed. The word would pass from one end of this enormous building to the other, and we would stop sorting. We let all the beans go through to the end, into the big bins, and then they'd have to be put through again.

Fraser Valley, B.C.

The Ontario Women's Land Army was provincially organized, like the Ontario Farm Service Force. High school students who worked for the O.F.S.F. during the summer were guaranteed a certificate for their school year if they stayed for the full thirteen weeks. TT 100-676

Japanese Canadians, Manitoba, 1944. After Japanese Canadians were forcibly removed from the coastal areas of British Columbia in 1942, some were sent to work on farms in the prairie provinces. WCPI 663-20357

Shredding cabbage at a dehydration plant, Vernon, B.C., 1943. Dr. Mary McArthur, a research scientist at the Dominion Experimental Farm, Ottawa, developed techniques for dehydrating vegetables for shipment to Canadian troops overseas. PAC PA 116079

PROUD OF UNIFORMS   As a uniformed service the schoolgirls have dress uniforms in the same way as any armed service. The uniforms are a plain blue tailored cotton dress with shoulder badges marked O.F.S.F. (Ontario Farm Service Force).

At first I was inclined to be skeptical over the need of a dress uniform. The cost, $6.90, although certainly not exorbitant, seemed unnecessary.

Actually, the dress uniforms are important to the girls. They are proud of them and like to wear them on their occasional visits from the farm.

The work was undoubtedly harder than most had anticipated, but after the first stiffening wore off the girls voiced few complaints.

My own impression was that it might have been in the interests of the girls' health to allow them to work for the first week in half-day shifts; ten hours a day is pretty hard on a girl of 16 or 17 who has had little experience of strenuous work.

Strangely enough, although the war was the cause of these young girls being in camp and on the farm, it was a subject which rarely came up. Like all young people, they were interested more in their friends, their homes and their pleasures. . . .

Jean Tweed,
Globe and Mail, Toronto,
1 May 1942

FARMERETTE QUEEN   Smiling beneath her crown of wax fruit and flowers, Pat admitted she was too excited to explain how she felt about representing the typical Ontario Farm Service Force girl. Chosen from among seventeen candidates, Pat was crowned farmerette queen at the armouries Saturday night, when farm placement officials and district fruit growers gathered to honour the 1,300 girls who serve in Government labour camps and on private farms throughout Ontario.

In the final competition judges placed Pat first on the basis of her service, personality and camp spirit. Although the final decision was not based on physical attractiveness, Pat would have little trouble to win top honours in any beauty contest with her dark curls and dimples. She admitted her ambition to join the Women's Royal Canadian Naval Service as soon as possible.

"I was going to study medicine next year," she said, "but now the war is so serious, I think it would be better for me to get into the service right away."

Miss Farmerette has saved $30. in her five weeks of service at Fenwick Camp and has invested the money in War Savings Certificates.

Toronto *Globe and Mail*, 27 July 1942

Picture Butte, Alta., 1944. Many women teachers, who had been obliged to quit their jobs when they married during the 1930s, were invited back to work during the war years. PAC PA 116075

WOMEN TAKE ON FARM WORK

Wives and Daughters Help with Production of Essential Food

The women living on the farms of Canada cannot go overseas and drive ambulances, nor wear uniforms, nor make bullets. Neither can they prove themselves heroines night after night in the face of death. Nevertheless, they are doing their bit to help win the war.

There is no regimentation, no organization, no publicity. There are no uniforms. The individual farms see work waiting to be done, so they do it. They have been mowing, raking and pitching hay, working sweeps and building stacks. They are even stooking.

I have not yet heard of them running threshing outfits, but just give them time. Then there are chores. Cows to bring in and milk. Calves, pigs and chickens to feed. Sheep to tend. Then for a change there may be cattle to ride after or a sick horse to doctor.

Women are doing all these things here in Alberta — not so much, perhaps, on the big grain farms where one man with power machinery can work a large tract of land, but on the mixed farms, where there is such a variety of work to be done.

They are not finding it very easy. In fact it is not easy at all. But that does not stop them. One woman was out mowing one day when the wheel came off the mower. The next day she went raking and the seat came off the rake. But these little accidents didn't bother her at all. She has two sons in the Air Force. . . .

Sheilagh Jameson, *Calgary Herald*,
October 1940

Near Medicine Hat, Alta., May 1943. PAC PA 116129

THE FAMILY RANCH   As soon as I was sixteen, Mother left me in Medicine Hat, in charge of my three young brothers. She went to work on the family ranch forty miles away. We had fourteen sections and there were no men available.

Mother was there from April to October, and I took my brothers to help out in the summer. The school principal let us go three weeks early in the spring, and we went back to school a couple of weeks late in the fall. That was okay, if you kept up your marks.

Alberta

A WHISTLE PUNK   First, I worked in a sawmill, a planing mill, but I didn't like the kind of men, and the noise. The men made jokes and suggestive remarks. And that was a dangerous place. There was a big bandsaw and you never wore any protection — goggles or steel-tipped shoes.

After that I spent five years as a whistle punk with logging crews. You were the signalman; you signalled for the logs to be lowered into the machine. You strung out the whistle wire — you had 300 or 400 feet of wire draped around your neck, and that was heavy. You'd unwind it as you went along. If you blew at the wrong time you could really injure a man. If there was a hang-up you blew one blast and it would mean something to the engineer at the machine.

You'd be scrambling up these steep hills, over logs and around logs. I remember one time I had a nice new pair of corks put on my boots. I was walking along this log and the bark was slipping, but it stuck to the bottom of my boots, with these sharp corks. Man, I took a nasty fall! I had some doosies, but I never broke any bones or missed a day's work through it.

I worked for a little outfit, to start with. They treated me as a sister. I was always just one of the guys. When I needed to go to the bathroom I'd just say, "I'm going."

One time we were working there was fire on the Comox side and we knew that the fire was getting pretty close. Three of these fellows came over to our side and said, "You'd better get out of here because the fire's coming right over, it's going to burn you out." Oh gosh, we were all upset. We had to leave everything. We went out onto a part that had been logged previously and sure enough the fire came over. It burned up our machines, blew up our diesels. It hit the tops of the trees and it jumped. It roared like a freight train going throught the forest. It was really awful.

We weren't hurt because we were out in a slashing. We had this driver, I don't know how he got through, I don't know why we didn't blow up. I couldn't breathe, there seemed to be no air, and tears were pouring out. We had quite a way to go, on a plank road. Can you imagine? The bridges were just two big logs crossing over a ravine. My goodness, when I think about it!

Nanaimo, B.C.

MANNING THE CONVOYS   The busiest spot on the [Sydney, Nova Scotia] waterfront was the Shipping Office; it was here the seamen congregated to be engaged and discharged from ships. Shipping Master throughout the war was Ethel Dickson, on behalf of her father. Her Deputy was Miss Kaye MacDonald. In addition to the complex problems of manning the convoys, it was here that Identity Cards, with photos and fingerprints, were issued. A crash course in the basic method of fingerprinting was given to the Shipping Office staff by the R.C.M.P.

Sydney Post-Record, date unknown

HE WAS A WOMAN!   One captain remarked, "I went to see the Shipping Master and *he* was a woman!" Until a convoy was ready for sea, Kaye and I were on duty. We had no special hours. Naturally, extreme secrecy was maintained about times of departure. Those grey, camouflaged ships sailed from our quiet harbour in darkness into the merciless attacks of submarines and dive-bombers. It was difficult to say "goodbye" to friends who sailed with the convoy vessels, many of whom found a watery grave in the Atlantic.

Letter from Ethel Dickson Dingwall, Sydney, N.S., 1984

WILD AND WOOLLY   If I'd been able to get in, I'd have joined the forces. I tried the Air Force and the Wrens, but they wouldn't have me because of my eyesight. Then I heard that a friend of mine had got a job working on the Alaska Highway project. They were hiring through the Ontario Civil Service, and the money was unbelievably good: one hundred dollars a month plus living expenses. I was a writer and they were looking for secretarial workers, crack typists. I was a phoney, that's what I was. But they took me on. For three wild and woolly years.

I was stationed in Dawson Creek, B.C., the southern terminus of the Alaska Highway, for the first year and a half, then I went to Prince Rupert. I worked in the truck dispatching office, making out bills of lading. A lot of the girls were from the States — from Texas, from Seattle. We formed friendships then that have lasted ever since.

The 1,600-mile Alaska Highway was built in twenty months during 1942-43 in response to the possible threat of a Japanese invasion. 35,000 American soldiers and a small number of Canadians worked on the highway, which runs from Dawson Creek, B.C., to Fairbanks, Alaska. Courtesy Dodi Robb

Wartime civil servants. NFB

Mrs. W. E. (Nell) West, Director Voluntary Services, Department of National War Services. A former welfare officer, West had been assistant to the Deputy Minister, Public Welfare Department, in the Ontario government. PAC PA 142397

We lived fifteen girls to a barracks, in an army camp in Dawson, with no running water, just a corrugated tub to have your bath in, right next to the stove. Somebody would bring the pails of water around. You had the choice of washing your laundry first, or your body, whichever you thought was more important.

There had to be guards on the door, to keep the fellows away. There were probably eighty women and eight hundred men, so it was highly dangerous. I was twenty-three. If I had a twenty-three-year-old daughter who wanted to go on a similar venture, I would chain her to the closet door. I came of a very conservative, Scottish family, and it was a form of insanity, in a way.

We had a great time. We were terribly amused because all of our dates were miraculously single.

Toronto

THE SMALL-TOWN GIRL IN OTTAWA

Doris Wenda Sherwood is a compact little bundle of Maritime freshness. Five foot two, wavy, light brown hair, blue eyes, a round, frank face, she comes from Campbellton, New Brunswick, where she was born twenty years ago.

Doris came to Ottawa in 1940 with a brand new commercial education behind her and ready to serve her country at war by filing for small pay. For two years she lived in the rush of wartime Ottawa, working for the Dependants' Allowances and Assigned Pay Branch. Crowded lodgings, a quick breakfast, the dash to the street car, the morning routine of the office, the Coke and sandwich lunch, the long afternoon, the homeward rush, supper in a restaurant and a date two or three times a week, with a bit of

bowling in between, fill Doris's daily calendar. Like thousands of other girls in Ottawa she finds a lift to her spirits in dancing and a good show. Her dates mostly are boys in uniform.

As a filing clerk Grade 2, in the Civil Service, she has a tough time with her budget, having a net income of about $80. a month after taxes and other deductions. Her food and clothes, she says, cost too much but her amusements are pretty well provided for by the boys in uniform who find her good company. She is one of the exceptions to the supposed rule that Ottawa's working women are lonely. She says she is too busy to ever feel alone or sorry for herself.

Doris is a war worker in a very real sense. Without her and thousands of girls who have come from the towns and cities of every province, Ottawa couldn't carry on with its warmaking. . . .

Eaton Maxwell, *Saturday Night*, 20 November 1943

Phyllis Turner was Administrator of Fats and Oils for the Wartime Prices and Trade Board and had worked as an economist for the Canadian Tariff Board before the war. She represented Canada at international meetings. Private source

NO. 8 TEMPORARY BUILDING

Anybody in Ottawa who could work in an office was more than wanted. When you went to the civil service you had to take an exam, but you had to be a real dope not to pass. I could type, and that was just about it.

I was told to report to No. 8 Temporary [building], at the corner of Preston and Carling. I took information about enlisted men from the files and typed it onto cards. Next door was the casualties office — they got all the telegrams coming in from overseas and they sent off messages to the next of kin. They were just run off their feet. It was depressing, all those people getting wounded and killed.

I was a Grade 1 clerk, and I worked half a shift, from seven o'clock to eleven [p.m.]. It was good to bring in some extra money. The children had come bang, bang, bang and they needed shoes. I took home thirty-five dollars a month, but if I'd worked full time it would have been seventy dollars.

At night that building was really something. What with the rats and the cockroaches, I don't know how it stood up and didn't run away. You'd hear the rats thumping around in the waste baskets in the office next door, looking for something to eat. And the cockroaches — I can see them yet. When you snapped on the light in the washroom you'd see all these little brown things in the basins. They used to spray the place every so often.

Ottawa

SO MUCH DEPENDS ON HOW YOU FEEL TODAY

Stenographer? Bookkeeper? Clerk? It really doesn't matter what type of work you do — it is essential to our war effort. Office work may seem a far cry from flying bombers over Germany, but vitally important communications can often be delayed or speeded up, depending upon the efficiency with which you do your work. You know yourself how your work is affected by the way you feel — how important it is to keep feeling your best, in order to do your best.

Here's a hint for those days when you get out of bed feeling listless and miserable due to the need of a laxative. . . .

Laxative advertisement, 1943

LADY DOING A MAN'S JOB

Women working in Assembly Lines, in Government Offices, in any of your country's Services, side by side with hundreds of other men and women . . . [our cream] is for you. It protects feminine charm and daintiness, even on a difficult man-sized job. And it protects the uniform you're proud to wear — Service or Munitions. Acts in 30 seconds. Just put it on, wipe off excess, and dress. Keeps underarms sweet and dry up to three days.

Deodorant advertisement, 1943

HER LINOLEUM FLOOR HELPS HER WORK FOR WAR!

Simplified housekeeping is a "must" with women on the home front. A full-time war job or voluntary service in hospital, Red Cross or other vital work takes precedence over housework. With Linoleum floors to slash hours from her housecleaning schedule, today's busy housewife can still find time to handle both home and war work capably. . . .

Floor-covering advertisement, 1943

One of several women hired by the National Film Board during the war, Evelyn Cherry directs a film on wartime nutrition. Other women were hired by the Canadian Broadcasting Corporation to work as producers in Winnipeg, Montreal, and Halifax.
PAC PA 116120

VERY SECRET   The personnel manager was a Torontonian, a man called Herb Roland, and he emphasized that the work was very secret, very important to the war effort. There was a typing test, but it was pretty simple. If you could recognize a typewriter, you got in. There was a security check-up, though.

You had to give a detailed family background, and list the schools you'd been to. The names you gave as references were checked out by the Mounties, I found out later.

I went to New York in December. They recruited in Toronto and Winnipeg, and two or three hundred Canadians were hired, primarily women. You had to be either British or Canadian to work for British Security Coordination. Their offices were at 630 Fifth Avenue, in the International Building, right opposite Saks Fifth Avenue. I was taken up to the thirty-sixth floor for fingerprinting, and to be photographed. You were given a great security talk: how there would be instant dismissal for any misdemeanour. Above all, we were never to explain to outsiders where we worked, what we did, or what our phone number was.

New York was the headquarters for Intercept [intercepted messages] from all over the world. Stations in different countries would pick up coded messages, decode them, recode, and relay them to New York. The office was open twenty-four hours a day, seven days a week, and many girls worked shifts.

I kept charts and graphs showing how many messages had been sent concerning a particular location. The U.S. Navy used British Intercept services during the war, and I billed them for information provided through my graphs and charts.

I was paid $35 a week, cash, in a plain brown-paper envelope. There was nothing inside it to say who I worked for.

Toronto

TO WORK FOR BRITAIN

A department of the British Government in New York requires several young women fully competent in secretarial work of matriculation or better educational standing. The chief need is for expert file clerks and for typists and stenographers. Those selected can expect to serve for the duration of the war....

Advertisement in the Toronto *Evening Telegram*, mid-1941

QUEER HOURS   There was a sense of danger about what we were doing, but there were no break-ins, or thefts, or bomb scares. The only thing I remember going wrong was my own fault. I smoked, and I left a lighted cigarette on the corner of my desk. It burned up a night's supply of flimsy intercepts, and that didn't go over too well.

There were no restrictions on where we lived, or with whom, as long as they were British or Canadian. I shared an apartment with three friends from the office in the Osborne, the second-oldest apartment building in New York, kitty-corner from Carnegie Hall. We had very little contact with Americans, but we told people we were nurses. That accounted for the queer hours we kept.

Stephenson would come into the office from time to time, and he'd bring in field officers from Europe to talk to us, men who'd been parachuted in behind the lines. They'd emphasize how vital it was that information got through to them as soon as possible. And important visitors came, like Noel Coward and Lord Mountbatten. But a lot of the work was pretty tedious. In fact, the work was quite secondary to being in New York. We were young, we were single, and we had a darned good time. Mind you, there was nothing against us being married—but your husband had to be British or Canadian.

Toronto

GERMAN SHIPS   The U.S. was not at war in 1941, and there were German ships docking along the Atlantic coast. My job in New York was to keep track of those ships and the people on them. It would seem like a hopeless job, but we knew the important names to look out for.

Toronto

Operator with coding machine. NMC 74-17527

INTREPID

He was most insignificant to look at. He was lightly built, not terribly tall, probably in his forties. He had neat hair and neat clothes; he dressed quietly, in grey or navy suits.

Toronto

Intrepid? He was a brilliant man, but he was very reticent, very Canadian: the perfect person for the job. He was nice-looking, with piercing blue eyes. He didn't miss anything.

Toronto

He was not formidable, but he was not familiar, either. He was very quiet, very unassuming. He had a tremendous ability to make himself almost invisible.

Toronto

GUATEMALA VIA MEXICO CITY   I'd been working in New York for one year, sorting out lists of names, and I was bored to tears. Then in July 1942 someone said, ''Does anyone want to go to Guatemala?'' I said, ''I'd love to,'' then I went and looked it up on the map.

I took coding and decoding before I went. The man I went with had been trained at Camp X [Scarborough, Ontario], but we left separately from New York. I went by train, and we met in Brownsville, Texas. Then we flew Pan Am to Guatemala, via Mexico City.

We had an office in the British Legation, and this man was called the Cultural Attaché, but that was a cover for MI5. There was no sense of bodily danger. There was no sabotage involved; this was a preventive operation, to check on the expatriation of Germans from Guatemala — the people who'd come to settle there in the 1930s or earlier. They were supposed to go back to Germany, or to camps in the U.S.

The F.B.I were already there, at the American Embassy, and they didn't take to our appearance very well. The U.S. was trying to keep Germans out of the Panama Canal area, and out of the Caribbean. Whenever we exchanged information, we always held something back.

The man I worked with recruited sub-agents to give us information regarding anyone of a suspicious nature. He was the perfect person for the job — he absolutely loved intrigue — but nothing very earth-shattering happened, and I began to wonder why we were there. Sometimes it felt ridiculous. In December we got an urgent message from London, and I rushed off to decode it. It said, ''Merry Christmas to you!''

Toronto

Saskatchewan, early 1940s. Farm work was considered high priority as of March 1942, and no agricultural worker could transfer to another job without a special permit, except to one of the armed forces. SAB S-B 6578

8

Officers All: The Nursing Sisters

PAC PA 501335

"**P**atriotism, that old-fashioned word, carried most of us into service," said one nurse among hundreds who immediately volunteered for service when war was declared in 1939. Besides "old-fashioned patriotism", however, there was also a sense of tradition. In the First World War there had been 3,141 nursing sisters in the Canadian Army Medical Corps, and 2,504 of them had served overseas. Six of those had been killed or mortally wounded on land, and another fifteen had died at sea, so nursing sisters were aware of the dangers to be faced.

The first contingent of nursing sisters went overseas in January 1940. Emma Pense, R.C.A.M.C. Matron, and a First World War veteran, left for London, England, in April to become Matron-in-Chief, Overseas. At Ottawa headquarters another veteran matron, Elizabeth Smellie, became Matron-in-Chief for Canada.

In 1939 the Army was the only service with a nursing division; after the First World War a very small nucleus of nursing sisters had been retained in the Royal Canadian Army Medical Corps, permanent force. But as the need for nurses grew, first the Air

Force and then the Navy established a Nursing Service, although on a much smaller scale than the Army.

The qualifications required to be a nursing sister were similar in all three services. Applicants had to be British subjects, twenty-five to forty-five in the beginning (age limits were extended later), unmarried, or widows without children of school age. They were expected to serve for at least one year and (initially) to resign upon marriage. They had to be graduates of a recognized training school and registered in the province where they qualified.

Every nursing sister was a commissioned officer. In May 1942, Canadian nurses became the first in any Allied country to have official officer status with the equivalent power of command. Women with related professional skills — physiotherapists, occupational therapists, dietitians — were also recruited and commissioned. They usually carried the same rank and wore the same uniform as the nursing sisters.

In the R.C.A.M.C., nurses enlisted as second lieutenants and were eligible to become full lieutenants once their military training was complete. The matron of a small army unit was a captain; if she commanded a large unit, she was a major. The R.C.A.F. and the R.C.N. used equivalent ranks for their nursing sisters.

R.C.A.M.C. nurses had the closest contact with Canadian military operations overseas. By the end of

Nurses of No. 5 Canadian General Hospital at Taplow on the estate of Lord and Lady Astor, 1940. TT 352-2330 the war, more than two-thirds of them had served abroad. They also staffed the two Canadian hospital ships that sailed between Britain, the Mediterranean, and Canada.

Most R.C.A.F. nurses worked in Canada on British Commonwealth Air Training Plan stations, where inevitably there were accident victims needing care. However, approximately one in seven served overseas, either in Newfoundland or in Britain. Two also served in continental Europe, with an R.C.A.F. mobile field hospital in Normandy. R.C.N. nursing sisters were posted to Canadian shore establishments on the east and west coasts, to St. John's, Newfoundland, and to Greenock, Scotland, where R.C.N.H. *Niobe* was located.

When the war ended, Canada's 4,480 nursing sisters had cared for more than 60,000 wounded Canadians, numerous Allied servicemen, and many enemy casualties. In recognition of their service, they received 386 awards of the Royal Red Cross and they were mentioned in over 100 dispatches.

I RAN ALL THE WAY   I hadn't finished my training when the war started. I thought: "Oh my, I do hope it's not over before I get there!" I graduated in 1940, then I worked one year before I wrote to the Army. They arranged an interview, and I ran all the way to the Bessborough [Hotel]. This Colonel said, "When can you start?" and I said, "When can I come?"

R.C.A.M.C., Saskatoon

BEDPANS TO HYPODERMICS   In November 1940 I was one of eight nurses from Toronto Military Hospital picked to go to Camp Borden. I was the sister in charge. There had never been nurses at Camp Borden before.

The hospital was a shambles. The wards were Nissen huts, with twenty patients down each side and a Quebec heater, a wood stove, in the centre. Then there was a barrack-room table with everything from bedpans to hypodermics all piled on it together.

The patients were all Canadian soldiers, and they were all sick—there were practically no injuries. A doctor would say that a patient should get up and go to the bathroom. He could have a temperature of 103 degrees, and he'd have to go outside in the cold, in November! We were able to change that, and we really piled in to get that place clean and nice. It was one of the most rewarding things we ever did, and there were just eight of us.

Nurses were officers, and we had supper in the Officers' Mess. We had our own cabin, of course, which we made quite comfortable, and a sergeant came over each night with a pail of cocoa for us. It was a nice cold, crispy winter with lots of snow.

R.C.A.M.C., Ontario

BOYS WITH ARMS OFF   When I first went into Army nursing I was at London Military Hospital. We got our first convoy of patients in from Italy; they'd been in hospital there and they were coming home for more treatment, or to be discharged.

They were boys with arms off and legs off, and it really upset me. There were about three hundred of them. I went around with the tears pouring down my face. But you learn to control your feelings, to adjust. If you can do something constructive for someone who is suffering, you can handle your emotions.

R.C.A.M.C., Ontario

WE LIVED IN HUTS   It was hard to get into the R.C.A.M.C. The pay was fantastic: $150 a month compared to $70 which I was making before, and our accommodation and meals were all paid. We were anxious to join for the money and adventure, but we were patriotic, too.

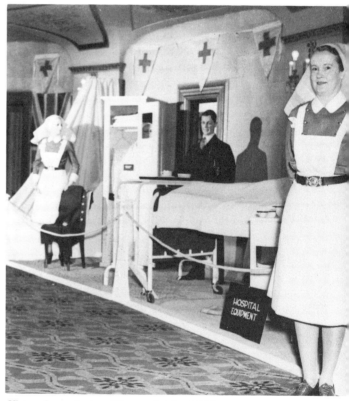

Victory Loan display, Ottawa, October 1942. PAC PA 128212

At Camp Sussex we lived in huts, and the conditions were fairly primitive. They were heated with round-bellied coal stoves, like in rural railway stations, and soldiers came in through the night to shovel coal. There were walls, but they didn't reach up to the ceiling.

We really had it made. Women were scarce, and we could have our choice of who we went out with. Except we weren't allowed to go out with N.C.O.s, like sergeants. That was an Army rule. So it was always officers. Today we'd laugh at a rule like that, but then we took it seriously.

R.C.A.M.C., Cape Breton

N/S J. E. C. Porteous was appointed Principal Matron of the R.C.A.F. nursing service in 1943, with the rank of squadron leader. By the end of the war the service had 481 members. DND PL 117352-2

Appointed Matron-in-Chief, R.C.A.M.C., in April 1940, Elizabeth Smellie was a veteran of the First World War. Since 1925 she had been Chief Superintendent of the Victorian Order of Nurses. The R.C.A.M.C. recruited 3,656 nurses before the war ended. In 1941 Smellie was seconded to select the first class of officers for the new Canadian Women's Army Corps. PAC PA 128225

SOMETHING MORE MEANINGFUL   I was a pacifist, with no wish to join the military. But my job in advertising with Lever Brothers seemed rather pointless in wartime, visiting textile manufacturers and persuading them to hang tags on material saying "Wash in Lux". I was thirty-two years old in 1942, and I wanted something more meaningful to do.

A friend persuaded me to become a Home Sister with the R.C.A.M.C. I had the rank of second lieutenant, but I was really the housekeeper in charge of a nursing sisters' residence in Chorley Park [Toronto].

R.C.A.M.C., Toronto

THE ONLY GIRLS   I was sent to Penhold, one of the B.C.A.T.P. [British Commonwealth Air Training Plan] stations just outside Red Deer. There were lots of Aussies, New Zealanders, and Brits. The doctors were British too, and it was almost like working in a foreign country.

Myself and another nurse, we were the only girls on the station. If they wanted something done, like sewing on a badge or a ribbon, they'd ask us. We were just like mothers to those boys away from home.

We were always welcome in the mess; we'd stand at the bar with them and have an aperitif before dinner. If they were having a stag, though, we knew enough not to go.

R.C.A.F., Edmonton

A HARD TIME GETTING IN   I'm Jewish and I felt keenly about the Holocaust. I wanted to do something active in the war, so I applied to be a nurse with the R.C.A.F. I was a trained nurse but I had a hard time getting in because I was only five feet tall, and you were meant to be at least five feet two.

I had quite a talk with that Medical Officer. I said, "When you get a medal in general proficiency, which I did, then there should be a place for you." I was accepted in September 1941 and I was discharged in March 1946.

R.C.A.F., Winnipeg

These R.C.A.F. nursing sisters were sent on a special secret training course in Kentucky, to prepare them for air evacuation work in front-line areas of Europe. Unlike the American nurses on the course, the Canadians were never permitted to put their training into practice. Courtesy Evelyn Hardwick Calow

UNDER BARBED WIRE   In 1943 I was one of six qualified flight nurses chosen for an air evacuation course in Louisville, Kentucky. The R.C.A.F. kept our course very hush-hush. None of us knew each other, and we travelled separately. I left from Dartmouth. It was a course for nurses and some doctors to be parachuted into combat areas.

We were taught to rescue wounded men by air, no matter where they were. We learned to crawl on our stomachs under barbed wire under fire — we were told they fired live ammo — and we were trained to make parachute jumps, although we never did jump.

The American girls went on to Europe, to the front lines, but the Canadians didn't. The R.A.F. wouldn't have women flying with them, and they set the rules for the R.C.A.F. The American girls pleaded with us to go with them, but it would have meant switching services, and we didn't want to do that.

As it happened, I did some air rescue work, but with civilians, when I was sent to Newfoundland. We'd be sent out to pick up patients from remote areas. One time, our plane was forced down ten miles from where we were headed in northern Newfoundland, and we went in with a dog team to pick up a man. But the only one of our group who made real use of her training was Evelyn Hardwick. She ran a course in air ambulance evacuation for male orderlies at Rockcliffe.

R.C.A.F., Winnipeg

THE STORM AND THE SUBS   When we were posted to [H.M.C.S.] *Avalon* [St. John's, Newfoundland], it was right at the height of the war in the Atlantic. Coming out of Halifax harbour we could see the ships which had been sunk.

We were eleven days going from Halifax to Newfoundland because of the storm and the subs. We were in a convoy of about forty ships, and we went to Bermuda and back. We were on a merchant ship, and it was not very large. The storm was so bad, the waves were breaking over the ship. I was in charge of five nurses, and by the time we arrived at St. John's I was the only one on my feet.

It was so sad to see these youngsters suffering from exposure. There'd be a whole wardful of them at *Avalon* with fans blowing on their feet to cool them. If they'd had ice packs it would have been easier, but we didn't have any. Later the Navy developed a method of treatment.

R.C.N., Streetsville, Ont.

IMMERSION FOOT   I didn't consider joining the Army or the Air Force — it was the Navy that appealed to me. When they started taking in nurses, in '42, you had to know somebody to get in. My mother did know somebody, and she wrote a letter on my behalf.

I signed up at [H.M.C.S.] *York*, and I was sent to Halifax as an acting sub-lieutenant. There were some Canadians in the hospital, but there were R.N. sailors, Russians, Free French. . . . There were a lot of infectious diseases, and some were very sick.

We got patients suffering from exposure. After a ship had been torpedoed the men would spend hours in the water sometimes, or even days in an open boat. One of the greatest worries was immersion foot — if they were in the water too long they lost the circulation. Their feet would be so swollen, there wasn't much to be done. There weren't the antibiotics then.

R.C.N., Toronto

Marjorie Russell was Matron-in-Chief of the Nursing Service Branch, Royal Canadian Naval Medical Service. Eventually the service numbered 343 members. Courtesy Grace Walker

WHEN THE TORPEDO HIT   We were asleep in our cabin when the torpedo hit. Agnes and I were going back to *Avalon*; we'd been on leave for two weeks and we were relaxed and happy.

There were about 240 passengers on the *Caribou*, going from Sydney to Port-aux-Basques, women, children, Newfoundlanders, and a lot of servicemen. There were just the two of us from the nursing service.

It was dark, terribly dark, in the cabin, and the door was jammed. But I had a flashlight and we managed to get out. We grabbed our life-jackets and went up on deck. I had a good sense of direction and we got to the lifeboat station, but the lifeboat was gone. The ship was sinking and we were washed off into the water. I thought we would never come up again, but we did, and we had our life-jackets on. At first the water felt warm. It was terribly cold up on the deck.

We were in the water for hours. Something burn-

ing drifted towards us, and I was terrified. Agnes and I held onto each other. An overturned lifeboat drifted by, and we got ourselves up on top of it and held onto the ropes. We were wearing pyjamas and our Burberrys but we had nothing on our feet.

There were about a dozen of us hanging onto the lifeboat, to begin with, but in the morning there were only three or four left. Each time a wave went over, someone was washed off. Agnes got cramped, and eventually she let go. I held her with one hand as long as I could, but in the end she just drifted away. She was a tiny, slender person, she'd have weighed maybe a hundred pounds.

It was daybreak when we were picked up by a minesweeper, the *Grand'mère*, but I don't remember anything about the rescue. They took us to Sydney, to the Army hospital there.

R.C.N. Nursing Sister Margaret Brooke,
Ardath, Sask.

Tea-time at Naval Hospital, H.M.C.S. *Avalon*, St. John's, Newfoundland. N/S Agnes Wilkie, second from right, was drowned after the ferry *Caribou* was torpedoed in October 1942. N/S Margaret Brooke, in white uniform on left, was awarded the O.B.E. for her brave efforts to save her colleague. Wilkie was the only nursing sister to lose her life as a direct result of enemy action during the war. Courtesy Margaret Brooke

WITH OUR GAS MASKS ON   Before we went overseas we had to get used to wearing gas masks. We congregated in Windsor [Nova Scotia] and we had route marches along the streets. One day we were marching along in our navy-blue skirts and blue blouses with our gas masks on. I heard one woman standing on a street corner say to another, "What do you suppose they are?" And the other person said, "Oh, they must be telephone operators!"

R.C.A.M.C., Ontario

YOU TOOK YOUR LIFEBELT

We boarded the *Queen Elizabeth* in Halifax. There were thousands of Canadian troops on board. It was like Christmas at Eaton's. We got two meals a day; you were given a card with the times on it, but you could take rolls and fruit away with you to your cabin.

There were twelve of us in a cabin on A Deck, which was first class. It would have been a large cabin for two people. We didn't travel in convoy because the *Queen Elizabeth* was so fast that speed was our protection. But we had drills all the time, and you took your lifebelt with you, always.

R.C.A.M.C., Nova Scotia

STARCHED CUFFS AND A VEIL

Our uniform was navy blue, a very pretty shade of blue for the shirt, with a navy-blue tie and a navy-blue hat with a little brim, and a caduceus pin, the medical insignia, which had a snake winding around a pole.

On duty our uniform was pale-blue cotton with a white bibbed apron, all starched, and a brass buckle on a leather belt. We had white, starched cuffs and a veil like the British nurses, and a white organdy veil. A person in a slightly faded uniform was a "vet"; you knew she'd been around for a while.

R.C.A.M.C., Cape Breton

PULLHEMS

Your physical category was based on the "pullhems": your *p*hysique, *u*pper *l*imbs, *l*egs, *h*earing, *e*yes, and *m*ental *s*tability.

I went overseas in 1942 to No. 8 Canadian General at Farnborough, an old British military hospital next door to Aldershot. We lived in cottages, five to a cottage.

It was a fantastic old hospital, with windows high up off the floor and fireplaces built back-to-back to heat the wards. In the old building there were wide plank floors which we washed down regularly. The newer wards, built out behind, had battleship-grey linoleum floors.

We got all the sick cases you'd normally get, plus accidents. There were many vehicle accidents, particularly motor cycles, because of the blackout.

The nurses' mess was in a Nissen hut, and it was *cold*. I wore an overcoat to meals.

R.C.A.M.C., Saskatchewan

Agnes Neill took the nursing sisters of No. 15 Canadian General Hospital to England in January 1940 as the unit's first matron. In 1942 she succeeded Emma Pense as Matron-in-Chief Overseas at Canadian Military Headquarters, London. Neill became Matron-in-Chief for Canada in 1945. Private source

First Matron-in-Chief, Canadian Army Overseas, was Emma Pense, a veteran of the First World War. Pense is seen here with the owner of Digswell Place, the Canadian Nursing Sisters' Convalescent Home and Rest Centre at Welwyn, Hertfordshire. PAC PA 142297

IN THE BALLROOM   In September 1942 we went overseas as No. 2 Casualty Clearing Station. There were eight sisters, twelve officers, one hundred men, and the officer commanding, and we were like one big family.

We were stationed in Surrey, not far from Guildford, in a large house belonging to somebody who was away in the R.A.F. There were greenhouses, and rose gardens, and a swimming pool. The nurses' mess was the children's nursery, and a dumb waiter brought our food up from the kitchen.

There was a ballroom with a balcony running round the top of it. We had forty or fifty patients in that ballroom, and the beds were not even close together. A lot of our patients were dispatch riders, motorcycle accidents, and it was nice looking after people who got well quickly, easily.

R.C.A.M.C., Ontario

A PUB OR TEAROOM   In our free time there was always plenty to do. We went bicycling on picnics, or to a pub or a tearoom. Some of us had bikes with us, smuggled on board the *Queen Elizabeth*, brought from Camp Sussex. And there was always a party, somewhere.

We had a pass on the railways when we were on leave, and we went up to London, and I went to Scotland a couple of times. After a while London was out of bounds because of the buzz bombs.

Watford was the nearest town, and there were beautiful concerts to go to. I heard Dame Myra Hess play there.

R.C.A.M.C., Ontario

HIT BY SHRAPNEL   You became very fond of your patients, particularly the younger ones. You felt nothing but pride in them. You very rarely got a difficult patient.

One particular patient was a French-Canadian chap by the name of Benoit, and he'd been hit by shrapnel. He had lost an eye, he had thirteen holes in his intestines, plus flesh wounds in his arms and legs, and he had had a kidney taken out. But the only time I heard him complain was when they gave him a glass eye, and he was so upset because it didn't match the other.

You couldn't despair when you were looking after men like that.

R.C.A.M.C., Toronto

WOUNDED MANY TIMES   We had a visit from a Major-General, who told us our first duty was to get our men well again so they could go back into action. That disturbed me. They were supposed to be sent home if they'd been wounded three times, but I had patients who were wounded many times and still they got sent back to the front.

R.C.A.M.C., London, Ont.

STUMPS   I never showed my feelings very much until I'd been at Horley in England for some months. Just after Christmas I went to see a patient of mine who'd been sent to the surgical ward. The man in the next bed had both legs off above the knees, and he had stuck the stumps in his Army boots and he was running up and down the bed. He said, ''Sister, I've been in the war for five years and the Red Cross never gave me anything. But this year they sent me a present.'' Then he held out a pair of socks.

R.C.A.M.C., Ontario

SEXUAL AFFAIRS   I learned about men, listening to them talk at night. There was a man from Vancouver with a wife and four kiddies, and he used to talk about how he missed them. One night he went out on leave and he was late getting back to the hospital. (After ten o'clock you could put them on charge and they had to see the Colonel.) When he got in he said, ''I've been over to see my girl in East Grinstead.'' I said I didn't understand how he could, and he was furious, because in his mind he didn't connect this girl with his family back home.

The war had a lot to do with it. People did things away from home they would never do back in Canada. My friends never talked about their sexual affairs, they never admitted or discussed their affairs, even if it was obvious. There was so much at stake. We didn't have the pill, and there was V.D. Not until we got penicillin was V.D. controllable. So there were lots of deterrents.

R.C.A.M.C., Ontario

I LOVED TO DANCE   It was a paradise as far as the nurses were concerned, even the most unattractive. I loved to dance, and we danced three nights a week when we were in England. Those were wonderful years. Our boys were so proud of us, almost as if we were their own sisters.

R.C.A.M.C., British Columbia

WHEN ANOTHER BOMB FELL   I took the tube to Cromwell Road, and as I came out of the station someone said, "The club's been bombed!" My room was just a shambles, with dust and rubble all over the place. I was standing there assessing the situation when another bomb fell near by and the dresser took a flying leap across the room and hit my hip. Fortunately the windows were all out already, but there was this one big piece of glass which had struck the mattress with such force, it had gone right through it. And the night before, I hadn't bothered to go down to the shelter when the alert sounded.

I had a dozen or so stockings hanging in the bathroom, and my whole treasured hoard of stockings was all ruined. You'd have thought someone had shot a pea-shooter through them. It was the shattered glass that did it. I never did find my slippers.

R.C.A.M.C., Alberta

THE BURN BOYS   There was no room for us to stay at the hospital in East Grinstead, so Lord and Lady Glendyne took the two of us at "Herontye". It was part of their war effort, they said. It also enabled them to keep some of their servants. Lady Glendyne was quite frank with us.

We lived in the attic; we had two very large bedrooms, a big bathroom, and a huge sitting-room. The younger butler brought our dinner up in a dumb waiter and set it up in the sitting-room. The helpings were small, but everything was beautifully cooked and served. If we were not going to be home for dinner, we had to be sure to tell the butler.

At weekends we were invited to dinner with the family. Lady Glendyne told us later she wanted to see what we were like. Dinner was at eight o'clock in the main dining-room, then at nine we retired promptly to the Oak Room, where coffee was served. They still had all kinds of maids and a personal cook. But they lost the younger butler; he was taken to work in a factory, and after that we ate with the family every night.

In the mornings we walked to work. It was over four miles each way, and Lady Glendyne offered her car, but neither of us could drive. The Hospital had three huge wards built for the Air Force boys, British, Canadian, South African, Australian, American — they were all brought there. We called them the "burn boys", but they called themselves "guinea pigs", because many of the operations were experimental; there'd been no extensive burn work done before. I worked in the operating-room and I loved the work, but it was upsetting to see boys so terribly burned. There were boys whose planes had burst into flames, and some had crashed in the ocean. They were very pathetic-looking sights, with their noses, ears, and eyelids burned off. And many had been handsome-looking chaps.

Some of the R.A.F. boys — their wives would come and take a look at them, and that would be it. But many English girls married the Canadian "burn boys".

R.C.A.F., Napanee, Ont.

Queen Victoria Hospital, East Grinstead, Sussex, specialized in plastic surgery for burns and jaw injuries. Courtesy Lenora Mardall

ON CHRISTMAS DAY   We arrived at Liverpool on board the *Mauretania* on Christmas Eve, 1943. There were eight of us who were leaving for Glasgow on Christmas Day, three nurses, some Wrens, and a male doctor.

We had Christmas dinner on board ship, on the twenty-fourth, but on Christmas Day all we had were our K rations: compressed, dehydrated food. It was terribly hard to find any restaurant open on Christmas Day.

Our train didn't leave for Scotland until nearly midnight, so we had time to put in. Then we discovered there was a Canadian ship anchored off Birkenhead, and they were thrilled when we made contact. They brought us on board and they gave us the remnants of their Christmas dinner. But the real thrill was seeing the Maple Leaf on the funnel of that ship.

R.C.N., Toronto

R.C.A.F. HQ London, WC 2
28/9/42

Dear Mother,

We spent the weekend in the country, and it was lovely. The three of us were invited to a dance at one of the Army Officers' messes. They were so very nice to us, so glad to hear Canadian accents again.

Our railway tickets were mailed to us, we were met at the station, there were rooms in a lovely hotel, then dinner and dance Saturday night, lunch, tea, and dinner on Sunday, and then we were put on the train for home. We couldn't have had more attention.

Oh yes, we were each given a package of marshmallows, a tin of peanut butter, and a jar of olives from their precious supplies. . . .

Officers' Mess, R.A.F. Station,
Houghton Green,
Warrington, Lancashire
3/1/43

Dear Mother,

. . . To go back to Christmas. I was lonely and wanted to be with you all so much and yet I knew how impossible it all was. Christmas morning breakfast was at 9.30. Great excitement — orange juice (contributions from home), real fried eggs (I often think of all the times I refused eggs at home, Mother), and bacon, toast, and coffee. Then the C.O. filled socks for all of us, in front of the fireplace. Molly and I each received half a dozen clothes pins, a beautiful (?) corsage, a chart on how to play the piano in one easy lesson, then Santa Claus gave me some cod liver oil capsules with a sign on them ''two capsules a day will surely keep that cough away''. All the boys had potatoes and brussels sprouts in their socks — the mainstay of the diet here.

R.C.A.F. ''R'' Depot
10/3/43

Dear Mother,

The night before we came down here, two American boys came over to see us and gave us each a real egg and a roll of toilet paper. It was funny — but we appreciated it more than anything else. My third egg since I left home [28 August 1942]. I'll never refuse another egg for breakfast, Mother.

Excerpts from an R.C.A.F. nursing sister's
letters to her family in Ottawa

A TERM OF AFFECTION   At *Niobe* [near Glasgow] we lived in each other's pockets, and we had fun. We knew more about each other than our families knew, but we learned not to encroach on another person's ''bubble of space''. If we were ill, we looked after each other.

The patients depended upon us. Men were used to women taking care of them. They would call us ''Sister'', where they called a Wren ''Ma'am''. ''Sister'' was a term of respect, but it was also one of affection.

R.C.N., Toronto

Occupational therapy for patients. Courtesy Grace Walker

REVOLVER PRACTICE   Before we left England for the continent we had to learn to defend ourselves. We all got a bang out of revolver practice. They hung targets from a tree for us to aim at. One girl had no strength in her right hand. She used two hands when the instructor wasn't looking.

One time the instructor saw a nursing sister smoking a cigarette and he said, "Are you game for me to shoot it out of your mouth?" He did, too. He was so cool and self-assured.

R.C.A.M.C., Ontario

EMERGENCY RATIONS   We went north to Yorkshire for a toughening-up period before D-Day. All our nice blue uniforms went into storage and we wore British-issue women's battledress.

We spent long hours marching. On route marches we carried large packs, with our respirators and tin hats and blankets. We wore beautiful leather-lined British boots, double-soled, with laces. We wore little leather gaiters around the bottom of our pants. We marched over the moors all day and we marched to the pubs at night.

We were going to be living outdoors once we got to Europe, so we were put under canvas in fields behind the house. It was springtime, and the meadows were full of buttercups and daisies. We had to learn to put up our tents and take them down in a hurry, and to pack our belongings — sleeping bags, collapsible canvas cots, wash-basin stands, and canvas buckets.

When word came for our unit to move south, we went to a staging camp close to Arundel, where we pitched our tents behind barbed wire. We went through "Woolworth's" — that was a tent where we got stuff to take with us: two 48-hour ration packs, cigarettes in a tin, and matches in a waterproof container. The emergency rations were in a tin like a sardine can, which you opened with a key — but only on order from a senior officer. We were issued with "invasion" francs, paper money with the red, white, and blue tricolour on it. And vomit bags, black ones with handles.

They called you with loud hailers when it was time for your unit to move. We went by truck to Portsmouth and onto a landing-craft with a front which dropped to let the tanks roll off. There were no tanks on it, though. And the crew were quite surprised to see us. They brought us great thick spam sandwiches and "compo" tea — it came in blocks, with milk and sugar in it. You broke a piece off and put it in your tin mug and poured boiling water over it.

We sat on the narrow decks, and when night came we slept against the canvas bulwarks. It was not very comfortable. At one point there was a tremendous crash as we rammed something — or something rammed us. I became sick and made good use of my vomit bag.

We were glad to land at a Mulberry dock, where great big lorries picked us up. They took us and our gear, all lumped together, to an orchard in Normandy, a beautiful Calvados orchard, full of sour little apples. When we got the tents up we started receiving patients right away.

R.C.A.M.C. Saskatchewan

Falaise, France, August 1944. PAC PA 132193

HIGHLAND DANCES ON DECK   Soon after D-Day eight of us went by boat from Tilbury to Ostend with a group of English nurses. There were men from the 53rd Highland Division on board, and as we pulled away from the dock these men got up on deck with their bagpipes and played Scottish laments. We started doing Highland dances on deck, till we were told it was against regulations and we had to get below.

R.C.A.M.C., Ontario

PENICILLIN DISCOVERED   We went to Normandy in August 1944. The hospital was set up in an apple orchard near Bayeux, where the famous tapestry is. You could hear the gunfire from where we were.

It was shortly after penicillin was discovered, and all I did, all day long, was give injections. We had to give them every three hours. We didn't have many needles. I had three. The best one I kept for Canadians, the next best for our Allies, the British and the Americans, and the one with the biggest hook on it I used for prisoners of war (it was hard to get that one out). According to the Geneva Convention, we had to treat prisoners of war the same as our men.

We got patients with grass and gravel in their wounds, and you saw people with terrible mosquito bites around their wounds. But it didn't get to me personally, I didn't become involved. I felt I had this job to do. It's easier when you are young.

We lived two to a tent, and one of our problems was rain. It was muddy inside — the tent had no floor — so you had to keep your boots ready to put your feet into when you got out of bed. But you watched for small lizards which got inside them. The mud bothered me. Sometimes your boot stuck in it, and your foot would come right out.

Despite the rain, drinking water was very scarce. Your canteen was filled each day, and you got a chlorine tablet to disinfect it. And you had a canvas bucket for washing, which you took to the community pump. That was all the water you got to keep yourself clean, and your clothes clean. And at one point someone stole my bucket!

We had all kinds of inoculations,mind you, and the

Nursing sisters of No. 10 Canadian General Hospital land at Arromanches in northern France, July 1944. Before they left for Europe, R.C.A.M.C. nursing sisters underwent a rigorous training program. PAC PA 128193

only disease in the camp was dysentery. We all had that. The "Normandy glide", it was called. If you were doing something for a patient, you might have to stop and run to the latrines. Everybody knew what the trouble was, and you weren't embarrassed, you couldn't be. But you hoped you wouldn't have to line up when you got to the latrines!

R.C.A.M.C., Nova Scotia

A FIFTY-FOOT SCRAMBLE NET   We were torpedoed at 6.15 p.m. We were on our way to Italy, with two thousand Canadian reinforcements on board. At the second meal of the day, the steward said, "The last ship I was on was torpedoed right here." An hour later we were torpedoed ourselves.

The officers and men had to swim to the rescue ship, because there were not enough boats. We were told to climb into the rowboats, but we found we had to row ourselves over, because the men didn't know their right oar from their left. Then we had to climb up a fifty-foot scramble net, to get on board the rescue ship.

We sailed for Naples, and we were put up in a hotel for the night, the Rock Palace or the Palace Rock. We went to bed exhausted, but we soon woke up. One after another we all sat up, scratching ourselves. There were bugs! We were being eaten alive with bugs! We spent the rest of the night sitting up draped in sheets, then we set to work cleaning the bugs out when it got light.

R.C.A.M.C., Ontario

SICKNESS AND FEVER   El Arrouch was a little place off the coast of North Africa, east of Algiers. It was pretty grim. The temperature was 120 degrees every day, and the first thing that happened was the Arabs blew up the water line which went into our camp. The British Army had to supply us with water.

There was an awful lot of sickness and fever. The soldiers with malaria had very high temperatures, and we didn't have enough to give them in the way of fluids. We had oranges and lemons, and we contrived what we could. At one point our camp was hit by a typhoon, and there was a dreadful deluge of rain which pretty nearly washed the tents away. The water swept down the hill and carried a lot of our things away with it.

I caught jaundice, and I was sent to England on a hospital ship.

R.C.A.M.C., Ontario

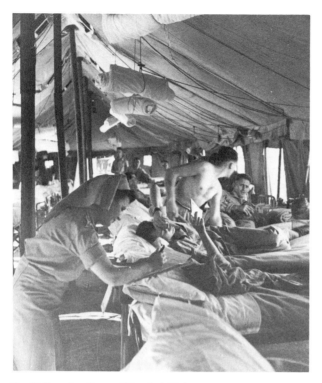

No. 15 Canadian General Hospital, El Arrouch, Algeria, August 1943. PAC PA 141498

It was hard to get used to the fact that money had no value in Italy. Cigarettes and chocolate were what the storekeepers wanted. And they didn't cost us a cent, because we got them in our rations and our food parcels from home. It was the same in the country districts, where I bartered cigarettes and chocolate bars for eggs and fresh vegetables. Nobody would accept our money.

We employed civilian help to clean and mend and supply wood for our camp stoves. One young man and his wife had a baby which was deathly ill. Their nutrition was so bad because we were near the front line. One of our doctors did what he could to help, but the baby died. Our Colonel arranged that one of our vehicles would be a hearse, to take the child to the cemetery. This little figure was laid on a board, almost like a piece of plywood, in a long, white dress with flowers around her head. Then she was put in a rough box, and we bumped along this terrible road to the cemetery. Then this little thing was tucked away in the wall—the bodies go into the cemetery wall, not into the ground. It was their first baby.

R.C.A.M.C. Messing Officer, Toronto

THAT'S SHRAPNEL!   Casualty Clearing Stations moved very quickly. When the troops moved, one of us was ready to go. In Lanciano [Italy] we had set up in an apartment building, and I was helping out in the operating-room. There was a sudden silence and I heard this funny noise up above. I said to the surgeon, "There's mice upstairs," and he said, "That's not mice. That's shrapnel!" That was the only time it happened. Usually we were protected by the huge Red Cross on the roof of a building, or on the ground, in the case of a tent hospital.

We set up in all kinds of places. After Lanciano we moved out to a tobacco factory, where we strung wires across the open space and hung grey blankets up, to make separate wards. The C.C.S. that replaced us in that factory got a direct hit.

R.C.A.M.C., Ontario

I BARTERED CIGARETTES   As Messing Officer I was in charge of the meals for the officers of No. 3 C.G.H. [Canadian General Hospital]. In Italy I could get the Colonel's jeep whenever I wanted to go foraging. The Americans had a much greater variety of food—not as much dried and tinned food as we had. I would take a military vehicle into Naples, and five or six cigarettes would get me what I wanted.

Nurses with this Canadian Field Surgical unit worked close to the fighting front in Ortona, Italy, April 1944. This caravan was built from the wreckage of a carriage from an Italian luxury train and a Messerschmidt bomber. TT 101-686 DND.

CEMENT DOWN ALL THE TOILETS   From Normandy we were sent to Belgium. We could hear the shelling. But nothing happened. The driver knew the mined spots on the road.

We spent the first night in a dreadful place. When the Germans left, they had poured cement down all the toilets. But the second night we were in Brussels, and we stayed in a hotel, in the lap of luxury. I had my first bath in six weeks.

The third night we were in Bruges, with our own unit. We moved into a home for retarded girls, run by a convent. The nuns were moving out as we moved in. We arrived on a Saturday night, and on Tuesday we started taking patients, after the bombing of the Scheldt estuary. When we got the operating-rooms set up, they were running nonstop. We were billeted in a hotel, and we got up at 5 a.m. The lorries took us to the hospital, and brought us back at 7 p.m. in the blackout. We did nothing but work, sleep, and eat in Belgium.

R.C.A.M.C., Ontario

THE V2'S STARTED TO FALL   When we got to Antwerp there was still fighting on the outskirts. We moved into a Belgian veterans' hospital — indoors at last! And we had the most magnificent house as our billet — a mansion with a marble entrance hall and a red, gold, and black Chinese room. The front doors were glass with wrought iron on them, and there were more glass doors at the back, leading out onto a glass-brick patio. The china cabinets in the dining-room were lined with mirror glass, and I had a beautiful stained-glass window behind my bed. We thought we were in heaven until the V2s started to fall, and then we found out that it was terribly dangerous to be anywhere near glass.

Eventually all the windows in our beautiful house were shattered. Injuries from blasts were awful. Great chunks of glass were embedded in people's bodies from the concussion. We were in Antwerp from September to December and the hospital was never hit, but the men said they felt safer at the front! I developed a tic — when a rocket fell my right arm jerked. The hospital which came behind us never set up in Antwerp because the C.O. refused, on account of the danger.

R.C.A.M.C., Saskatchewan

GERMAN WOUNDED   In Holland the German prisoners who came in to us were mere boys.

During the second battle of Arnhem I was matron of a large hospital with two wings. The area in between them was just laden with German wounded. But priority had to go to the Allies. You just hoped they'd survive.

They cried. They were just sixteen or seventeen, and we cried inside for them.

R.C.A.M.C. Matron Evelyn Pepper

WHEN THE RAID BEGAN   In Holland we were very close to the Germans. When the bombers came over we'd run for shelter. The maddest I ever got was one night when I'd been invited down to the male officers' mess for dinner. I'd put on my best silk uniform, and I was on my way when the raid began. I had to lie down flat in the dirt, in my best silk.

We knew the danger was always there, and we hoped if a bomb fell that we'd be hit square, and not have an arm or a leg blown off.

R.C.A.M.C., Ontario

REPLACEMENTS GOT YOUNGER   In Nijmegen the nurses kept getting younger. The WOOFs (women of over forty) were taken from the units and sent back to Canada. Their replacements got younger and younger, and we felt responsible for them.

Nurses were always being asked out to dances, and I knew it was important for our boys to see Canadian girls. But I worried about the distances they had to go. So I spoke to some English officers, engineers, and said I wanted to create an area where the girls could happily invite their friends to *our* unit.

The engineers got some big black and white chequered tiles and built a tile floor outside the mess, with canvas tenting around the sides and little tables. They strung lights around, and made a beautiful beer garden. From then on I slept at night!

R.C.A.M.C. Matron Evelyn Pepper

No. 1 Canadian Hospital Ship, the *Lady Nelson*, crossed the Atlantic thirty-seven times during the war. Between them, the *Letitia* and the *Lady Nelson* evacuated 28,000 Allied casualties.
Private source

CHILDREN SEARCHING THE GARBAGE
We were in Holland just before Christmas 1944, and we set up in a boys' school on the Mons River. Word got around that the last great push was about to start. At Christmas dinner the Colonel said there was a ship standing by to take off the sisters, if necessary.

Three battalions came for Christmas dinner in the Auditorium. Some nurses were very clever at making decorations. They made snowmen with cotton batting wrapped around bottles. Black paper or X-ray film made hats and belts and shoes. They saved silver paper from cigarette packets and made it into chains.

Everybody got an orange and a bag of hard candies after dinner. But when the troops came out to pick up their gear, they gave all their treats to some little Dutch kids standing around outside in the cold. They were in an awfully bad way in northern Holland. Sometimes we saw children searching through the garbage at the back of the hospital, and that was heartbreaking.

R.C.A.M.C., Saskatchewan

ANTICLIMAX We were in Ghent till after VE Day. On my way to work, I saw local women who'd had their heads shaved because they had gone out with German soldiers. The houses of collaborators were marked with swastikas, and the contents were smashed and burned by the Belgians.

I worked for an ear, nose, and throat specialist, and truckloads of patients with facial injuries came to the clinic. The moment we heard that the Germans had surrendered, the doctor said, "Tell them they can go back to their units to celebrate. They don't have to wait for treatment today."

I was so pleased, so excited. I told them the war was over, but there was no response at all! I expected them to cheer. Maybe it was an anticlimax. They were tired, they had been through so much, some of them were deaf from blast injuries. They just wanted to stay for treatment. So we had to stay in the clinic and work till all hours. But we had a party afterwards.

R.C.A.M.C., Nova Scotia

SO MANY PARTIES When VE Day came, you couldn't relax because there were so many parties going on. We worked hard but we played hard, too. There were so many invitations for "x" number of nursing sisters when such-and-such a [Canadian] regiment was having a party. We were all young and the men wanted girls from their own country.

We used to drive miles to go to parties. All the bridges in that part of Holland had been blown up by the Germans, and the British had built Bailey bridges to get across. But they were raised at night, to send the food barges through, and they weren't lowered again until 7 a.m. So many a night, after a dance, we spent on the floor of an officers' mess. But the boys always woke us in time to get back. We'd drive over the bridge as soon as it was lowered and we'd be back at the hospital, ready to go on duty when we were supposed to.

R.C.A.M.C., Ontario

OH MY GOD, ANGELS! I was asked if I would go to South Africa, and it sounded great, but when we got to Saint John and I saw the ship, I thought, "My God! What am I doing?" It was a 10,000-ton cargo ship, one of the Castle Line, a British ship, and there was no convoy. We were all alone, taking cargo from Canada to South Africa.

There were just ten of us young nurses and, boy, were those officers thrilled. They said we'd soon be lounging on deck, in the sun. But the third day out we picked up twenty-eight survivors from a torpedoed ship; they were British merchant marine, and they'd been six days and six nights in an open boat. It was very dangerous for a ship to stop anywhere where there might be U-boats, but of course we did. Those men looked up at us lining the rail and one of them said, "Oh my God, angels!" There'd been ninety-four to start with, but many had died, we found out later. Four others had been picked up by another ship. The men couldn't let their families know they were safe until we got to Cape Town thirty days later.

The boys in the hospital at Baragwanath were British, South African, Polish. Many of them had been burned, terribly burned, in tanks in North Africa. And we had blinded men, legless men. When you're young, you just cope. They were brought down the coast on hospital ships, then by train and ambulance to Baragwanath. By the time we got them, their initial wounds had been looked after. They came for further treatment, for skin grafts.

We worked under the South African Military Nursing Service, and we were treated royally. People opened their homes to us; they felt it was wonderful that we'd come so far to serve. The South African V.A.D.s [Voluntary Aid Detachment] looked after us; they were high-class girls, and they brought us tea in bed!

Ontario

TAKEN PRISONER   Hong Kong fell while we were working at the British Military Hospital. That word "surrender"! I can't tell you what it does for you. There had never been a Canadian nursing sister taken prisoner before.

There were two of us Canadians and fourteen British nurses from Queen Alexandra's Imperial Nursing Service at the British Military Hospital. We kept on working there as prisoners of war for the first eight months. There was not enough food, and we didn't have proper medication for our patients. The casts smelled badly and they should have been changed, but we hadn't supplies.

On August 10, 1942, we were sent to a civilian

These Canadian nursing sisters left Saint John, N.B., for South Africa aboard a freighter in April 1942. Three hundred Canadian nurses responded to a call from the South African Military Nursing Service to help care for Allied soldiers wounded in North Africa and shipped down the coast for treatment. Nurses signed up for one year, but some stayed longer. Courtesy Joan Riley

Lt. Kay Christie, R.C.A.M.C., meets her father in Montreal, December 1943, after her release from a Japanese internment camp in Hong Kong. PAC PA 141659

internment camp on the south side of the island, and we had to leave our patients without nursing care. We were loaded into trucks just like cattle going to market.

There were 2,400 internees in Stanley Camp, men, women, and children in different buildings and compounds, and there was nothing for us to do. There were some schoolteachers in the camp, French-Canadian nuns, and every afternoon I went to one of them for a French lesson. And I learned to play bridge: that was my great accomplishment. I could become quite oblivious to my surroundings, and it made the greatest difference to my life.

We had very little food, two meals a day, if you liked to call them meals. The greens they gave us had to be ground up, they were so coarse and rough, and the meat or fish had to be made into stew or hash for supper. At ten in the morning we got half of our rice and some soup, which was the water the fish or meat had been cooked in. If it was fish, there would be fish eyes floating around in it.

There was a small hospital in Stanley Camp, and after a while the nurses who ran it asked if we service sisters could help out with night duty. We were very glad to do that.

In September 1943 the Americans and the Japanese agreed to exchange civilian internees through the International Red Cross, and the U.S. agreed to bring out the Canadian civilians from Hong Kong, at the request of the Canadian government. The British nurses were not allowed out, and neither were the Australians and New Zealanders; they had to sit it out for another two years. A great many of them asked the two of us to write down the names and addresses of their families, so that we could get word to them.

The Japanese wouldn't let us bring out anything written, and we were warned about the consequences if we were caught. I wrote the names and addresses down, and then I learned them all by heart, while we were waiting. When we were lined up, eventually, to board the Japanese exchange ship, I very deliberately and obviously threw my notes away, scattering them in the wind, while I repeated and repeated those addresses to myself, in my head.

When we boarded we were handed an unusual thing, a roll of orange-coloured toilet paper, and as soon as possible I wrote down as many of those names and addresses as I could remember.

Kay Christie, R.C.A.M.C., who, with
Anna May Waters, was taken prisoner after the
fall of Hong Kong

9
Over There

"I felt I had to get over to England to be part of the war," said one Red Cross volunteer from Montreal. Many other Canadian women, particularly those of British extraction, felt the same strong urge to identify with the British war effort. Rather than waiting to see whether or not the Canadian armed forces would admit women, they enlisted in one of the British women's services, or signed up as nurses.

One alternative to enlisting in the women's services was to join a paramilitary organization like the British Mechanized Transport Corps or the Women's Transport Service, which provided cars and drivers to military and civilian groups. The W.T.S. was a division of the First Aid Nursing Yeomanry (F.A.N.Y.).

In 1940 and 1941, when women's paramilitary groups were active in Canada, at least two of them inquired about sending members to Britain. The British Columbia Women's Service Corps was interested in service with the Auxiliary Territorial Service, the official women's auxiliary of the British Army. The Women's Auxiliary Corps wanted to respond to Lord Beaverbrook's 1941 appeal for five thousand women to serve as radio technicians in Britain's defence against night-bombing attacks. But both groups were told that, through an Order-in-Council dated June 1940, the government had banned the movement of Canadians to Britain and the European war zone unless they were members of the armed forces or the civil service.

The Canadian ban on trans-Atlantic travel was lifted, however, on certain occasions. In June 1941 the government allowed the British Mechanized Transport Corps and the Women's Transport Service to recruit in Canada. (The number of women involved was small, and all were expected to pay their own fares.) A handful of women pilots, frustrated by the R.C.A.F.'s refusal to allow women to fly, joined the

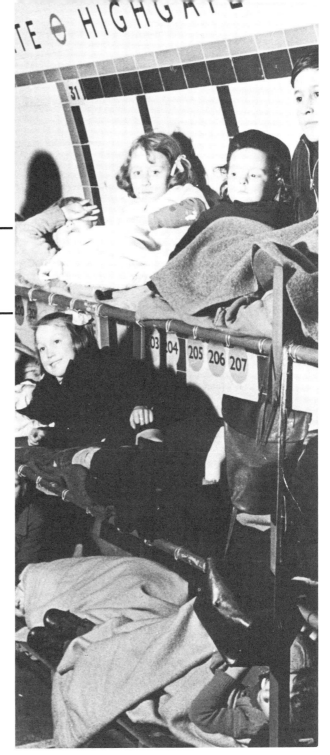

Hundreds of people slept underground each night on London tube station platforms during the blitz. In 1943 the St. John Ambulance Brigade in Canada recruited women to work in British hospitals and various first-aid posts. By 1945, 221 St. John Ambulance volunteers were working overseas as nursing auxiliaries, speech therapists, physiotherapists, and ambulance and transport drivers. In charge was Mrs. Thomas (Kathleen) Gilmour, Lady Superintendent-in-Chief of the Brigade in Canada. LT 16829, Album 5

British Air Transport Auxiliary as ferry pilots. Other women went overseas as volunteers to help run services for the Canadian armed forces, or to work in military hospitals in Britain, Europe, and Asia.

AT WORMWOOD SCRUBS At the end of 1939 I was back in London looking for something useful to do. A friend of mine had been recruited by MI5 and she said she could get me in as a filing clerk. That's where I started, working in the registry, keeping the files tidy for £2 2s 6d a week.

At that time MI5 was at Wormwood Scrubs [a former prison]. They'd scooped the prisoners out, and people worked two to a cell. The graffiti were still on the walls. It was full of the most extraordinary women with pearl necklaces from terribly county families, all "don't you know" and "actually". They had wonderful names like "Mims" and "Mumbles". I was the only one with a degree.

The registry was housed in the central block, four or five floors with iron stairs, and it was completely covered with glass. When the bombing started, one landed right on the roof and demolished all the written records of MI5. But three or four days before, we'd finished putting the records on film, and the film was saved.

After that we were ordered to move to the country, but I said, "Not me, kid." I was damned if I would go; I was in love with somebody, and passionate about London. Three months later, though, I succumbed. MI5 went to Blenheim Palace, from the prison to the palace.

My first job was in the great library of Blenheim, reading films of MI5 records and remaking them all. The registry was deep in Churchill's bedroom [where he had slept as a child].

Intelligence Officer, Toronto

A "SAFE HOUSE" Back in London [1944], three of us shared a flat. The house was used by S.O.E. [Special Operations Executive], and when agents were getting ready to be dropped they'd come around for a touch of warmth. We were allowed to run a "safe house", and they'd come to have a beer, to relax. One woman who came, she was very glamorous, received everybody in bed. The whole house rocked at night!

Toronto

A REAFFIRMATION The whole sexual thing was fascinating in London. Everybody wanted to go to bed with somebody—they didn't care who. It was a feeling of *life*: the war was so terrible, so many people had been killed, it was a reaffirmation.

I remember standing in a doorway with a beau one night during a raid, when we were on our way to dinner. All this stuff was raining down, but I was young and I felt mildly immortal. He was a pilot—he was killed later on—and he said, "I think this is the most frightening thing I've ever done." "Heavens," I said, "you're a fighter pilot!" "But in a plane I'm doing something active," he said, "not just waiting here like a sitting duck."

Toronto

The British Mechanized Transport Corps included several Canadian drivers. Established to serve both military and civilian organizations, the corps was allowed to recruit Canadians in Canada during the war. CWM 85-3036

B.C. WOMEN VOLUNTEER

Hard work, long hours and no pay—that's the kind of war job voluntarily picked by seven B.C. women who are leaving for England some time next month. They were chosen this week to accompany Ensign Janet Carruthers of the Mechanized Transport Corps to England, where they will sign away their personal freedom for the duration.

They may drive ambulances for the Red Cross; they may be attached to the Embassy and chauffeur foreign diplomats; they may drive cars for the army intelligence department, or be appointed to the wheel of army staff officer cars. Once they have begun their transport work they will not be allowed to have passage back to Canada, but they may be sent anywhere in the Empire. They must stay in service for the duration.

The corps buys its own uniforms copied from the army officers' tunics, with skirts, soft-crowned peaked caps and flat-heeled tan oxfords. They may wear silk stockings if they have any, but after they get to

England only thick lisle ones will be available. They will be entirely self-supporting and have guaranteed an income of $100 a month to take care of their living and personal expenses.

For four of the women, going to England means a possible brief reunion with their husbands, Canadian officers on active service....

Vancouver Sun, 4 October 1941

CARRYING WOUNDED SOLDIERS   Betty Murphy of Westmount, Que. joined the Mechanized Transport Corps in January 1940, and when they asked for names of girls who would like to go to France, Betty volunteered. She was driving there until France fell.

She was working near Bordeaux driving ambulances and carrying wounded soldiers and airmen to hospitals or, as in the last days before the French collapse, transporting casualties to the coast for embarkation. Besides driving ambulances, the M.T.C. worked in conjunction with the French government and helped to disperse the refugees who took to the roads in Northern France.

Betty and other M.T.C. members used to meet evacuee trains with their cars and as quickly as possible find places for them to live in the country districts. When the refugees were aged or infirm the girls took them to homes and hospitals.

"I guess I must have driven something like 12,000 miles during the five months I was in France," Betty said. "On my last journey to the coast I carried 13 wounded soldiers and airmen to the port from which we left for England."

Montreal *Gazette*, 15 February 1943

NIGHTMARE OF AGONY

(The following eyewitness story of the evacuation of Paris was written by Gladys Arnold, former Regina newspaperwoman, who for the last three years has acted as Canadian Press correspondent in the French capital.)
LONDON, June 24 (CP Cable) — London looked like heaven, Sunday, as I arrived after spending ten days travelling from Paris with the human stream that flowed southward. I left Paris twenty-four hours before the Germans entered its northern gates.

And yesterday, looking upon this haven after ten days of agony, seeing buses circulating normally and people going about their Sunday occupations, I couldn't help thinking, Heaven, yes, but for how long? Paris

looked almost exactly like that two weeks ago.

I wanted to shout to everyone I saw here: "For God's sake, wake up, every man and woman, and turn England into a fortress, so that what I have seen in those two weeks may never happen here."

No trains, no cars, no taxis, no bicycles available, and the stream of human lava flowing out toward the south of France. Only luck and a seat in a friend's car saved me from leaving like hundreds of thousands of others — afoot.

Twelve Hours — Five Days
Even at that, the trip from Paris to Bordeaux, normally twelve hours, took five days. There was no food in the villages or towns, where soldiers gave their rations to hungry mobs. Women, babies strapped to handlebars on bicycles, rode by. Bordeaux was swollen from 300,000 to 2 million overnight. There was no news, only wild rumors and talk of capitulation. Britons began an exodus to Le Verdon, where boats awaited them. After hours on a tender, I was taken aboard the "Stad Haarlem", a Netherlands cargo boat with 300 other passengers.

Before we left, three German planes dropped mines into the mouth of the Gironde. Shore batteries and Royal Air Force fighters engaged them. After one mine was dropped 50 yards away and the German plane crashed in flames, the explosion rocking our 8,000-ton ship, the captain decided it was time to sail.

For three days we slept in the coal hold, the crew serving soup and tea once daily. The remnants of a British brigade rested below decks among sacks of linseed and corn.

Almost everyone aboard had lost everything they possessed beyond what they were wearing, except an actress from Cannes who in some way had managed to get aboard 11 trunks and suitcases and her pet pekingese.

Regina *Leader-Post*, 25 June 1940

STENOGRAPHERS FOR OVERSEAS

Miss N. M. Pullen, new recruiting officer in Canada of the British Women's Mechanized Transport Corps, said today the Corps is seeking stenographers who are willing to enrol for service in England. Miss Pullen said the applicants must be financially independent and will be accepted from any part of Canada. She asked stenographers who are interested to get in touch with her....

Canadian Press news item, November 1941

Canadian Violet Milstead, seen beside a "Mosquito", was an Air Transport Auxiliary pilot in Great Britain. WCAM

Helen Harrison was the first Canadian woman to fly with the British Air Transport Auxiliary, a civilian organization within the British Ministry of Aircraft Production whose function was "to keep a flow of new aircraft moving to the services".

Flyers from many different countries joined the A.T.A. The first women's section was formed in January 1940 under Commander Pauline Gower. By April 1943 ninety women had joined: three of them are known to have been Canadians — Helen Harrison, Marion Orr, and Violet Milstead. WCAM

CANADIAN GIRL LEADS WORLD AS FIRST MILITARY AVIATRIX

A winsome Canadian girl, born in Vancouver and least known in her own country, Helen Harrison is the first military aviatrix in the world and is licensed to fly in four countries. She has a record that would turn most male pilots green with envy.

With over half a million miles of flying to her credit on 49 different types of aircraft, many of them military, Miss Harrison is back in Canada after a tour of ferrying R.A.F. planes with the A.T.A. in England.

Although she was born in Vancouver, Miss Harrison's family moved to England when she was nine years of age. . . . Not until June 1939 did Helen Harrison return to her native land, and obtained a Canadian Limited Commercial license and instructor's ticket in July — the first woman instructor in Canada.

At the outbreak of war she transferred to the Kitchener Flying Club to train Air Force pilots, and turned out many provisional pilot officers for the R.C.A.F.

Then she came to Toronto and offered herself to

the Air Force for a more active part in the war effort. After months of interviews and letters to officials in Ottawa she arrived exactly nowhere. The Air Force refused to recognize her status, evidently because she wore skirts. What she wanted specifically was an instructor's job or ferrying duties in Canada or in England.

She taught at the Island airport, Toronto, for some time and attempted to form a Women's Auxiliary Airforce such as those operating in Australia, England and South Africa. Here again she met official deafness.

Finally, in October 1941, Miss Harrison, after instructing at the London Flying Club, joined Jacqueline Cochrane's group of American girl pilots and went overseas, joining the Air Transport Auxiliary in England in 1942.

She was the first Canadian girl to join the group.

From 1942 until April 1944, except for a short trip back on leave during 1943, incidentally returning to Scotland as a co-pilot on a Mitchell, she served in the A.T.A. on almost every type of aircraft.

Excerpts from an article by Keith Edgar in *Canadian Aviation*, October 1944

THE EVACUATION DEPARTMENT

Dr. [Clarence] Hincks and Dr. [William] Blatz gave us our orientation. We had our shots, and we were fitted for our uniforms. We had two skirts and a suit coat, a greatcoat, a felt hat, and a tie, all navy blue. There were twenty-eight of us, plus a chaperone. I was the only married woman, and I was aged twenty-seven. Most of us were in our twenties. Our salaries were to be paid by the British Ministry of Health, and they were considerably less than what I'd been earning in Canada.

The first few days I spent at the Ministry of Health, and then I was sent to Poole [Dorset] as an aide in the evacuation department. Then I went to High Wycombe, where I was in charge of the kids still remaining there in billets. They'd been evacuated from London after the first bomb scare, and their parents had never claimed them. They either didn't want them, or they had disappeared. Some children never did get back to their parents.

The evacuation office was in a Tudor building in the High Street, on the third floor, in the old servants' quarters. There was beautiful linenfold panelling on the stairs, and bottle glass in the doors, but it was so cold in that building that I wore overshoes and gloves and a scarf when I sat at my desk.

Manitoba social worker

Canadian Children's Service members in London, 1942, with the Parliamentary Secretary to the British Minister of Health. The C.C.S. established and ran a model day nursery in Birmingham, where British child-care workers were trained from 1942 to 1944. In charge was Dr. W. E. Blatz of the Institute of Child Studies, University of Toronto. Blatz had earlier devised a special nursery for the Dionne quintuplets and developed a daily program for them.
Courtesy Glen Sharpe

THE SLUMS OF BIRMINGHAM

We were given this gutted school, which we turned into a model day nursery. The day the school opened, on Dominion Day, 1942, forty children arrived from the slums of Birmingham. The moment we got them in, they scattered to the four corners of the playground. They found a hole in the fence, and immediately escaped.

Few of them had ever eaten at a table, or sat on a chair to eat, or had a plate to put food on. Some of them put their heads down into their plates, and all of them ate with their fingers.

Meat, potatoes, and vegetables were strange to them — they preferred a piece of bread. They'd put their hands in the air and call for "a piece, a piece, a piece". However, we used our good old nursery-school methods of minute servings and letting them go back for more.

These children hadn't learned to play games, or to use language other than for demand needs. We had to bath them, because they had bugs — and pretty soon the parents came too.

Child psychologist from Toronto

NO WAY WE COULD BE SAVED   There were nineteen of us women, from Toronto, Montreal, and Halifax, and we sailed from Montreal, but on two different ships. There were seven of us on my ship, a Manchester liner, and there were twelve passengers altogether, two to a cabin.

The Captain was very strict and wouldn't allow us to speak to any of the officers except the chief steward. We got reported to the Captain if we got caught fraternizing! We found out later that the group on the other ship had a whale of a time.

We stopped at Three Rivers and took on a load of TNT. We never had a boat drill on the voyage because the Captain said if we got hit, there was no way we could be saved. We sailed out of the St. Lawrence and down to New York to join a convoy. There were 165 ships and we were right in the middle. We flew a red flag to show we carried explosives. When the rest of the convoy took part in exercises, the Captain made us all go to our cabins and sit on the floor.

We were twenty-three days on that ship before we landed at Liverpool.

St. John Ambulance volunteer, Toronto

THE CREW LOOKED LIKE PIRATES   We had been told our ship was a good one and very fast —but we had not been told that it was very small, or that it was French. I have a liking for British ships and British sailors—and my heart sank when we went aboard and heard French spoken all round us. In peacetime she carried only twelve passengers, but extra bunks had been built in each cabin so she carried twenty-four on this trip.

Even the Captain doesn't know whether he is to take a northern route or a southern one until twenty-four hours out when he opens his sealed orders. We evidently went north, because it snowed and blew and it got very rough. We were told not to worry until the water went down the funnels. One night our ship rolled so far that as I lay in my bunk my feet went six feet higher than my head—my pillow flew out into the corridor and all the furniture made a rush for the door. I felt sure some water went down the funnel that night!

We were all seasick—some very badly, but in spite of that we managed to have some fun. We got to know all the officers and had plenty of chance to brush up on our French. They were all very happy-go-lucky. We were going to have no boat drill—but I protested. I thought we should at least know which boat to go to in case of need. So we had one boat drill

View of a convoy in mid-Atlantic, seen from H.M.C.S. *Skeena*. In 1942 both the Canadian Red Cross Corps and the St. John Ambulance Brigade were authorized to do voluntary work in Canadian military hospitals abroad. About 900 members of the two organizations paid their own way to Britain and guaranteed to cover their own basic expenses while serving abroad. PAC PA 128200

and when I saw the crew I was horrified. They were Negroes and Chinamen and French who looked like pirates. They all carried knives in their belts and we were told the officers carried guns because the crew would rush the lifeboats if anything happened!

Our first sight of land was a big thrill and as we drew close to shore the sea became calmer and everyone revived rapidly. The morning we came into harbour I was up on the bridge. The pilot was there —he spoke no French, the Captain spoke a little English, and the wheelman spoke only French. I went below to get packed and a few minutes later there was a tremendous bump and our ship lurched heavily. I rushed up on deck to find we had collided with another ship which was towering over us. A great piece was taken off our bow and the cabins were stove in all along the side of the other ship. I suspect the Captain had not understood the pilot's English.

From a talk given by Mrs. Barnston Tudball, National Commandant, Canadian Red Cross Corps, Toronto, May 1944

INSIDE THE FORTRESS   I was a V.A.D. —
Virgins Almost Desperate, we used to say — a nurse's
aide in a hospital twenty miles out of London. I was
twenty in 1944, but I was a child, very young and
impressionable. I felt I had to get over to England, to
be part of the war, like the people who went to fight
in Spain. It was a compulsion. It wasn't patriotism for
Canada. I had an English father; he'd been in the
British Navy in the First World War, and he'd been
decorated. And we were steeped in English history
at school.

It was indescribably exciting, arriving in London in
the winter, in a pea-soup fog, in the blackout. I was
inside the fortress, I was part of it. London was black
with soot, dirty, smelly — but I thought it was heaven. I
was cold most of the time, sometimes you had to go
to bed with all your clothes on, you had to manage
with one inch of water in the bathtub — but none of it
mattered.

Red Cross volunteer, Montreal

I SAW CHILDREN KILLED   It was during the
time of the buzz bombs and rockets in London. I was
attached to Civil Defence, and I drove a Light Mobile
Surgical Unit, a Hillman sedan. We carried a doctor, a
nurse, and a V.A.D. We covered Westminster, Buckingham Palace, Park Lane, all the area round Victoria
Station, from Victoria to the river. We were on duty
twenty-four hours on, twenty-four hours off, from 10
a.m. to 10 a.m.

When a bomb dropped, we'd go out. One headlight
was covered and the other had slits, so you couldn't
see very well. It was quite scary. We were equipped
so that the doctor could amputate right away if the
only way to get somebody out of the rubble was to
take off a mangled leg. I went along with the nurse
and helped out wherever I could. What bothered me
most was when I saw children killed. One night it was
two children who'd just been brought back from
Scotland. They'd been evacuated, but their parents
missed them so much, they'd brought them home
again. There was a broken teddy bear beside them. I
was all right at the time, but afterwards the nerves
would be bad.

On my day off duty, I'd go to Leicester Square tube
station at eight o'clock, to man our first-aid post
there. Twenty-five hundred people slept on the station platforms every night during the bombing, and
by a sort of gentlemen's agreement they came back
to the very same place every time. There was a place
where they could store mattresses.

People came to the tube station after work if they
had no place to go, and there was quite an air of
neighbourliness down there. Whole families would be
there together, and often mothers would ask you to
heat up a bottle for their babies. Older people liked to
go down there and talk — they made so many friends.
They'd take flasks of tea and food with them. But it
was a terribly dirty place. There was nowhere to
wash, and people just took turns at the toilets.

The trains ran until 10 p.m., and people getting off
would step over all these bodies.

St. John Ambulance driver, Toronto

WINDOWS AND FLYING GLASS   When the
siren goes, say at two in the morning, you tumble out
of your warm bed and put on slacks, sweaters, tin
hat, and greatcoat, sling your haversack over your
shoulder containing your papers and valuables, and
with your flashlight take yourself down to the cellar.

The cellar is the safest spot if the house gets a
direct hit, as you are away from windows and flying
glass down there. About ten minutes after the siren,
the gunfire starts. If many planes get through to
London, the barrage is tremendous and the noise
simply deafening. The girls sing to drown out the din.
It's cold and drafty in the cellar, as the doors to the
street have to be kept open. It's tiring, too, standing
down there leaning against the wall, especially if the
raid goes on for an hour or so. One's tin hat gets
awfully heavy. When the gunfire dies down, the girls
are allowed to go up and sit in the lounge and wait for
the all-clear.

Eggs are very scarce. It's a great treat to get
one for breakfast every two weeks. Once in a while
oranges appear on the table. Margarine is used instead
of butter. It's really quite good and looks just like
butter. There is no cream in England and only two
and a half pints of milk a week. Bread is a wartime
bread and always brown. The sugar doesn't seem to
sweeten, and salt and pepper make little difference.
The meat ration works out to about a quarter of a
pound a week per person. You find that you eat a lot
in England but don't feel satisfied. Everybody craves
sweet things, and candies from home are most welcome. The candy ration is a quarter of a pound per
month. Some of the girls put on a lot of weight the
first month or so. . . .

From a talk given by Mrs. Barnston Tudball,
Canadian Red Cross Corps, Toronto, May 1944

By the end of the war, there were 641 Canadian Red Cross Corps volunteers overseas. Besides driving ambulances and other vehicles, they worked as dietitians and cooks, recreation aides, and office workers and administrators. The majority, however, worked as nursing auxiliaries or as welfare officers in hospitals. The first senior officer in London was Mrs. Margaret Lee of Toronto.
TT 100-677

BURNS TO BASINGSTOKE   I was assigned to AVAC as it was called, air evacuation of wounded. It was a joint project of the British Red Cross and St. John. You went to the airfields to pick up "bods" flown from the Continent in DC3's or Dakotas — I think they got eight stretchers into a DC3, but maybe it was a dozen.

We'd had a few weeks' training in such things as maintenance of our vehicles, trouble-shooting, and taking apart fuel pumps, things like that. Then we were assigned to a camp at Liddiard Millicent near Swindon and we had a railhead which we serviced. I believe a lot of the men we picked up at this time were casualties from Arnhem. We'd go in a convoy of

ambulances, anything from a dozen to maybe thirty or more. The airfield would signal how many they needed.

We drove two-ton Austin ambulances, which were terrific. You loaded the first two stretchers, then they were cranked up by a wonderful elevator arrangement to make room for two more.

Certain ambulances were assigned to ferry patients from the tarmac to the casualty clearing centre, and the rest of us were assigned to transport men to the appropriate place. It was burns to Basingstoke, heads to Oxford, eyes to Stratton St. Margaret, lungs to Shaftesbury, and the rest to the railhead. They were shipped to some other centre from there.

Nearly always we were called out at night, and we had just a little slit in a painted-out headlight to see by. But I remember very clearly that the British Red Cross woman who took us round told us, "You'll know you're approaching the railhead when you smell rotting cabbages."

I was very lucky, I never had anyone die in the back of my ambulance, but some of the women drivers did have very unhappy experiences. You didn't have anyone with you, that was the real problem — you didn't have a co-driver or an orderly. But the worst part was that you couldn't do anything for the injured men, except give them an Aspirin; and they often made the assumption, because of the insignia, that we were nurses, which we certainly were not. A man would cry out in pain, saying, "Please, Sister, please, Sister, give me something," and you just felt miserable when you had to say, "You'll be all right. Now, just take an Aspirin."

Our camp was made up of Nissen huts. The Americans called them Quonset huts. They were made of corrugated iron, no insulation, and there was a stove in the middle of the hut which radiated heat for a distance of four inches.

You'd come in from raw weather, all wet, and people's socks would be festooned around this nasty little stove. You'd huddle round it, eating your supper and trying to get yourself warm enough to go to bed.

Red Cross ambulance driver, Victoria

BATTLEDRESS LIKE THE MEN   We loaded hospital ships at Liverpool. It was a dismal city, very badly bombed. We were based at Chester.

On long trips you had a co-driver. It was cold driving in the winter, because the front of an Austin ambulance was not closed in. There was just a canvas flap, which you hooked up. I wore a long sleeveless leather jacket with sheepskin lining over my uniform, and boots with a fleece lining. St. John Ambulance drivers wore brown battledress, like the men, although we had started out in dark blue.

We had to do all our own maintenance, and that meant getting underneath and doing a proper grease job, for inspection. We couldn't change the tires, because they were too big for us to handle.

Later on I was based at Knutsford [Lancashire], where there was a German prisoner-of-war camp. We'd go in every day to drive a group to a hospital in Preston. We had a British guard with a gun sitting with us, but there was never any trouble. They seemed quite happy to be prisoners, to be out of the fighting, but they missed their families. They'd show us pictures of their wives and children in the ambulance. But we never talked about the war, what the fighting was all about.

There didn't seem to be much wrong with those prisoners, and eventually I found out they all had V.D., and that's why they had to go to the hospital, for treatment. We scrubbed out our ambulances very thoroughly, I can tell you, after each trip. The prisoners did all their own cooking, and they used to sing in the kitchen. That's where I first heard the song "Lili Marlene".

I drove some German prisoners to a camp near Crewe, a huge place on an English lord's estate. High-ranking German officers were billeted there, and they looked like they'd come out of the movies, with their smart uniforms, their high boots, and their coats slung over their shoulders.

St. John Ambulance driver, Toronto

"HURRAH! WE'RE WINNING!" Dressed in a blue smock, I sailed down the corridor, carrying a tray full of books, toilet articles, Red Cross comforts, and handicraft materials. It wasn't exactly Florence Nightingale stuff, but I knew, in her own way, the Lady with the Tray could mean a lot to men who were lonely and sick. . . . in a few minutes I would be seeing pale faces light up as I paused to chat . . . hearing broken words of thanks for Red Cross gifts. . . .

It wasn't like that at all.

Pushing open the door, I saw a sea of faces, all turned for a good look at the something new which had been added to their lives. At once there was a deafening outburst of those AWFUL whistles and wolf-calls! I had never been whistled at in mass formation and I felt absolutely frozen to the floor. How

that first hour passed I really can't remember, but I vaguely recall going to one bed and saying timidly, "How would you like to embroider a cushion cover?" More hoots and yells burst out all over the place. The first covers we received were ghastly things, having the face of a bulldog resembling Churchill with a cigar in his mouth painted on one side. The patient was to outline the face with black embroidery cotton. Other cushions had a pair of flags painted on them, with "There'll Always Be an England" written across the bottom, while still others had some warlike scene, with "Hurrah! We're Winning!" flaunted in large letters.

I blushed the first time I faced one of those grown-up men and suggested that he embroider anything, least of all those horrors. Yet in the end they proved extremely popular. Once one of the lads started something, the rest were distributed like wildfire. . . .

Jean M. Ellis, Red Cross welfare officer, *Facepowder and Gunpowder*, Toronto, 1947

Canadian Red Cross Corps welfare officers give cigarettes and reading material to convalescing soldiers at No. 8 Canadian General Hospital, Normandy. PAC PA 141885

SCHOOL FOR THE BLIND

St. Dunstan's ran a training school for the blind in Church Stretton in Shropshire, high up in the hills. There were servicemen from all the Commonwealth countries there. Many of them came straight from hospital, but they were trained from the very beginning to be independent.

The men lived in various houses, and they got around by putting a hand on the wall and following it to a doorway. They found their places in the dining-room by counting the tables and the backs of the chairs. Later, when they went outdoors, they used wires which ran from the back of each house down the hill to the training centre. They learned to put their canes on the wires and to follow them downhill.

It was a wonderful place to work. You could tell that you were helping. We read their letters to them, and we listened when they needed somebody to talk to. We were on duty all day, and in the evening we'd bring them down to some entertainment, in the valley. Sometimes we'd have four men on each arm, and we'd sing all the way down. It was a very cheerful place.

We went to dances with them, and we took them to concerts. Famous singers and bands used to come, from London. I remember the night Max Miller came. He was a comedian who told off-colour jokes. Matron wouldn't let us go inside to listen. We took the boys to the door and we had to leave them there!

St. John Ambulance volunteer, Toronto

St. John Ambulance volunteer at St. Dunstan's rehabilitation centre in Shropshire with two blind servicemen. Courtesy Constance L. Hutcheon

The four Maple Leaf Clubs in London, operated by Canadian Red Cross Corps volunteers, were open to men and women in the Canadian services. CRCS

Arromanches, Normandy, shortly after D-Day, 1944. Following the Allied advance through France, Belgium, and Holland, Canadian Red Cross and St. John Ambulance drivers drove wounded troops to casualty evacuation aircraft. The loading and unloading of planes was done almost entirely under cover of night; enemy attack from the air was frequent. Courtesy Claire Watson Fisher

"THAT'S A PROSTITUTE!"　　I joined the Y.M.C.A. War Services in the spring of 1944, when they were getting short of men. The Y sent me to Greenock, a naval station near Glasgow, and they made me Assistant Supervisor of the leave centre. I took over a little biscuit factory, and it became the Y clubhouse. I wore a civilian uniform, a grey suit with a blue shirtwaist, and a little peaked cap.

We put on dances, and one of my jobs was to bounce out any camp-followers. The boys would bring girls in to these dances, and then leave them to their own devices. Sometimes, somebody would come up and say, "Miss F——, that's a prostitute over there!"

Another thing I did was to send telegrams home for the boys. It was done by code, and each number I phoned in to the operator would mean a certain message. One number meant "I'm fine", and another meant "Happy Birthday". One fellow sent two exactly the same—one to his wife in Canada, and another to a girl in Ireland, saying "Missing you terribly, all my love till we meet again"!

Y.M.C.A. volunteer worker, Toronto

"MAPLE LEAF UP"　　The afternoon of July 13, we anchored a few hundred yards off Courseulles-sur-Mer in Normandy. My heart was very full as I waited. Just a few weeks before on June 6 the Third Canadian Division had landed on this very shore and established its beachhead at frightful cost.

Approaching shore, we could see a surging mass of people on the beach, who waved and shouted and surrounded us the minute we landed. There were uniforms from all branches of the Canadian army; French boys in berets gaped at us open-mouthed, touched our Red Crosses and said "Qu'est-ce que c'est?"; gendarmes beamed; abbés in long robes smiled at us. Everyone cheered, everyone tried to shake our hands.

Soon all of us were loaded into several open lorries, sitting where we could on top of bedrolls and packs, clutching our bags and steel helmets. We drove through town after town amid lines of cheering lads, while French people leaned from upper-storey windows to throw flowers and kisses, calling out "Vivent les Canadiennes!" At last we were on the famous road "Maple Leaf Up", main highway from Normandy to final victory in Germany. Orchards and fields all along the way were occupied by some Army or Air Force unit. Nearly every kilometre we sang "The Maple Leaf Forever" and "O Canada", to let any lads still unaware of it know that sixty Canadian girls had come to share their job.

We were completely overwhelmed by the reception we got. In the midst of it, we suddenly noticed two airplanes circling just overhead, then gunfire burst from one of them.

"A dog-fight, girls! On with your tin helmets!" somebody shouted.

This was a new experience for us—enemy aircraft without a warning siren! We felt we really *were* in it now, and we watched the fight with bated breath until the planes disappeared from view. Further evidence of our closeness to grim realities were the overturned or badly burned vehicles we saw, still flaunting weird camouflage paint; pieces of aircraft scattered on the ground; dozens of dead cows and horses along the road, horribly bloated, lying on their backs with their four legs in the air and giving off the most ghastly smell. . . .

Jean Ellis, Facepowder and Gunpowder, 1947

AN AWFUL AMOUNT OF BLOOD　　The stretcher-bearers would bring the men in. They were not a pretty sight. There was an awful amount of blood, clothes were stuck to wounds, and some men's boots hadn't come off in a week. Some men would be gasping for breath. Everything known about a man's condition was on his tag, so if it said you could give him something to drink, you did.

But often you couldn't do anything except hold his hand and say, "You've been admitted to a Canadian hospital. My name is ——''. The Padre would be there, and he was a lot of help. As soon as you could, you got them admitted to a ward. What they wanted most, once they'd been attended to, was for you to write a letter home for them. Often it would be to someone's mother: "Just tell her I've been wounded, and I'm in a Canadian hospital, and I'm okay now."

In three or four days the serious cases would be shipped back to England.

As the hospital area was plainly marked, it was supposed to be safe from attack. But when enemy planes passed over at night there was a terrific barrage of anti-aircraft fire, and our own shrapnel flew around us. Since there was a large hole in our tent torn by shrapnel, I never went to bed without pulling my sleeping bag around my head. Sometimes I put a steel helmet on too, and slept with an extra pillow over my stomach for protection. It didn't seem crazy in the morning when you got up and found new pieces of shrapnel all over the place.

Jean Ellis, *Facepowder and Gunpowder*, 1947

FLYING GLASS November 26 [1944, Antwerp] was a day I shall never forget.

Just one V-2 bomb had caused a tremendous number of casualties when it fell at an intersection in the heart of Antwerp. A streetcar full of people was demolished. The N.A.A.F.I. [Navy, Army, Air Forces Institutes] canteen, operated by the British, collapsed while full of men on leave. Buildings for hundreds of yards around were shattered or had all their windows blown out. Many people would not have been casualties except for the flying glass, but even one small piece hurtling at great speed after such a tremendous explosion could do severe damage, especially to the face.

Rushing past the wounded into our Admitting Room, I threw coat and beret on a table, and went to one of the M.O.s for orders. "Do anything you can to get patients ready for examination, and serve hot tea whenever they can drink it," he advised.

There were nearly a hundred beds in that long, narrow room, all of them full, and many stretchers besides. Moans and cries formed a horrible symphony; faces were distorted with pain. Orderlies hurried from one bed to another, bathing the eyes of the appalling number who had face wounds. Nursing sisters and medical officers worked at fever pitch to relieve agony, and gradually the groans subsided a little. Every Army nurse and doctor in Antwerp was there, whether on leave or not, as a general call had

been sent out for all of them to return to duty. The hospital was crowded beyond capacity, surgeons working night and day without stopping for food. Nursing sisters carried on beyond the breaking point.

New arrivals reported that blood was running in streams down the gutters, while headless bodies and pieces of arms or legs were lying about the streets. Undoubtedly it was no exaggeration; when I visited the intersection next day, blood could still be seen all over the pavement.

Just a few days later another direct hit was scored on the Rex Theatre, open only to the services. Again the hospital was full to overflowing and beyond. It was a sad week, and I scribbled many a message to the next of kin of dying men. They didn't want to die that way, so far from the firing-line, and on a leave! If they had to go, they wanted it to be on a battlefield. We who were left felt our hearts torn and bleeding, and raged against the stupidity of Authority, which made such a vulnerable town a leave centre. Very soon afterwards the military hospital there was moved and Antwerp was closed as a leave centre, but it was too late to save many precious lives.

Jean Ellis, *Facepowder and Gunpowder*, 1947

SO CLOSE TO STARVATION People from the forced-labour camps were streaming into Belgium and Holland — there were swarms of people everywhere. It was a terrible winter, 1944-45, and the food situation was terribly bad, particularly in Holland. Even so, the Dutch were mad for cigarettes, the wartime medium of exchange, and we'd be offered an egg for two cigarettes.

We were told never to exchange cigarettes for food because the people were so close to starvation. We could exchange food for food, though, and we had our food parcels. Nearly all of us got them from Canada, from our families, and we were happy to swap cocoa and sardines. You'd far rather have a fresh egg than a tin of sardines. Sometimes we got asked for other things. The Dutch women craved our shoe polish, not for shoes but for their furniture!

We were in Holland, then Belgium, and then our hospital went to Germany. We went to Oldenburg, and set up a tent hospital in the grounds of an old hunting lodge. Our hospital had taken over a camp for Russian prisoners, and many of them were suffering from malnutrition and T.B. They were moved into our tent hospital, but they'd go out into the fields at night and make home brew with potatoes they dug.

A three-woman team from the Canadian Red Cross Corps distributed relief supplies in Villers Bocage, Normandy, in 1946. The project was organized by Mme Pauline Vanier, wife of General Georges Vanier, Canadian Ambassador to France. Courtesy Claire Watson Fisher

Then they came back half-drunk. The nurses were horrified.

The Russians wouldn't accept that their men could be taken prisoner. Our Colonel got in touch with the Russian officials and asked them to bring a hospital train onto the siding at Oldenburg. But the Russians sent no train, and the Colonel took the men back to the hospital. Eventually, when we packed up to go, we had to leave them behind. They were all killed, because the Russians didn't want them back.

Red Cross welfare officer, Ottawa

PRISONERS OF WAR   We were the only female personnel at No.1 convalescent depot at Salerno [Italy]. Officers had to salute us, though we had no real rank — it was a disciplinary measure.

When the Canadian Army pulled out of Italy, two of us were left behind to help round up stray Canadian servicemen in British or American hospitals, who were too sick to be moved right away. We were also sent to meet prisoners of war, Canadians who'd been taken in Crete. And I remember meeting a ship from Odessa, and one particular soldier who was very agitated. He had a kitbag over his shoulder and he asked me to take charge of it. Inside there was a girl! He wanted to take her to England with him. Well, first I had to get her deloused, but in the end we did manage to send her off. She didn't speak any English, and I never knew where she came from — Yugoslavia? Russia?

Red Cross welfare officer, Toronto

NAZI THUNDER CUT TO WHIMPERS AS JODL SIGNS SURRENDER TERMS

REIMS, FRANCE, May 7 (delayed), CP — Without ceremony, without drama in today's predawn hours, Colonel General [Alfred] Jodl, newly created Chief of Staff of the German Army, and General Admiral Hans George von Friedeburg, Commander-in-Chief of the German Navy, grimly scrawled their signatures to documents of unconditional surrender.

I watched the Germans sign the death warrant of the Third Reich in the oppressively hot room of Allied Supreme Headquarters as they sat on cheap deal chairs at a black-topped ordinary table.

The Germans tersely fulfilled their part of the signing ceremony and departed with bows and clickings of heels. When they had left the room, General Eisenhower broke into his famous grin and exchanged a joke through an interpreter with the Russian commander. Then he turned to the other officers, correspondents and photographers pushing into the tiny room and said:

"I'm glad to get rid of those damned Germans!"

From Thunder to Whimper
The world conflict which Hitler had launched with such thunder ended with a whimper in the small stuffy room crammed with about 60 persons dripping with perspiration.

The whole scene in itself was unbelievably mundane after years of war and the tenseness of the last

Canadian Press Overseas correspondent Margaret Ecker Francis receives a gold medal in 1944 from the Hon. Vincent Massey, Canadian High Commissioner to Great Britain. In May 1945 Francis covered the German military surrender to General Dwight Eisenhower for CP. PAC PA 128185

24 hours. I, like the other 15 correspondents, was allowed to witness the ceremony and we crowded together, peering over one another's shoulders under the glare of photographers' lights. We could not believe the sheets of common paper passing from hand to hand were really the documents of surrender and meant an end to the war which had devastated millions of lives.

There was no dramatic hush when Jodl took the khaki-colored pen in soft pink hands that shook to sign his name.

Flight at Sunrise

It was sunrise when it finally was over and when we had experienced probably the most historic moment in our lives.

In the chill morning, the first day of peace, our transport plane lifted us off Reims airfield, bound for Paris, where we would try to write a story for which no words seemed appropriate. . . .

Margaret Ecker Francis,
Canadian Press correspondent

WE SCROUNGE CARDBOARD

September [?]. Nijmegen — We are now stationed in the C.W.A.C. Barracks at 1st Canadian Leave Camp in Nijmegen, at the end of a long line of barrack buildings for men. When we walk the approximate mile to get to the Mess Hall, the hoots and hollers, the comments, etc., are all rather nerve-wracking. You would think we would be used to it now.

September 17. Nijmegen — Wednesday and Thursday we were out at 13th Btn., a Repat. [Repatriation] Depot, and the camp is completely under canvas. So were we. We put on our show in a tent and it was an immense thing. The audience was 600 or 700 fellows and they were packed in like sardines. It was really alright except that it rained. Thru' the spotlight we could see the water dripping through on to the audience. We didn't see anyone leaving. We kept stepping in the mud puddles. It isn't very good for dance shoes.

Shoes! I've worn through the soles on both pairs of tap shoes. We scrounge cardboard or even the envelopes from our mail and put it in the soles.

September 27. Wilhelmshaven — When we visit with any of the fellows we can tell they are all very anxious about what they will do when they get home. What will it be like? Where will they get jobs? Some have

been over here so long they really feel out of touch with civvie life completely. At first, they just wanted to hear us talk. They wanted to hear about frivolous things — the movies, the latest music, what people are dancing to, what they are wearing. Now they are asking us definite questions.

October 2. Dene Lodge, Ashgreen, Hants, England — Here I am back in the land of hedges, pubs, double-decker buses driving on the wrong side of the road, tea, and broad accents.

Cathy and I shone our buttons, polished our shoes, and were all set to venture forth this afternoon. At Brookwood there is a huge military cemetery. We went to visit the grave of two fellows Cathy used to know. One was her best girlfriend's fiancé and the other was a boy who lived down the street from Cathy's home. Both were killed returning from operational flights. I've never had such a feeling in all my life as I did this afternoon. There were just row on row of white crosses. The place just seemed a white blur, there were so many.

Excerpts from the letters and diaries of a
member of the Sun Life "Eager Beavers"
Concert Party, 1945

A GRIM MEMORIAL   We left Paris at noon on the 5th, travelling through the "Falaise Gap" battle-ground, and in spite of the lush green grass and the apple trees bursting into bloom, one's heart ached to see the desolate, stark ruins of what once were peaceful Norman towns. From Argentan on, not one village was untouched by the hand of war. Many were completely flattened fields of rubble with only a church spire or a grey stone wall standing as a grim memorial to the life that had formerly surged around it. The majority of these villages now have flimsy prefabricated huts to house the people. These have been sent from at least four or five countries, so vary in size and shape. Some with flat roofs and composition walls have wilted a bit under the rainy Normandy climate. In these, as many families as possible have crowded. Household utensils are in very short supply, so a family of nine or ten may have only three plates, four glasses and one cooking pot to its name. Frequently, gorse or boughs are pressed into service as mattresses, sheets are rare and luxurious and there are never enough blankets. . . .

Excerpt from a Report on the Civilian
Relief Project, Normandy, May 1946, by
Marion K. Bigelow and Claire Watson,
Canadian Red Cross Corps

WHO DID THIS?   Local people would ask us to make speeches, sometimes, at places where the [Allied] invaders had lost their lives. I would look at the utter devastation, and I'd ask myself, "Who did this?" People wouldn't say it to us, but we knew it was us, the Canadians, the British, who'd done this.

Red Cross volunteer, Montreal

BELSEN   You could smell Belsen seventeen miles away. It was a peculiar odour, on the wind. The Germans had been burning bodies, but there were thousands and thousands of bodies decomposing, and they hadn't had time to cremate them.

I went into Germany from Belgium, as a welfare officer with the 29th British General Hospital, a 1,200-bed hospital. We were sent to Belsen in May 1945, just as the war ended. I was the only Canadian V.A.D.

When we got to Belsen, we were not allowed in for a week, until the British Army had removed all the bodies and burned the camp. Sometimes they said they couldn't tell the dead from the living.

When we were allowed in, there were still sixty thousand unburied bodies, and I witnessed the burial. The bodies were put into pits dug by German prisoners of war, they were laid out, and lime was put on top of them. When we went in to the camp the Army made us wear hip waders, because of the ash—there was so much of it—and because of the vermin. We had to be hosed off whenever we left the camp.

The prisoners all wore pyjamas. It was a long, long time before I could look at a pair of blue-and-white-striped pyjamas again. One of our jobs was to collect clothing for the prisoners. Harrods of London was what we called the clothing depot.

We lived outside the camp, under canvas, and to begin with there were two hundred of us, nurses and physiotherapists and V.A.D.s in one huge marquee. There was no room for our cots. We put our mattresses down on the canvas floor, and our sleeping bags on top. But the wet came through the canvas floor. It rained for four days after we arrived, poured down as if it would never stop. When the sun did come out, you could see the steam rising from this huge marquee. Later, though, we moved into tents, four girls to a tent.

We were at Belsen for seven weeks. First we had to segregate the prisoners, the dying, the T.B. cases, and those who were still healthy because they hadn't been there for very long. We put them into barracks which had been occupied by the Germans.

Quite a lot of the children had T.B. and a number were bordering on mental cases. I still worry about the children — a child always remembers.

Elsie Deeks, St. John Ambulance
volunteer, Winnipeg

A war artist's view of Belsen concentration camp shortly after it was liberated. A St. John Ambulance V.A.D. was one of the first civilians to work with the survivors. Painting by Donald Kenneth Anderson. CWM 10759 PL 47004

BEGGING FOR FOOD

We went by sea to Calais and then by train to Hanover. We wore British Army khaki uniform, with UNRRA [United Nations Relief and Rehabilitation Administration] patches on the shoulders, and a little beret.

We were given K rations to eat on the journey— sandwiches and the hardest chocolate that I ever tried to eat: you could only lick it! We sat up all night on the train; it was very uncomfortable. But it was nothing compared to other trains we saw in Germany, jammed with people. People who couldn't get inside were riding on the top, or on the couplings— anywhere they could hang on. When our train stopped, children swarmed around with baskets, begging for food, anything they could get. We threw our sandwiches into their baskets, and the chocolate too.

Conditions were distressing, but the worst was over by the time we got there. The Germans we met were stunned, numbed, they'd been through so much bombing. We weren't allowed to fraternize with them, but you felt an acceptance of what had happened to them.

A lot of the people we came to help were living in quarters the Nazis had built for the slave labour they brought into Germany. They were badly constructed buildings, with roofs that leaked. Water dripped onto the beds through the ceilings. There was lots of T.B. We rehoused these people anywhere we could find room, including a former dynamite factory, and a former cavalry barracks. Everywhere was overcrowded. Families were separated from one another in these buildings by blankets hung between them.

UNRRA was very disorganized. We'd get Red Cross supplies in the refugee camps, and there'd be thirty toothbrushes and so many pairs of children's boots—and we had to decide which of several thousand people should get them. We got six sewing machines, but no needles, and large sheets of leather for making shoes, but no nails. We had to buy these things on the black market with cigarettes—we were each issued a ration of 150 cigarettes a week, and I didn't smoke.

There were Polish, Baltic, and Ukrainian camps arranged by nationality. I remember one camp with Poles and Jews in two separate barracks, and they fought constantly, with water hoses. These people had been through such traumatic experiences, life was very difficult for them, and there was not a psychiatrist in sight.

Welfare officer, Toronto

Five Canadian St. John Ambulance volunteers outside their London headquarters before leaving for the Far East in May 1945. St. John nursing auxiliaries and welfare officers served in India, Burma, Malaysia, Hong Kong, and Singapore. Courtesy Constance L. Hutcheon

UNDER COVER OF DARKNESS

Before the war with Japan ended, British and American prisoners of war were being liberated from camps in Burma. There were special trains to bring the men out, but serious injuries were flown back to Calcutta, and I made four plane trips to the Burmese border to pick up sick patients. It was a very well-organized operation, and a lot of the work was done under cover of darkness. We took twenty or twenty-five patients on each plane, some sitting up, some in cots. These men had been under great strain, and they could have gone berserk on the plane, putting everybody in great danger, so they were heavily sedated.

Immediately after the war ended, I went to a leave centre in Darjeeling on sick leave. I was on a train on my way back to Calcutta with some English nurses when the Military Police came to tell us that rioting had broken out between the Hindus and the Moslems. The doors of our compartment were locked from the outside, and the Police told us to stay away from the windows, which were all barred.

When we reached Calcutta, the train was surrounded by masses of angry people, swarming around like ants do when you spill honey on the ground and suddenly there's a seething mass of them. Fortunately, I had arranged with my American boyfriend to come and get us at the station. The rioters were mad at the British, rather than the Americans, and Joe told us to take off our nurses' tunics immediately, so that the rioters couldn't tell what we were. He got the six of us into his small station wagon, and he drove through the mob, with his hand on the horn. It was a very frightening experience, with the people spitting at us as we went. But we got out of the city and back to the hospital.

We left India soon after. I hated to leave at that time. There was still a lot of work to do. But India was in turmoil, and for safety's sake they wanted us out.

St. John Ambulance V.A.D., Saint John, N.B.

REGINA GIRL COMMANDED JAP SOLDIERS

V-J Day meant little to 1,700 white prisoners of the Japanese at jungle-hidden Bangkinang internment camp in interior Sumatra. Their prison was not listed in Allied records and their chances of immediate liberation looked far from good.

When a husky, dark-haired, medium-height Canadian woman arrived on the scene and, practically single-handed, transported the 1,700 prisoners 280 miles through hostile Indonesian territory to safety on the coast, the liberated POWs were, to say the least, incredulous.

The woman is Miss Joan Bamford Fletcher, 30, formerly of Regina and now of Vancouver. For her Sumatra exploits she has been made a member of the Order of the British Empire (MBE).

Miss Fletcher's story is one of the most unusual and heroic to come out of World War Two. During her Sumatra exploits she was nearly killed by a big army truck. Later she developed swamp fever which settled in her jaw, necessitating removal of part of the bone.

In evacuating the prisoners she used 70 Japanese soldiers as truck drivers and guard. She is believed to be the only white woman ever to command a party of Japanese army men. She won the respect of the Japanese and one of their officers paid her a tribute by presenting her with his 300-year-old sword.

Miss Fletcher earlier had been sent into the Southeast Asia area with a detachment of FANYs (Britain's First Aid Nursing Yeomanry). Daughter of a Regina dairyman, Miss Fletcher trained as a transport driver with the Canadian Red Cross. Paying her own way to Britain, she joined the FANYs and was posted as an ambulance driver and general worker in a unit operating with the Polish Army in Scotland.

In the spring of 1945 she was posted to Southeast Asia, as a lieutenant. In October of last year she landed on Sumatra to evacuate the Bangkinang prisoners.

Arriving at the POW camp in a jeep, she conferred with the Japanese officials, secured 15 trucks with Nipponese drivers for them, and made arrangements to take the first convoy of prisoners to Padang. Later, Miss Fletcher increased her convoy capacity to 25 Japanese vehicles, manned by 70 drivers and guards.

At the beginning, the convoy went fairly smoothly, but [soon] the Indonesians grew steadily more hostile. By the time the last convoy rumbled down to Padang, Japanese with mounted machine-guns on the

Joan Bamford Fletcher of Regina was a member of the British Women's Transport Service. In 1946 she was awarded the M.B.E. for services rendered in Sumatra shortly after the war with Japan ended. CWM

trucks were guarding the liberated prisoners.

Miss Fletcher had been evacuating POWs for three weeks before British troops reached the Bangkinang area. Then, according to regulations, she should have turned the job over to the troops. "I should never have been allowed to continue if it hadn't been for Brig. Peter Hutchison, who was in charge of the troops," she recalled. General Hutchison offered her some British soldiers for assistance, but she was getting on so well with the Japanese that she retained them for guard duties.

Later, in an effort to stop her evacuation, the Indonesians began piling road blocks across the highway to Padang. The roads in the area, built originally by the Dutch, had been kept in good order by the Japanese.

To counteract this, Miss Fletcher had a heavy vehicle rigged out with bumpers that would lead the convoy and smash through these obstructions. The Indonesians made no actual attacks on Miss Fletcher's convoy, but at times it was nip-and-tuck. "It was fatal to stop on the road," she recalled. "Those boys didn't waste much time if they got you."

Montreal *Standard*, 16 November 1946

10
When the War Was Over

DND PL 37168

When the war was over, "everybody was in the same boat, picking up the pieces," as one woman put it. "Picking up the pieces" had another dimension for the wife of a returning serviceman. Sometimes the reunion was joyous; sometimes it meant starting all over again. The "boy" who had gone away to war five or six years before returned a man who was in some ways a stranger to her, and to their children. And after five or six years running a household single-handed, and working as a volunteer in the community war effort, she was not the same "girl" he had left behind. There was even more adjusting to do for women whose husbands or sweethearts returned badly maimed or emotionally scarred, or did not return at all.

Servicewomen, like servicemen, found it difficult at first to settle down in peacetime Canada. All three women's services were disbanded in 1946, although many women indicated their interest in staying on. Only a small nucleus of nursing sisters was retained in the permanent force. Upon their discharge, servicewomen were entitled to certain immediate benefits, just as their male counterparts were.

There were under fifty thousand servicewomen at the end of the war, but there were over one million working women in Canada. All of them found that women's employment prospects changed profoundly with the end of the war and the return of three-

quarters of a million former servicemen to the labour market. The fear of many people that the war would be followed by an economic recession was expressed by one delegate to the Trades and Labor Congress convention in 1943: "Women have no business in industry, except in wartime. After the war women are going to be in competition with their fathers, sons, and future husbands."

Peacetime was clearly going to be a different era.

WELCOME-HOME SERVICES   Whoever has seen a railway station in Winnipeg just before the arrival of a troop train is not likely to forget the picture. Flags and "Welcome Home" banners give an aura of gaiety and expectancy to the great rotunda; the Band is ready to strike up the music at a signal from the Master of Ceremonies; long, white-covered tables are laden with plates of doughnuts and cups are set out to receive the steaming coffee; young hostesses, their faces bright with excitement, are waiting to pass refreshments or hand out souvenir packages and magazines; the Canadian Legion guides, with their official "Guides" armbands, go about their job of directing relatives, answering questions or leading the parade of returning men through the station to the reception; the Mayor stands by the Public Address System ready to welcome home these special citizens, and to give a word of greeting to those who are passing through.

In a specially prepared, quiet room set apart from the crowded rotunda, the wives and children of the men who are coming home at last wait in a fever of joy and anticipation. It is a thrilling moment, and thrilling, too, for the men themselves as they swing off the train and down through the station passages to face the almost unbelievable fact that they are home again. . . .

Gertrude Laing, *A Community Organizes for War*, Winnipeg, 1948

DOES ANYONE KNOW JIMMY?   I was in Halifax in August 1945, when the *Île de France* came in with ten thousand returning servicemen. It was a very exciting day. The ship was absolutely packed, and there were hundreds and hundreds of men lining the rails. It took at least a day to unload the troops. They were brought off in lots and put onto special trains, at the station behind the Nova Scotian Hotel.

I went down to the dock with a friend, who was looking for her brother. He'd been away for six years. We climbed up onto the roof of one of the immigration sheds, right beside the ship. She wrote, "Does anyone know Jimmy Duncan?" on a cigarette package, and tossed it to the nearest group by the rail. Incredibly, someone did find him, among all those men, and he came to the closest point on the rail to greet her.

Wren, Ottawa

End of war parade, Regina, 1945. SAB R-B 9395

TELL ME WHAT HE LOOKS LIKE!   My best friend met her future husband in Windsor [Nova Scotia] before he went overseas in 1943. They were together just for a week, but afterwards he wrote her such beautiful letters, saying he wanted to marry her when he came home.

Jean and I were working in Walton [Nova Scotia] when Grant came back in 1945. He came straight from Halifax to the house where we were staying, and he knocked at the door. Jean said to me, "You go down and answer the door, and tell me what he looks like!" I came back upstairs and I said, "He looks just fine to me." They were married in Windsor very soon after, then he took her home to Sarnia with him.

Halifax

TREMBLY AND EXCITED   When Joe's regiment came back to Toronto the men were marched into the Coliseum. I'd been told to go down there, and I sat in the "S" section, for Smiths and Samuels, or whatever. When Joe was dismissed he looked for me there.

We saw each other right away. I felt strange, trembly and excited, and a bit frightened too. He said afterwards he felt the same.

Joe got thirty days' leave with pay and he wore his uniform all that time. If you sat down in a restaurant, somebody would be sure to come and sit with you, and say, "Did you know so-and-so?" We went to New York for ten days, and we went to a show every single night. It was our second honeymoon.

Toronto

VJ-Day celebration dance, Vancouver, August 1945. VPL 44917

PICKING UP THE PIECES

My engagement didn't survive the war. He was in India, I was in Alaska. You got the feeling after four or five years that there was no point. The whole thing became irrelevant to my life.

Then the war ended, and it was back to Toronto, back to unemployment, back to all my friends home from the war, all of us five or six years older. Everybody was in the same boat, picking up the pieces. For the last few years we'd all had such purpose, such excitement in our lives. It took time to find a new direction. For me, the break came when I went into advertising.

Toronto

ON A HOSPITAL TRAIN

I came home as a patient myself, with T.B. I was on a hospital train to Regina. All along the route this train would stop and people would get off. Many men hadn't seen their families in years.

The emotional scenes when they met were hard to watch, all the way from Halifax to Regina. Some of those men had lost limbs. Some were blind and couldn't see their children waiting for them. The reunions were heart-breaking sometimes.

R.C.A.M.C. Saskatchewan nursing sister

Wounded servicemen on board a hospital train receive candy and cigarettes from a Red Cross volunteer. CP 8135

CONSPIRACY OF SILENCE

There was a tremendous amount of propaganda — you have to call it that — before the men came home. Our role was clear. We were to be utterly supportive. We were to make the adjustments because we were the fortunate ones. We had been on the cosy home front, and we knew if anything went wrong with this reunion it was the wife's responsibility.

Men came home from such varied experiences, and there was — among close friends, even — a conspiracy of silence. Someone would say to you, "I hear John will be home tomorrow, isn't that marvellous?" and the only possible response was, "Yes, it's going to be the most glorious day of my life." Well, it wasn't the most glorious day, usually. It was the scariest day. It meant beginning again — it wasn't just picking up threads, because when a boy goes away when he's twenty and comes home when he's twenty-six, having had a war experience, he's not the same boy who went away.

Jim was still a baby. He was supposed to be a boy when his father came home, but he was still a baby, not talking really, not responding to deep male voice commands except with utter fear and horror. I'm sure that John was very disappointed in the manliness of his eighteen-month-old son.

And when a woman is alone with two or three children for six years and has learned to handle money, and how to make the furnace work better than it used to work, it isn't easy to give up those skills.

Jobs weren't always up to the men's expectations after the war. It was hard, and the trouble was, it wasn't supposed to be hard.

Winnipeg

TO MY DARLING MAY

My husband's best friend married his sweetheart on his embarkation leave — and then he went overseas, and he was gone six years. She used to write and tell him she was lonely, and he'd write back and say, "Go out and have a good time."

Well, he got back and he found books lying around inscribed "To my darling May, from John", and this other man's bankbook in her purse. He never really forgave her. But can you imagine? She was nineteen when she married him on a forty-eight-hour leave, then he went away for six years.

Toronto

MEN WERE HARDER   Men were harder when they came back. They felt we'd been so coddled and sheltered, while they'd seen women and children really suffering overseas.

My brothers didn't want to talk to us about the war, but they'd sit around the kitchen table and talk among themselves. They were just carefree boys when they left; they were different when they came home.

Toronto

WAR WIDOWS   VE Day was a bad time for me. I expect it was for a lot of other war widows. Everybody else seemed to be celebrating, but our husbands weren't ever coming back.

I had been living with Noel's parents and going out to work each day, but shortly after VE Day my job folded up and I had to decide what to do next. I loved his parents dearly, but I was afraid if I stayed with them I'd be forever living in the past. I'd always be the wife of their dead son.

I decided to take up occupational therapy, and the University of Toronto was the only place to go for that. So I started a new life in a new city.

Newfoundland

Returning prisoners of war are welcomed by members of the Canadian Red Cross Corps when they arrive in Montreal. CRCS

A PRISONER IN HONG KONG   VJ Day was the worst time. John had been a prisoner in Hong Kong since 1941, and there was a long delay before the liberators went in. When they did get in, there were no messages right away. October came, and I still hadn't heard a word.

One night I went to the movies with my sister to take my mind off things. When I came out, my father and mother were waiting for me. They said, ''Go down to the cable office right away.'' He was on his way back to Victoria on an American ship, and he was arriving in a couple of days.

My husband had been taken out to Manila, to a huge camp for Americans, and he had sent me a message via Sydney, Australia. But it was three and a half weeks before I got it.

On the day he came back I went to Admiralty House with the kids to wait, but then a great bank of fog came up and the ship couldn't get in. I had to send the kids home. Finally, at eleven o'clock at night, the fog lifted.

When he came off the ship I didn't recognize him. One of my friends told me it was him. He'd had beriberi, a disease which makes you look blown up, and he'd always been so thin. He was wearing a very strange collection of clothes — American battledress and a Glengarry cap, which someone had given him.

Victoria

Dear Family:

The *Aquitania* docked Tuesday evening, and we watched the ship come in. The band played ''O Canada'' and ''Here Comes the Bride'', and the wives threw down English coins to those on the dock (like us) and everyone was happy, despite the drizzle.

Wednesday noon I left with the first train of four. Each was ten cars long, filled with brides, two trains for the west, two trains for Montreal and Toronto. There were three army officers, one medical officer, one W.D. officer, and varying numbers of Red Cross [volunteers] — never more than four — on board each train, so you see, Pop, I didn't do it all myself.

We had a fairly easy trip across as these trips go — the worst is getting up at all hours to dump people into the arms of waiting husbands. I could almost write an essay on styles and ways of greeting long-separated husbands and wives. Our worst worry was that whenever we stopped 20 minutes or more at some small town they would rush out to buy things — fruit, clothes, shoes — anything. Some of them went completely berserk because they didn't need coupons and it was pathetic the things they bought and the

Family reunion. DND PL 34522

C.W.A.C. officer escorts war brides and their children on their way to Canada from London in 1945. WCPI 653-20074

prices they paid. Naturally they weren't used to handling Canadian money and unfortunately all our shopkeepers weren't the honest type.

Also there was too much country for them—they got bored with trees, then lakes, then prairies. Just too much of them, they said.

Letter from a W.D., 6 May 1946

WE HAD LOST TOUCH When our ship docked at Halifax there was a group of women, a reception committee, and one of them was wearing this crushed-raspberry, pinky-red suit. I hadn't seen anything like it for years, and I couldn't take my eyes off it. Overseas you got so used to drab colours, to uniforms and the drab clothing the civilians wore.

The Army did bring in some civilians before we were demobilized to tell us how to dress, what was in style, and something about makeup. We had lost touch in three and a half years.

Demobilization was a real anticlimax, but it took two or three months to hit you. When you got home, you found you had no friends, nothing. You didn't fit in anywhere. Prisoners must feel the same sort of thing when they come out. It was a different world.

In the Army you never have to think about what you're going to eat, where you're going to live, what you're going to wear. Your whole life is programmed. I remember finding it was dreadful to make the simplest decisions.

I toyed with the idea of going back to school, but I was offered a job and I took it, not knowing what else to do. When I got married a year later I used my Benefits to buy pots and pans, a bedroom suite, a sewing machine, and this chair I'm sitting in now.

CWAC, Calgary

GIRLS HAVE NOTHING   Hard though it be for the men, there is no doubt that for many girls, post-war adjustments may be impossible.

Most of the men have wives and homes to return to, but the girls have nothing. Even their careers will be broken. I suppose they must realize it all, but for the present life is jolly enough. There is comradeship and plenty of fun. ''After the war'' will continue to sound unreal until it becomes an actuality.

Letter from a married servicewoman overseas
quoted by Marion V. Royce in *The Effect of
the War on the Life of Women*, New York, 1945

JUST ANOTHER BUBBLE IN THE BATH
When I had these stripes on, everyone talked to me. Then, all of a sudden, I was out of uniform and nobody talked to me. I was just another bubble in the bath, and it hurt. There was no rehabilitation school, no easing back into civilian life for me.

I didn't want to go back home to Victoria, so I stayed in Vancouver, but I was so lonely. I became a steno in the C.P.R. legal department.

Pipe Major, C.W.A.C. Pipe Band, Victoria

WRENS MODEL WARDROBES COSTING $95 IN OTTAWA

A fashion show, designed especially for them, delighted several hundred Wrens of H.M.C.S. *Bytown* in the fo'c'sle of Wallis House last evening, when six of their own members donned practical and attractive outfits to illustrate what could be done with the $100 clothing allowance they will get on demobilization.

Modelling the budget wardrobe (which actually cost $95.39 in Ottawa stores) were six Wrens of the same size, who drew cheers of admiration from the crowd of Wrens with their finished performance as mannequins. They were Wren Georgina S. Hall of Guelph, in a brown topcoat, brown accessories of standard classic style; Leading Wren Molly R. Bird of Victoria, in a green wool suit, same brown coat and accessories; Leading Wren Dorothy McMaster of Toronto, combining the green suit with the brown hat, shoes and bag, but dressing it up a bit with veil, flowers and pretty blouse; Wren Nancy Harold of Paris, in a ''date'' dress of pale green with polka dots, draped lines and dirndl skirt with pockets (which, incidentally, brought oh's and ah's from the Wrens, especially when they

heard the low price); and then Wren Lillian Messenger of Calgary showed a pretty blue print dress, with flowers in her hair and at the neckline, light gloves and brown pumps.

Then they were shown the piece de resistance —a made-over navy blue suit and smart hat, converted from a Wren skirt and jacket and a round sailor hat loaned by a Wren. There were gasps of unbelief from the crowd when Betty Hook modelled the stunning outfit with its perky trim of pink taffeta.

Clipping from Ottawa newspaper, 1945

NOT PEACE-TIME SKILLS   It was strange to be home again after wartime England. I came back on a ship after VE Day, supposedly to get ready to leave for the Far East, but VJ Day put paid to that.

I'd been getting up at 4 a.m. for so long, to meet bomber crews returning from raids over Germany. I woke Mum and Dad three times in a row at 4 a.m., telling them it was time to go for interrogation! Dad said, ''It's time you went out and found out how the rest of the world lives.''

I was twenty-six. I didn't want to go back to school, but it was tough finding a job. Our skills were not peace-time skills. It was more difficult for some of the men, the bombers and gunners. Eventually I found a job in personnel with Goodyear Tire.

W.D. Intelligence Officer, Toronto

R.C.A.M.C. nursing sister's wedding, Ottawa, May 1945.
PAC PA 128247

PAC PA 128258

THEIR REAL LIFE'S WORK   By far the greater majority being discharged intend to stay at home. They are married or about to be married and they are interested only in setting up their home and starting housekeeping.

The next largest number seek training as stenographers or some other kind of office work. The next largest group take up hairdressing.

It would seem unfortunate that so many women take stenography or hairdressing because when those still in the Armed Forces and the Civil Service are finally released there will be excessive competition in these particular occupations. The same argument applies to Beauty Treatments. The first thing any sensible woman cuts when hubby's pay envelope is not so fat is beauty treatments.

Married women can take training [Canadian Vocational Training] exactly the same as men. We try to counsel married women to make the home and raising their family their real life's work. If they insist on taking C.V.T., then we try to persuade them to learn something that would provide a livelihood in case she was widowed or forced to keep herself. Married women with dependent children must satisfy the authorities that good and satisfactory arrangements have been made for the care of such children while the mother is taking her course.

On the other hand, we encourage unmarried mothers to take C.V.T. because they often have to support a child as well as themselves. The child must be properly cared for before training starts.

Mrs. Grace L. Arrell, Senior Women's
Counsellor, Department of Veterans Affairs,
Hamilton, 1946

I DIDN'T WORK AGAIN   My big idea was to get married after we were both demobilized. We'd waited a long time. We took advantage of the Veterans' Land Act; we pooled our gratuities and we built our first house.

I didn't work again after we were married. It never occurred to me. Thank goodness I never needed to.

Wren, Manitoba

Dear Family:
. . . It may be some time yet before I am "rehabilitated", Pop. It seems that people have to be fed and it takes a large number of airwomen to help keep everyone's records straight, and what with all the people coming back we are busier than ever.

One doesn't mind one's friends and relatives asking that question, but the attitude here in Ottawa towards girls in uniform is getting such that the kids hate to go downtown in uniform because of the rude remarks and the number of times complete strangers ask them why they are still in uniform.

Partly I think it's housing conditions and they want our barracks, but it's a mighty poor show when service personnel are given that feeling so soon after the end of the war. It gives you anything but a feeling of security and pride in your work to feel you don't matter at all.

Letter from a W.D., Ottawa,
16 September 1945

SHOWING INITIATIVE   Some people seem to think that the only kind of training available to ex-servicewomen is hairdressing and clerical work. That, of course, is an entirely mistaken idea. Women are in training for more than eighty-five different occupations, ranging from the highly skilled and professional occupations which require several years' training, such as Law, Architecture, Medicine, Pharmacy, and Social Work, to those occupations requiring shorter periods of training such as Book-binding, Linotype-operating, Photography, Egg-grading, and even Frog-farming. At the end of January there were more than 1,000 women attending university or taking matriculation classes preparatory to university training; more than 1,200 were taking various kinds of vocational training.

On the whole I think it very encouraging to find that so many women are showing initiative in pursuing and preparing for occupations which are a bit off the beaten track. For instance, some women are in training as Watch- and Clock-makers and one is in training for an Embalmer. Could you suggest any occupations which are less likely to go out of business than these, or any reason why they are not suitable occupations for women?

Lest you think I am forgetting the importance of Home-making as a career for women, I wish to state that in several centres in Canada a special course of training in Home-making and family living has been designed for ex-servicewomen. I am glad to be able to announce that in some centres evening classes in this subject are also being provided for those men who recognize that they too need training. . . .

I am very much aware of the importance of home-making, but let us not forget that women have demonstrated their ability to perform all sorts of tasks hitherto not open to them, and we should see to it that opportunities for them to use their talents to the full are never closed again.

Olive Russell, Superintendent of Women's
Rehabilitation, Department of Veterans Affairs,
in a CBC interview, Vancouver,
25 March 1946

Physics lecture at the University of British Columbia. Ex-servicewomen could use their Re-establishment Credits to enrol in university or vocational training after the war. They were also eligible for business and professional loans. PAC PA 116069

TUITION WAS FREE   I stayed on in the Service until 1946, working in the sergeants' mess at Rockcliffe. I was discharged after all the laddies came back.

Tuition was free for retraining, and I got sixty dollars a month for each month I served in the forces. That meant I could study art at O.C.A. [Ontario College of Art] for four years after the war.

W.D. cook, Toronto, later a commercial artist

THE SAME RIGHTS   I spent a year doing discharge counselling, preparing the girls for civvy street. Servicewomen had all the same rights and privileges and benefits as men. They got rehabilitation credits and Veterans' Land Act benefits.

No ex-servicewomen had a difficult time if they knew what they wanted to do. Veterans' rights were very much to the fore. That's probably how I got the job I did. I'd been an English teacher before the war, and I went back to the same high school as librarian.

CWAC, Halifax

BACK TO SCHOOL   I never married. A considerable number of us didn't. Many of us were in our late twenties or older after the war. By the time I got back from overseas, most of the men I knew were married.

Many ex-servicewomen became interested in careers. There were re-establishment credits for education or setting yourself up in a business. I went back to school, to university, and finally I went into social work.

CWAC, Winnipeg

THEY HADN'T EXPECTED A WOMAN   The university required you to find a place to article before you began studying law. The Law Society of Manitoba had said any returning service personnel would be assured of a law office in which to article, but they hadn't expected a woman to apply. They told me this quite frankly.

I was sent to three different offices which said they needed an article clerk. But not one of them offered to take me. One said they wanted someone to do shorthand and typing. Another told me to get back into teaching, that's what I was trained for.

Since I couldn't find an office which would take me, I didn't turn up at law school. But I heard later that my name was called on the first day. They were apparently expecting me. In the meantime, I had found an opening as a personnel officer, and I made that my new career.

W.R.C.N.S. officer, Winnipeg

WE WERE FURIOUS   During our last few months in the Army, Hazel and I had many discussions as to what we were going to do next. I was anxious to go back to the west coast, more specifically Vancouver Island, and she was anxious not to go back to Toronto, where she had grown up and worked before joining the Army.

We decided we would have a turkey farm. We acquired some acreage and a shack and then went to see the Veterans' Land Act people about a loan to complete the deal and buy stock and equipment. Of course, they just gave us the brush-off and said no dice. We were furious, and, having made up our minds that we were going to do this thing, cast about for the next step. So, for starters, we wrote to the Superintendent of Women's Rehabilitation, who was an ex-CWAC and knew us quite well. She inquired of the Veterans' Land Act office as to why we were not even able to put in an application for assistance, and I suppose they got in touch with Victoria and we found that we were to appear before a Board. After that, they were very helpful and we were able to get going. However, as they were convinced that two women could not possibly get along without a frightful row, they insisted that the land should be surveyed and divided into two equal parts so that we each had our own bit and the buildings that we put up. It was a good thing in a way, as we each got the full amount of the loan (all $6,000 of it). We have now been together for 37 years and have not had a row, so they didn't really have to worry.

Letter from a former C.W.A.C. officer,
Sidney, B.C., November 1984

CWACs board the *Nieuw Amsterdam*, England, September 1945. Discharged servicewomen received a clothing allowance, a cash rehabilitation grant after six months of service, a gratuity based on length and place of service, life insurance, medical care for one year, and dental treatment. They could return to their former jobs, and if they had served overseas, they were given preference for civil service jobs. MA 189

DIFFICULTY SETTLING DOWN   War doesn't encourage a person to plan ahead, so when the war was over and suddenly I was back from overseas, I was in a state of shock.

I decided to get out of the Nursing Service. It never occurred to me to do anything else. But I had no plans. I wasn't sure *what* I wanted to do.

In January 1946 I went back to Toronto General [Hospital], but I had great difficulty settling down. A friend and I decided just to chuck it and go west, maybe to get work out in Vancouver. But we didn't stay there. When we got to Vancouver we saw a Greyhound ad for a bus to California and off we went. We came back to Toronto with very little money.

I took a job in the radium clinic at the Cancer Institute, then I left and went to university for a year to study public health.

R.C.N. nursing sister, Toronto

WE WERE FORTUNATE   Those of us who remained in the Service, we were fortunate; we were a small nucleus within a group of men who knew us and respected us.

R.C.N. nursing sister, Streetsville, Ont.

DAMES AT DESKS

Well, girls, it looks as though we're getting the push again. Straws in the wind? How about the demobilization of the Women's Division of the R.C.A.F., married women first? How about Civil Service job ads, in which the little postscript, "Preference will be given to a qualified male applicant", is frequently added to advertisements for jobs, male or female? How about the Civil Service Association's statement that married women will be barred from employment as soon as replacements can be found after the war?

It begins to look as though the old game of employment by sex, rather than by merit, is on the books.

It's my contention that women in employment have failed miserably in a crucial test. They seem to have missed the opportunity to break down masculine prejudice against women with pay envelopes. The women who have the best chance to do this are the women who work side by side with men in white-collar and executive positions.

Women to Blame
Many businesswomen lack dignity and poise. They tend to be too shy or too friendly. Many of them seem to find it difficult to be comradely without being

Right: Edmonton factory workers. PAC PA 116122 *Above:* Veterans' housing under construction, Ottawa. NFB

gushing, to be reserved without being stand-offish, to be dignified without being high-hat.

They accept the men's estimate of their importance, and too many of them exhibit well-marked inferiority habits, are deferential where they should be positive, apologize when they are owed apologies, express gratitude for things they should take as a right, accept patronage for their work and try to get a man to sponsor their ideas instead of presenting them forcefully themselves.

Women in trade unions have a chance to make themselves heard, and women's organizations can raise a voice in the male wilderness. But there should be no need for women to have to band together *as women*. They should be able to act on an equal basis as workers. It took war before jobs were allotted to those best prepared to fill them. Will we have to wait until the next war for awards of jobs on merit? Until then women will have to fight all along the line for a policy of equal employment opportunity.

Kathleen Kent, *Maclean's,* 15 January 1945

MUCH RATHER BE HOME If a married woman with means of support is crazy enough to want to earn a living — let her go to it!

But I do not believe many women will want to keep on with the daily grind of earning a living after the war, when their men are home to do it for them. I do not believe any woman really *likes* to dig out of her home, be it ever so humble, morning after morning and spend the rest of the day in the business world, being bossed around by someone else. She'd much rather be home where she can do some first-class bossing herself.

I do not believe women can take the place of men in the business world, so there's no danger of the ones who go on working stealing jobs from the men.

I do believe the majority of Canadian women now working will return to their homes after the war. The business experience they have gained in the past five years should make wives more interesting to husbands (God bless them!), more understanding of husbands, too. It should help women become more efficient housekeepers. And, also important — lead women to taking a more active part in the affairs of their country.

Claire Wallace, radio commentator,
in the Canadian Women's Press Club
Newspacket, November 1944

"THE PARTY'S OVER, LADY!" I stayed at Fairchild's [Aviation] till VE Day. There was a gorgeous celebration, then the pink slips started to be delivered. I became a Workers' Education Association representative for a while, and then I was research director of the textile workers' union. I wrote up petitions to labour boards. But when the men came back from overseas I lost my job.

I went looking for factory work, and I was offered forty-five cents an hour. When I protested, because I'd been earning sixty-five cents at Fairchild's, they said, "The party's over, lady!"

Montreal

TEMPORARY We were hired as temporary, for the duration. When the war was over, Alcan [Aluminum Company of Canada] laid all the ladies off and brought the men back. When you were laid off it was understood that the young girls, the unmarried ones, would be called back first, if there were jobs.

It didn't bother me. I was ready to settle down then and raise a family.

Kingston, Ont.

MAD AS HELL An awful lot of women were mad as hell when the war ended. They were earning good money and they knew they'd never do that again. They didn't want this bloody war to end.

You have to remember there'd been a Depression before the war. Very few jobs, very little money. They remembered what it was like to be poor.

Former employee, General Engineering
Company, Scarborough, Ont.

Toronto clothing-factory workers. Many older women who took jobs during the war lost their source of income when the war ended. PAC PA 116091

Factory workers, Toronto. NFB

WANTED A REST   At GECO [General Engineering Company] work was phased out, but not abruptly. The large majority of women went back home. They had done their patriotic bit. They had sons and husbands coming home and they wanted a rest. These women had kids, they were running households single-handed, they had to nurse family members when they were sick.

I stayed on to close down the recreational program and dispose of the facilities, then I went back into social work, to the Children's Aid. I found the experience at GECO invaluable. I understood what working mothers faced.

Employment officer, then recreation
director, General Engineering Company,
Scarborough, Ont.

HE WANTED ME OUT   I stayed at C.N.R. [Canadian National Railways] until they kicked us out. I remember the superintendent coming round one day and saying, "Well, you're a good-looking man!" I knew what he was getting at — the boys were coming back, and he wanted me out. I would have stayed on if I could.

Toronto

OF MAJOR IMPORTANCE   What happens to women in the general employment picture . . . is a question of major importance — one that will affect, and is already in fact affecting, our social philosophy, the survival of our rural economy, our birthrate, many of the foundations in short of our present society. . . . We can probably count on over 100,000 in industrial employment alone, for whom we must, in one way or another, prepare an economic future in postwar Quebec.

Neither marriage nor a return to the family unit can be counted on to reduce the problem appreciably during the first years following the war. . . . The average age of marriage in Quebec is the highest in Canada (25½ years) and our proportion of marriages to our population is the lowest. Over 45% of our women between 20 and 40 are not married.

Renée G. Vautelet, *Post-War Problems
and Employment of Women in the
Province of Quebec*, Montreal, 1945

MUCH FLOWERY TALK   After the war we may expect, from those who want to go back to the good old days, much flowery talk glorifying home-making and a lot of talk about "taking men's jobs". Let us talk rather about the good new days. The old days are not coming back for any of us. Full employment, not depression and unemployment, is our hope and aim.

Dorise Nielsen, M.P., *New Worlds
for Women*, Toronto, 1944

"GET OFF THAT DARNED JOB"   I was still working on the streetcars after the war was over, and people would come up and insult you: they said you were taking jobs away from the men. It wasn't only men that said that, a lot of women said it too. It was just deadly. They didn't even ask if my husband had come back from overseas, or whatever—no, it was just "Get off that darned job."

Vancouver

UNION HITS LAYOFF OF WOMEN WORKERS

Strong objection to the laying off of North Burrard's last 14 women workers was voiced today by officials of the Marine Workers and Boilermakers Industrial Union (CCL). W. L. White, president, charged the company with "rank discrimination".

An official of the company told the Vancouver Sun he would like to keep the women but "according to government regulations" they would have to maintain the plant's special women's building with its staff and provide the various other services required for women employees.

Cost Too High
He said continued employment of the women would necessitate an overhead cost out of all proportion to their value in view of the fact that they can be replaced by men.

He declared that when women are employed in a shipyard, nurses, special first aid rooms and restrooms must be provided, in addition to day and night supervisors.

Vancouver Sun, 18 December 1945

THEY WANTED TO BE INDEPENDENT   At John Inglis there were a lot of older women who worked all through the war because they were needed —and then there was no work for them. They didn't want to depend on their children, on their families, they wanted to be independent. It was very hard on them.

Toronto

THEY GOT RID OF US   We were working in the mail-order department at Eaton's after the war, and we got our wages cut, with no explanation. That's how they got rid of us; they didn't actually give us notice.

Toronto

ROSIE THE RIVETER'S JOB HONEY-MOON OVER

The era of Rosie the Riveter has passed.

The comely miss who trekked off to work in white coveralls, her hair tucked in a snood and a tin lunch box swinging in her hand, is off to conquer other fields.

Unfortunately for Miss War Worker, those fields will probably be very old and familiar ones. For Rosie seems destined to return to the domestic scene.

Would Shun Kitchen
And how does she feel about it?

Frankly, not so good.

Rosie isn't going back to laundry tubs, cooking three meals a day and minding babies without putting up a fight.

She has grown too familiar with the unionists' cry "Equal pay for equal work, regardless of sex."

She's ready to fight to stay out of the kitchen and, apparently, her male companions intend giving her plenty of support.

The Selective Service announcement that 1200 domestic jobs are available for women has been coldly received by women at Boeing's.

Can't Get Wartime Pay
Naturally, they say housework can't provide them with the same pay they received in war work and they don't want any part of it.

Not all women can return to their homes now that peace is here once again, Aeronautical Lodge 756 points out.

Many have responsibilities to their families or have to provide their own living.

They don't think they can do it very well washing dishes in someone else's home.

Rosie faces the future with trepidation. In the shipyards these past few war years, she has been making from 53 to 95 cents an hour.

They're Homemakers
Not all of Rosie's pals are complaining.

Some of the big army of war workers, who range in age from 17 to 70, are looking forward to going back to their own homes, to get back to a job which they know is every bit as important to peace time as the job they were doing in the war.

"They can send my man back from the army. I'm ready to go home," one young mother of two children declared emphatically today.

Vancouver Sun, 18 June 1945

WOMEN FROM WAR PLANTS   Although they were given much patriotic urging to enter the war plants, now that war industries are finished, women are being dismissed with no thanks. The impression is given that they have been paid so well for war work, while otherwise they might not have had jobs at all, that *they* should be the thankful ones. . . . Take this headline which appeared a few days after VJ Day: "Women Already Yielding Jobs to Veterans". The article plainly undertakes to make women believe that to give up their jobs to veterans, and take an inferior job at lower pay, or better still, go home and stay out of employment, is the proper attitude for women in the immediate post-war period.

This attempt to make women believe that taking a job away from one person and giving it to another will solve rehabilitation is vicious.

Laura E. Jamieson, *Women Dry Those Tears*, Co-operative Commonwealth Federation publication, 1945. (Jamieson was a C.C.F. member of the British Columbia legislature.)

HIGH-PRESSURE PROPAGANDA   For women, the threat of post-war unemployment is a two-edged sword. Those who desire or need to continue in employment not only fear the loss of their own jobs but are haunted also by the spectre of keeping a man out of a job. Moreover, women who do not wish to continue in gainful work outside the home stand in so great a fear of there being no jobs for their husbands and sons that they vigorously oppose women's continuing in the labour market in competition with their menfolk.

A certain apprehension lest the wartime exodus of women from the home may have undermined their home-making instincts is apparent in high-pressure propaganda on behalf of their return to the home. Yielding to the hysterical emotions of war, large numbers of writers, publicists and even persons in official posts of authority — both men and women — malign the character of women who wish to combine work outside the home with marriage. They attack with equal venom efforts toward economic policies of full employment which would allow women the choice of occupation outside the home. Women must be on their guard against their propaganda, which capitalizes on their normal desire for husbands, homes and children but disregards their dignity, rights and obligations as persons, workers and citizens.

Marion V. Royce, *The Effect of the War on the Life of Women*, New York, 1945

THE RIGHT TO CHOOSE   The right to choose what occupation she will follow must be conceded as a right to which every citizen is entitled. She must also have the right to equality of remuneration, working conditions, and opportunity for advancement.

We believe that the right to choose is not going to operate to make every woman, or even much larger groups of women, want to leave their homes for the labour market. It is the right to choose which is demanded. Happier homes, and, therefore, a happier democracy, will result from the recognition that women choose or do not choose marriage as their vocation. . . .

Report of the Subcommittee on Post-War Problems of Women, to the Advisory Committee on Reconstruction, Ottawa, May 1983

WHO AM I?   A crisis like the War brings out emergent leadership. All kinds of unlikely people surfaced because they were needed. Women were already being educated past the point of marriage and housekeeping, and they responded to the opportunity.

A new self-awareness developed during the War. Many of us began to ask "Who am I?" and to question our role in life. Many of us were fundamentally changed. If it had not been for the War, I would not have increased my participation in public life to the degree I did. I would probably have continued to be an unpaid volunteer, and I would probably have had more children. But by the end of the War I was teaching full-time, at the University of Manitoba.

It was difficult for my husband to come back and find a home situation which had changed so much — his wife, his family, his home, his community had all changed. It was a situation which we had to work through together.

Gertrude Laing, Executive Secretary, Greater Winnipeg Co-ordinating Board for War Services

HOW DOES MOTHERHOOD STAND UP IN THE WORLD TODAY?

Those who are the most shiftless and least capable of making plans for the future, the feeble-minded, the thriftless, the diseased, still continue to drift into parenthood and to propagate the species at an appalling rate.

Motherhood has been relegated [by working women] to a secondary place. To counterbalance the hard realism that war has engendered, we need . . . to make motherhood attractive to women with the

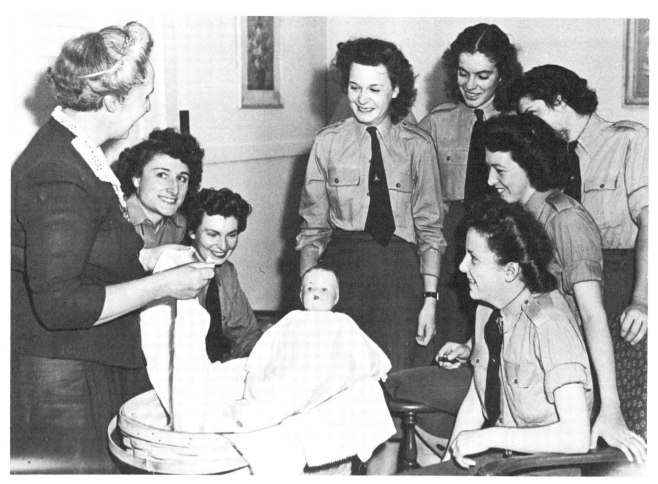

Weekly classes in homemaking were given at the C.W.A.C. barracks, Long Branch, Ont., in September 1945. All veterans were entitled to Re-establishment Credits, to help them purchase a home or business, tools, implements, or home furnishings.
TT 101-680

clear visions, the good physiques, the bright and practical intellects. . . . We need a state endowment of motherhood, with economic security guaranteed.

Hilda M. Ridley, *The Post-War Woman*,
Toronto, 1941

LET WOMEN WORK   The only answer men can give as a solution to industrial problems is: let the women go back home and the men will then have plenty of work to do. "We need more children; let the women fulfill their role by bearing more children. That's all they have to do."

That's all they have to do!

It is not right that one half of the human race should live under the dictatorship of the other half.

Why should women bear children, knowing full well that men in their blindness and stupidity will set the stage for another world war?

Let women work. Let there be no barriers against them because of their sex. First and foremost they are citizens, neither superior nor inferior to men.

High officials are worried about the declining birth rate. Their solution is "send the women back home", or provide family allowances. Another palliative.

How to encourage childbirth? Remove economic fears. Give a woman worker full pay for 10 to 12 weeks; four weeks before her child is born and six to eight weeks after. Have scientifically established nurseries available for women workers and their children.

Let there be free pre-natal and post-natal care, with minimum medical and hospital charges.

Give a decent standard of living to every family; establish more parks and playgrounds for children and adults.

Consult and take advice from women on all subjects that appertain particularly to the welfare of mothers and children.

The old grey-beards won't have to worry about the declining birth rate if they will do a little progressive thinking and take some progressive action.

Dora Dibney, Saskatchewan journalist,
Canadian Women's Press Club *Newspacket*,
August 1944

MY GENERATION   I'd been a teacher in Montreal before I enlisted and I had a job waiting for me, but I didn't take it. I was married overseas and my husband didn't think a wife should work, particularly when we were starting a family. My generation accepted that.

The women involved in World War Two [as servicewomen] were active afterwards in community work, whether or not they returned to paid jobs. They were involved in canvassing for the Red Cross, in committee work for the church, the Home and School. They accepted positions on school and hospital boards, set up self-help groups. . . . They accepted an opportunity to be part of the War — their generation's challenge. When it was over, they were more mature, and had possibly a sense of proportion which came with their respective experiences.

Servicewomen had experienced hard work; separation not only from their men-folk but also from their families and "home". They experienced Army food; North Atlantic voyages in wartime; irregular mail; uniform clothing; the uncertainty of postings; the need to make links with others, knowing that a posting-list might at any time separate newly-made friends or change the make-up of the group; the recognition that sexual harassment on the job could exist, even if one had no direct experience of this; the acceptance (necessarily) that, like or not-like, one's superiors gave orders, and these had to be followed . . . that the orders came from higher up, and that any of the nonsense of "feminine wiles", tears, etc., wouldn't affect the orders in the least; the never-ending confusion, changes in plans, countermanding of orders and so on was no one person's fault, but "the System", and the sooner one learned to hang loose, the better. . . .

All these kinds of things tended, I think, to reinforce qualities which were probably already there. So that after the war those women were not likely to settle *only* for coffee-parties and bridge (although those too!). I suspect they were more apt to cut through to the basic issues, with a new sense of what might be important. It is just as true, with modifications, for women on assembly lines, working shifts, carrying lunch-pails, becoming involved in unions.

None of these women could return unchanged either to domestic life or/and to a job. For women the War was SO different a way of life, the stresses were so different, they had so much farther to go (than men) in terms of leaving home and fireside.

Letter from Mary Buch, a former W.D.,
Brockville, Ont., 1984

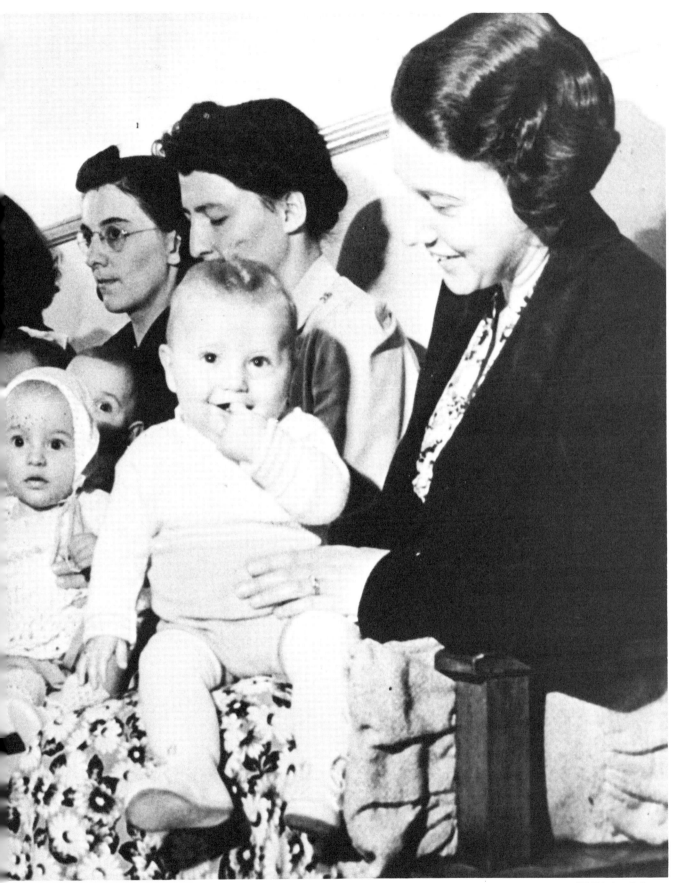

Well-baby clinic. NFB

Epilogue

"With the closing down of war industries, many women, particularly married women, have made no effort to seek other employment," Minister of Labour Humphrey Mitchell told the House of Commons in November of 1945. "This trend is particularly marked among the wives of returning veterans."

The last chapter provided many conflicting views and plenty of evidence of the pressures women were subjected to at the end of the war—pressures applied by other women as well as by men.

Did significant numbers of women workers really want to stay on in the labour force, whether or not they were married? One survey conducted by the Canadian Institute of Public Opinion in September 1945 provides some indications—although it was a survey of the public at large. In September 1945 respondents across Canada were asked whether men and women should have equal job opportunities. Only 20 per cent of those surveyed opted for equal opportunities, and 60 per cent said men should have preference. Among women surveyed—and they were not, of course, all working women—25 per cent opted for equal opportunities, but 62 per cent thought men should have preferential treatment.

The C.I.P.O. poll probably reflected an overwhelming urge to "return to normal" after six years of wartime disruption, following ten years of severe economic depression. The urge was shared by women as well as men. In 1945 the dream of "returning to normal" meant returning to both a prosperous and a stable society, with the family as its cornerstone. Women had been persuaded to join the armed forces or to take a job in war industry as part of their patriotic duty—but they had always been told this was a special effort, "for the duration". This message

came from senior women as well as from men—women like Mrs. Rex Eaton, Associate Director of the National Selective Service, and the senior officers of the three women's services. In 1944 Colonel Alice Sorby, the Officer Commanding all CWACs in the United Kingdom, was quoted in Canadian newspapers as saying that service overseas would not rob women of their domestic qualities. "I'll be delighted to go home to my own fireside and so will the rest. I think they'll be as eager to marry and settle down as ever—and they'll be better wives for the experience." Colonel Margaret Eaton, Director General of the C.W.A.C., served as a role model when she married after leaving the service in 1946. So did Wing Officer Willa Walker of the W.D.s, who resigned as Senior Staff Officer, R.C.A.F., W.D., in October 1944 to await the release of her husband from a German prisoner-of-war camp. Neither woman sought further employment.

It is interesting to find that a government-appointed Subcommittee on the Post-War Problems of Women raised the issue of women's right to choose paid employment in its report to the federal Advisory Committee on Reconstruction in 1943. "The right to choose what occupation she will follow must be conceded as a right to which every citizen is entitled." But the subcommittee was convinced that the majority of women would choose to raise a family as their main life's work, and its view was supported by its 1943 survey of working women which showed that more than half of them intended to stay home after the war. So the subcommittee's main recommendations were for measures that would improve the quality of family life: family allowances paid to the mother, well-planned housing, half-day nursery schools,

NFB

and a supply of domestic labour (to be assured by upgrading the status of household workers). Day nurseries were not recommended — they would not have improved the quality of family life as perceived by the subcommittee.

Household help was necessary if women were to participate in voluntary work, which the subcommittee said was "of incalculable value to the community". But, interestingly, it was also essential "if highly trained professional and business women are to make adequate return to the state for their expensive education". For all women who needed or wanted to work outside the home, the subcommittee recommended the right to choose an occupation, the right to equal pay and working conditions, and equal opportunities for advancement. Working women should have vocational guidance, placement assistance, retraining, and social security measures such as unemployment insurance, workers' compensation, and old age and disability pensions.

Contemporary observers noted that only those recommendations concerning home and family were given attention after the subcommittee delivered its report. In the immediate post-war years few married women, and even fewer married women with children, were employed in business, industry, and the professions, and almost none in the federal government. There were exceptions, of course. One was Gertrude Laing, who appears in the book as wife, mother, author, and Executive Secretary of the Greater Winnipeg Co-ordinating Board for War Services. After the war, Laing taught at the Universities of Manitoba and Calgary. In 1963 she became a member of the Royal Commission on Bilingualism and Biculturalism. Appointed to the Canada Council

in 1974, she served as Chairman from 1975 to 1978.

For some single, or widowed, professional women there were interesting career possibilities. Judy LaMarsh, a member of the C.W.A.C., became a lawyer, a Member of Parliament, and a cabinet minister in the Pearson government during the 1960s. Helen Hunley, another ex-CWAC, sat in the Alberta legislature and was a cabinet minister in the Lougheed government during the 1970s. She became lieutenant-governor of Alberta in 1984. Adelaide Sinclair, Director of the W.R.C.N.S., became Assistant to the federal Deputy Minister of Health after the war, and later was appointed Deputy Director of the United Nations International Children's Emergency Fund (UNICEF).

Marion Royce of the World Y.W.C.A. joined the federal Department of Labour in 1954 as first Director of the new Women's Bureau, with a mandate to promote equality of opportunity for women in the work force. CBC commentator Florence Bird, known professionally as Anne Francis, who began her radio career in wartime Winnipeg, took a particular interest in women's issues. In 1967 she became Chairman of the Royal Commission on the Status of Women. She was later appointed to the Senate.

All these women were exceptional, however. The majority of women who served in some active way during the war "returned to normal" after 1945: they stayed home to raise their families, and they devoted their considerable talents to voluntary organizations and community work. "My generation accepted that," said a one-time Montreal teacher and former W.D. intelligence officer, "and we had a great deal to offer." One can only guess at how much richer a society post-war Canada would have been had they involved themselves on a much wider public scale.

Sources

Advisory Committee on Reconstruction, VI, Post-war Problems of Women, Final Report of Subcommittee, November 30, 1943. Ottawa: King's Printer, 1945.

Auger, Geneviève, and Lamothe, Raymonde. *De la poêle à frire à la ligne de feu: La vie quotidienne des Québécoises pendant la guerre '39–'45.* Montréal: Boréal Express, 1981.

Bobak, Molly Lamb. *Wild Flowers of Canada.* (A personal history.) Toronto: Pergamon Press, 1978.

Bowman, Phyllis. *We Skirted the War!* Prince Rupert, B.C.: P. Bowman, 1975.

Brandt, Gail Cuthbert. "Pigeon-Holed and Forgotten: The Work of the Subcommittee on the Post-War Problems of Women (1943)." *Social History/Histoire-Sociale,* Vol. 15, No. 29, May 1982.

Broadfoot, Barry. *Six War Years, 1939–1945: Memories of Canadians at Home and Abroad.* Toronto: Doubleday, 1974.

Bruce, Jean. "Women in CBC Radio Talks and Public Affairs." Canadian Oral History Association *Journal,* Vol. 5, No. 1, 1981–82.

Casgrain, Thérèse F. *A Woman in a Man's World.* Toronto: McClelland and Stewart, 1972.

Chenier, Nancy Miller. "Canadian Women and War: A Long Tradition." *Oracle,* No. 54, National Museum of Man. Ottawa: National Museums of Canada, 1984.

Christie, Kay. "Behind Japanese Barbed Wire: A Canadian Nursing Sister in Hong Kong." Royal Canadian Military Institute Year Book, 1979.

Collins, Robert. "When Canadian Women Went to War." *Star Weekly Magazine.* September 23, 1961.

Conrod, W. Hugh. *Athene, Goddess of War: The Canadian Women's Army Corps. Their Story.* Dartmouth, N.S.: Writing and Editorial Services, 1984.

Diamond, Sara. *Women's Labour History in British Columbia: A Bibliography, 1930–1948.* Vancouver: Press Gang Publishers, 1982.

Dougherty, Chris. "Photographic Evidence and Interpretations of the Role of Canadian Women during the Second World War." M.A. research paper, Concordia University, Montreal, 1981.

Ellis, Jean M., with Isabel Dingman. *Facepowder and Gunpowder.* Toronto: S. J. Reginald Saunders, 1947.

Gaffen, Fredric. *The Home Front: Canada, 1939–1945. Canada's Visual History,* Vol. 68. National Museum of Man, National Museums of Canada/National Film Board of Canada, 1984.

Gibbon, John Murray, with Mary S. Mathewson. *Three Centuries of Canadian Nursing.* Toronto: Macmillan, 1947.

Granatstein, J. L. *Canada's War: The Politics of the Mackenzie King Government, 1939–1945.* Toronto: Oxford University Press, 1975.

Gray, James H. *Troublemaker!: A Personal History.* Toronto: Macmillan, 1978.

Greer, Rosamond "Fiddy". *The Girls of the King's Navy.* Victoria, B.C.: Sono Nis Press, 1983.

Hodgetts, J. E.; McCloskey, William; Whitaker, Reginald; and Wilson, V. Seymour. *The Biography of an Institution: The Civil Service Commission of Canada, 1908-1967.* Montreal: McGill-Queen's University Press, 1972.

Hodgins, J. Herbert; Crombie, David B.; Crawford, Eric; and Huestis, R. B., eds. *Women at War.* Toronto: Maclean Publishing Co., 1943.

Jamieson, Laura E. *Women Dry Those Tears.* Vancouver: Cooperative Commonwealth Federation, 1945.

Laing, Gertrude. *A Community Organizes for War: The Story of the Greater Winnipeg Co-ordinating Board for War Services and Affiliated Organizations, 1939-46.* Winnipeg: 1948.

Lennon, M. J., and Charendoff, Syd. *On the Homefront: A Scrapbook of Canadian World War Two Memorabilia.* Erin, Ont.: Boston Mills Press, 1981.

McIntyre, Linda. "Nursing Experiences in the Second World War: Continuity and Enrichment in Nursing Professionalism at Home and Overseas." M.A. research paper, Carleton University, Ottawa, 1982.

Mathews-Klein, Yvonne. *How They Saw Us: The Women's Archival Film Study Package (Introduction).* National Film Board of Canada, 1978.

Metson, Graham. *An East Coast Port: Halifax at War, 1939–1945.* Toronto: McGraw-Hill Ryerson, 1981.

Mitchell, Miriam C., and Deacon, Florence C. *641: A Story of The Canadian Red Cross Corps, Overseas.* St. Catharines, Ont.: Advance Printing, 1978.

Morton, Desmond. *Canada and War: A Military and Political History.* Toronto: Butterworths, 1981.

Nash, Theresa M. "Images of Women in National Film Board of Canada Films during World War Two and the Post-War Years (1939-1949)." Ph.D. dissertation, McGill University, Montreal, 1982.

Nicholson, G. W. L. *Canada's Nursing Sisters.* (Historical Publication 13, Canadian War Museum, National Museums of Canada) Toronto: Samuel Stevens, Hakkert, 1975.

———. *The White Cross in Canada: A History of St. John Ambulance.* Montreal: Harvest House, 1967.

Nielsen, Dorise. *New Worlds for Women.* Toronto: Progress Books, 1944.

Niemann, Lindsay. *Wage Discrimination and Women Workers: The Move Towards Equal Pay for Work of Equal Value in Canada*. Ottawa: Women's Bureau, Labour Canada, 1984.

Ontario Rehabilitation Committee, *Digest of Rehabilitation Conferences (Second Series) sponsored by the Governments of the Dominion of Canada and the Province of Ontario*. Toronto: 1946.

Pierson, Ruth Roach. *Canadian Women and the Second World War. Canada's Visual History*, Vol. 66. National Museum of Man, National Museums of Canada/National Film Board of Canada, 1983.

_____. *Canadian Women and the Second World War*. Canadian Historical Association, *Historical Booklet* No. 37.

_____. " 'Jill Canuck': CWAC of All Trades, but No Pistol Packing Momma." Historical Paper, presented at the annual meeting, Canadian Historical Association, London, 1978.

_____. "Women's Emancipation and the Recruitment of Women into the Canadian Labour Force in World War Two." In *The Neglected Majority: Essays in Canadian Women's History*, edited by Susan Mann Trofimenkoff and Alison Prentice. Toronto: McClelland & Stewart, 1977.

"Reflections on the Service: Records of W.R.C.N.S. Organization and Problems" (internal document), 1946.

Ridley, Hilda M. *The Post-War Woman*. Toronto: Ryerson, 1941.

Robertson, Heather. "The Education of Madeleine Parent." In *Her Own Woman: Profiles of Ten Canadian Women*, by Myrna Kostash, Melinda McCracken, Valerie Miner, Erna Paris, and Heather Robertson. Toronto: Macmillan, 1975.

Robson Roe, Kathleen. *War Letters from the C.W.A.C.* Toronto: Kakabeka Publishing Co., 1975.

Royce, Marion V. *The Effect of the War on the Life of Women*. New York: World Y.W.C.A., 1945.

Shaw, Rosa. *Proud Heritage: A History of the National Council of Women in Canada*. Toronto: Ryerson, 1957.

Sherwood, Ronald H. *Pictou Parade*. Sackville, N.B.: Tribune Press, 1945.

Stacey, C. P. *Arms, Men and Governments: The War Policies of Canada, 1939-1945*. Ottawa: Queen's Printer, 1970.

_____. *Six Years of War: The Army in Canada, Britain and the Pacific*. Ottawa: Queen's Printer, 1970.

Stewart, Margaret, and French, Doris. *Ask No Quarter*. Toronto: Longmans, Green, 1959.

Vautelet, Renée G. *Post-War Problems and Employment of Women in the Province of Quebec*. Montreal: Local Council of Women, 1945.

Wadden, Marie T. "Newspaper Response to Female War Employment: *The Globe and Mail* and *Le Devoir*, May-October 1964." B.A. research paper, Memorial University, Newfoundland, 1976.

Wade, Susan. "Joan Kennedy and the British Columbia Women's Service Corps." In *Not Just Pin Money: Selected Essays on the History of Women's Work in British Columbia*, edited by Barbara K. Latham and Roberta J. Pazdro. Victoria, B.C.: Camosun College, 1984.

Wartime Information Board. *Canada at War* (monthly reference booklet). Ottawa: King's Printer, 1943-44.

Whitton, Charlotte E. *Canadian Women in the War*. Toronto: Macmillan, 1942.

Ziegler, Mary. *We Serve That Men May Fly: The Story of the Women's Division, Royal Canadian Air Force*. Hamilton, Ont.: R.C.A.F.(W.D.) Association, 1973.

Archives, Libraries, and Museums

PUBLIC ARCHIVES OF CANADA
Federal Archives: Department of Labour; Department of National Defence; Department of National War Services; Wartime Prices and Trade Board
Manuscript Division (collections of papers): Kate Aitken; Canadian Women's Press Club; Co-operative Commonwealth Federation: Jean Flatt Davey; Imperial Order Daughters of the Empire; Agnes C. Macphail; National Council of Women; Katherine A. Peacock; Mattie Rotenberg; Olive Russell
National Film, Television and Sound Archives: Canadian Broadcasting Corporation; Joan Williams collection

BRITISH COLUMBIA PROVINCIAL ARCHIVES
Manuscript Division: British Columbia Women's Service Club; Burton Women's Institute; North Shore Council of Women; Janet and Noel Thompson Peters
Sound and Moving Image Division: Sara Diamond collection

MANITOBA ARCHIVES: Aileen Rebecca (Small) Odor

PUBLIC ARCHIVES OF NOVA SCOTIA: H. B. Jefferson

ARCHIVES OF ONTARIO: General Engineering Company

SASKATCHEWAN ARCHIVES BOARD, REGINA: Saskatoon Council for War Auxiliary Services

NATIONAL LIBRARY OF CANADA: Hansard; Canada *Labour Gazette*, 1940-45

ROBARTS LIBRARY, UNIVERSITY OF TORONTO: W. E. Blatz

CANADIAN WAR MUSEUM, NATIONAL MUSEUM OF MAN, NATIONAL MUSEUMS OF CANADA: Sunny Johnston; Betty and Wilbur Naylor

Acknowledgments

Over the past five years I have received much help and support from friends, fellow-researchers, family, and the women whom I interviewed. Nancy Miller Chenier, guest curator of the long-running Women and War exhibition at the Canadian War Museum, National Museums of Canada, shared many sources and ideas with me, and offered a critique on the first draft of my manuscript. Jan Andrews and Alison Taylor volunteered their help as researchers early in the project. During the past nine months much additional research and checking were undertaken by Kathleen O'Doherty and Claire Watson Fisher. Without their assistance and encouragement, and the unflagging personal support of my family, Gordon, Ellen, and Matthew Bruce, I could not have met my publisher's deadline. Credit is also due to my editor, Kathleen Richards, and to designer Catherine Wilson.

Many of the women I interviewed generously lent me their wartime letters, scrapbooks, and personal photographs and diaries, and introduced me to their former colleagues and friends across Canada. To each and every one of them I extend my grateful thanks.

Most of the interviews in this book were done by me personally, but I was fortunate to have access to additional oral-history material in the Joan Williams collection, Public Archives Canada, and the Sara Diamond collection, Provincial Archives of British Columbia.

I am indebted to the Canada Council, Explorations Program, and to the Ontario Heritage Foundation, for financial assistance.

Key to Photo Credits

AA	Provincial Archives of Alberta
ACA	Air Canada Archives
BCA	Provincial Archives of British Columbia
CN	Canadian National
CP	Canadian Pacific
CRCS	Canadian Red Cross Society
CWM	Canadian War Museum, National Museums of Canada
DND	Department of National Defence
GA	Glenbow Museum: The Archives
GECO	General Engineering Company Collection, Ontario Archives
LT	London Transport Executive
MA	Manitoba Archives, Canadian Army Photo Collection
MTL	Metropolitan Toronto Library, Broadside Collection
NBM	New Brunswick Museum
NFB	National Film Board, Multimedia Division
NMC	National Museums of Canada
PAC	Public Archives Canada
SAB	Saskatchewan Archives Board
TT	York University, Toronto Telegram Collection
TTC	Toronto Transit Commission
VPL	Vancouver Public Library
VSWG	Victoria Status of Women Group
WCAM	Western Canada Aviation Museum
WCPI	Western Canada Pictorial Index
WFP	Winnipeg Free Press

INDEX